Byways and Bylines
32 Trips
With Harvey Currell

Also by Harvey Currell
Where the Alders Grow
The Mimico Story
Thirty Trips Around Ontario
More Trips Around Ontario

 www.trafford.com

North America & international
toll-free: 1 888 232 4444 (USA & Canada)
phone: 250 383 6864 ♦ fax: 812 355 4082 ♦ email: info@trafford.com

DEDICATION

To JUDITH AND BOB,

My daughter and son

AND

JOHN BRADEN

My son-in-law and editor

Introduction

Ontario is a huge province, roughly 1,800 km (1,125 miles) wide from Kenora to Ottawa, and roughly the same distance from top to bottom. It stretches from Pelee Island in Lake Erie, at the same latitude as northern California, up to and beyond Polar Bear Provincial Park on the western shore of Hudson Bay. For 49 years, in what he called "the best job in the world," Harvey Currell, my father, travelled Ontario from top to bottom and side to side, seeking out places for readers of two big-city newspapers to visit. In this book, you will go with him on many of these trips, the ones he enjoyed the most and remembers best.

For every trip in the book, Dad has re-researched the facts to make sure the places and attractions still exist and are still open to visitors.

Besides inviting you to visit little-known spots in Ontario—and sometimes other parts of Canada—Dad also takes you back in time to a childhood in the Toronto of the 1920s and 1930s, through World War II and into the newspaper world of the 1950s and 1960s where he began as an office boy and eventually rose to become a senior editor.

Bob Currell
February 2009

Author's Note

Welcome To "Town And Country Trips"

That's the name of a column that was my journalistic home for forty-nine years—first for thirteen years in The Toronto Telegram and then for thirty-six years in The Toronto Sun. I welcomed readers to it every week and tried to make them feel at home and like family, introducing them to many hundreds of congenial people as well as to interesting and beautiful spots around Ontario and sometimes further afield. I got to know lots of the readers personally. They'd track me down, find my phone number and call me either at the newspaper or sometimes at home with unanswered questions about Trip columns or with suggestions for new trips.

Two books of the columns were published when I worked for The Telegram. Their titles were *Thirty Trips Around Ontario* and *More Trips Around Ontario*. Both sold out their first printings and went into second press runs.

I felt that my readers were friends and I still do. I dropped the weekly columns at the end of March 2007 for two major reasons: one, at age 85 I had grown tired of having to drive to some new place once a week, often in a winter snowstorm; two, I felt I should quit while I was ahead and still able to write well enough to hold readers.

For this book, I've selected and updated thirty-two of the Trip columns that I enjoyed the most. If you're an old reader who read the columns in their heyday, Welcome back! If you're a new reader, Welcome especially!

Sandwiched between groups of my Trip columns, I've inserted my own life story, featuring anecdotes about my experiences in 1920s and 30s Toronto and about my training and work as a writer and editor over sixty-eight years. I hope you have the patience to read this. But if it bores, just skip my life story and read about the trips.

Now at age 86, after a career in which I looked forward to going to work every single day, I've put this book together—mostly to give myself the pleasure of re-living those trips, but also to share a picture of life in Toronto and Ontario through the Great Depression of the 1930s, six years of World War II, and the period of explosive growth in the second half of the twentieth century.

During my journalistic career, I worked thirty-two years full-time for The Toronto Telegram. For thirteen of those years I wrote a Trip column every week. After The Telegram folded in 1971, I switched my Trip column to The Toronto Sun, which came to life immediately after The Telegram died. For thirty-six years I wrote a weekly Trip column from 1971 to 2007.

The first trip I'm going to suggest in this book is a walk on the Bruce Trail. To introduce you to this 885-kilometre (553-mile) footpath, I'll tell you how it began as the dream of a small group of naturalists and hikers and how it was built by volunteers, with

the consent of landowners, along the most rugged
terrain in southern Ontario.

On The Trail

Six members of The Telegram walking party trace
their way along an unopened road allowance in Mono
Township. One of the walkers, Dr. Aubrey Diem, was
missing this day because of a bad blister. The others are:
(left to right) Harvey Currell, Harry McCartney, Chuck
Harris, Ray Lowes, Bob Crosson and Robert Bateman.

Part One

Chapter 1

Clinging To A Cliff

It was late afternoon on an April day in 1962. My son Bob, 11, was clinging to a cliff at Devil's Glen Provincial Park on the Niagara Escarpment near Singhampton, Ontario. With one hand, he was using a wooden crutch to lever loose the limestone fossil of an incredibly ancient creature called a trilobite. With the other, he was swinging a geologist hammer to hasten the process. What made the scene almost blood-chilling to anyone who knew Bob was the fact that less than two weeks earlier he had been released from three months in a neck-to-ankle plaster cast following a major operation in which bone had been removed from my pelvis to be grafted into Bob to fill the cavity left by a large bone tumour.

That is the part that I now remember most vividly from what came to be called The Toronto Telegram Bruce Trail Expedition. It was the first-ever hike on the Bruce Trail, the real beginning of the Trail.

Since that time, the Bruce Trail has become famous as the first citizen-built long-distance hiking path in Canada. It runs for some 885 km (553 miles) along the length of the Niagara Escarpment from Queenston Heights at Niagara to Tobermory where the Bruce Peninsula juts into Lake Huron like an arrow pointing northwest towards Manitoulin Island and Sault Ste. Marie.

Now, back to that rock face at Devil's Glen Provincial Park and how Bob came to be clinging there. It happened just after an almost miraculous recovery from what his mother and I feared would be a crippling disability.

In 1962, I was Suburban and District Editor of The Toronto Telegram, a position which sometimes seemed to me to be also the result of a miracle. I loved that job, which I held more than ten years. As chief of a staff of twenty full-time reporters and photographers and many part-time correspondents or "stringers", I was responsible for filling one full newspaper page six days a week with news and feature stories from an area ranging outward from the city limits of Toronto to about 130 km (about 80 miles) of suburban and rural Ontario.

At that time, from the end of World War II in 1945 through the 1940s, 1950s and into the 1960s, the Toronto-centred area was the scene of explosive growth. In the immediate suburbs of Scarborough, East York, North York and Etobicoke, farm and market-garden land was being carved into hundreds of new housing subdivisions and covered with thousands of what some people called "strawberry-box" housing. My family—Josephine, my much-loved wife, Judith and Bob, our two kids—and I occupied one of the new suburban homes at 6 Springbrook Gardens in Etobicoke, a couple of miles west of the Humber River. From there I leaped out of bed around 5 A.M. every working day to drive downtown to Bay and

Melinda Streets where stood the Victorian red-brick building that John Ross Robertson had built in the 1890s to house his fast-growing populist newspaper.

In a later chapter of this book, I'll tell you how I came to be part of that newspaper and the czar of its suburban and regional coverage.

Right now, I'll skip to 1958 and an interview with Laurie McKechnie, then the Managing Editor of The Telegram. Over coffee one day in the makeshift cafeteria—housed in one of the old buildings along Melinda Street which The Telegram had acquired next to John Ross Robertson's original 1890s palace— Mr. McKechnie said to me, "You're always telling us about fascinating places you visit across Ontario. I think you should write a weekly column about them. We could call it 'Town and Country Trips'. Each week you'd suggest a destination for a family expedition. If it proves to be popular, we might even print a book of the columns. We'll pay you extra for the trip columns and you can do the trips yourself on weekends and holidays. You'll also get 10 cents a mile (6.25 cents a kilometre) car allowance for your travels."

That's how the Town and Country Trips column was born. In addition to my regular work as an editor, I was to continue writing a Trip column every week for forty-nine years.

Now we jump through time again to the autumn of 1961 when Jean Burlington, the boss's secretary, phoned to summon me to a meeting in the office of Doug MacFarlane. Doug was The Telegram's Editor in Chief and a legendary figure in Toronto newspaper circles. In Doug's southwest office I found Baz Mason, the Promotion Manager, and Laurie McKechnie, the Managing Editor. They were talking about something called the Bruce Trail.

I was familiar with the Bruce Trail project. In fact, I had already played a part in promoting it, along with a man named Ray Lowes, from Hamilton. By profession, Ray was a metallurgist on the staff of Stelco, the giant steel corporation that dominated Hamilton industry. By avocation, he was a naturalist, a director of the Federation of Ontario Naturalists, and a leader of the Hamilton Field Naturalist Club. I had met Ray while gathering material for my Town and Country Trips column and discovered that we had many interests in common. We had both hiked on the Appalachian Trail in the eastern United States. We had both walked many parts of the Niagara Escarpment and compared it to the Appalachian Mountain range in the U.S.

Somehow, with Ray Lowes, myself and other hikers and nature buffs, the idea had taken hold that it would be wonderful if Ontario could have a walking trail up the Niagara Escarpment—from the U.S. border at Queenston Heights all the way up to Tobermory, at the top of the Bruce Peninsula. I had suggested this in some of my Trip columns when I wrote about scenic spots up and down the Niagara Escarpment.

It's difficult to pin down the idea to any one person, but Ray Lowes was probably more responsible for the Bruce Trail concept than any other person. He has rightly been revered as the Father of the Trail. And he was the one, I think, who came up with the name—

The Bruce Trail. He once told me it was inspired by a book called *The Bruce Beckons* by Dr. Sherwood Fox of the University of Western Ontario. By 1961, the idea of a Bruce Trail was under active discussion. The Board of Directors of the prestigious Federation of Ontario Naturalists had formed a committee to investigate the concept. The Toronto Star newspaper had also jumped into the act and had announced that The Star's Atkinson Charitable Foundation was about to make a grant to enable the Bruce Trail to employ an organizer to plan and organize the building of the trail.

That's why Doug MacFarlane had summoned me to a meeting. The Telegram's plan was to outdo The Star by sponsoring a Bruce Trail Expedition. We would invite a group of natural scientists and hikers to walk the proposed route of the trail. Organizing and leading the expedition would be The Telegram's Town and Country Trips columnist and District Editor, Harvey Currell. This was news to me. Coming suddenly out of the blue, it set me back on my heels, and for a few minutes I was at a loss for words. Doug filled in the silence by telling me I could easily do this in addition to my regular job. The date set for the Expedition was six months away, in the week of the Ontario school Easter holiday the following spring. There would be lots of time to plan and organize.

This was a typical Doug MacFarlane decision. It reminded me of a similar one some seven years earlier when The Telegram had hired famous Lake Ontario swimmer Marilyn Bell for $15,000 to swim the English Channel.

It was fun to work for Doug MacFarlane but could also be a little daunting. He had a way of picking out people he considered promising and giving them massive responsibilities. That's how I, a lowly suburban reporter, had become the first Night City Editor of The Telegram and later the District Editor. MacFarlane rewarded good work and initiative, but he stamped hard on foolish errors. If an egregious grammatical goof found its way into the paper, it was likely to appear next day in Doug's daily Assessment Notice with a pointed query: "Who Done This?"

McFarlane also kept a keen watch over his reporters' expense accounts, but he had a sense of humour. As the son of a United Church Minister he had, like Winston Churchill, a habit of quoting the Bible in messages to staff members. Once when Bob Pennington was in Italy covering the Olympics, Pennington cabled the office to send more expense money. This was before the widespread use of credit cards. In reply, MacFarlane fired off a biblical admonition: "From every man shall be required an accounting." Pennington cabled back another Biblical quote. I think it was from Proverbs: "Muzzle not the ox that grindeth out the corn." Pennington got the expense money, and MacFarlane posted both cables on the bulletin board for the edification of staff.

Chapter 2
Organizing The Expedition

Well, to get back to The Telegram Bruce Trail Expedition: After thinking about it for a while, I was elated about being made responsible for carrying out a great idea and wished I had thought of it first. Three questions popped into my mind:

One—Where exactly are we going to walk on this expedition? There was no trail in existence, not even as a line on a map.

Two—Where are we going to eat and sleep?

Three—Who are "we"? Who would be the walkers on the expedition?

With the help of Ray Lowes, I tackled the first question, the one about the route. He put me in touch with Dr. Aubrey Diem, a geography professor at Waterloo Lutheran University. (It later became Wilfred Laurier University.) Dr. Diem, it appeared, had students working on a study of the Niagara Escarpment. I got in touch with Dr. Diem and invited him to become one of the walkers on the expedition. He proved to be enthusiastic about the whole project and became a most valuable member of the planning group. After equipping teams of students with topographic maps on a scale of one inch to one mile—Canada was still using the old measurement system—he sent them out on weekends to investigate a route from Burlington to Craigleith, following unused road allowances, crown land, conservation areas and reforestation tracts whenever possible. The route Aubrey Diem and his students worked out was to become the first route of the actual Bruce Trail.

For the answer to the second question about where we were going to sleep and eat, I turned to two members of my district staff at The Telegram. They were Bob Shannon and John H. (Tiny) Bennett. Both were outdoors people who had often accompanied me on fishing and hiking expeditions. Tiny (a giant of a man) later was to succeed Pete McGillen as The Telegram's Fishing and Outdoor columnist. Bob Shannon, son of a Barrie country doctor, I had hired a few years earlier as our Simcoe County reporter.

To Tiny, I gave three jobs. The first was to rent, borrow or buy enough camp equipment (tents, air mattresses, cots, sleeping bags, etc.) for about ten people. The second was to locate seven overnight camping sites along the route of the expedition. And the third was to get permission from the various landowners for us to cross their property and to camp at the sites selected.

Bob Shannon's assignment was to provide meals for ten people for seven days, to assemble outdoor cooking equipment, water supply, dishes, cutlery and utensils and to draw up menus and shopping lists. Besides being a reporter-photographer, Bob was— and still is—an excellent cook. Now retired, he and his wife Betty run a widely known Bed and Breakfast inn at Mount St. Louis. It's called Inn the Woods and has become famed for gourmet meals. You'll read about it later in these pages.

After consultation with Telegram brass, Ray Lowes and I decided that the expedition would walk about 250 kilometres (160 miles) from Burlington to the Collingwood area, that it would take place in the seven days of the 1962 school Easter holidays and that a total of seven walkers would be invited to participate. Following further discussion, we chose seven people who we thought would be interested and would be able in future to assist in the creation of the Bruce Trail. All of them enthusiastically accepted our invitation. They were:

- Ray Lowes, of course, a naturalist and chair of the Bruce Trail Committee.
- Bob Bateman, a friend of Ray Lowes. He was then a Burlington high school teacher and a recognized naturalist and traveler who was already gaining a reputation as a wildlife artist. He is now world-famous.
- Bob Crosson, another naturalist high school teacher and a friend of Bob Bateman. Both Bob Bateman and Ray Lowes especially asked that he be invited.
- Dr. Aubrey Diem, because of his work with students in laying out the route. He was actually to serve as guide for the expedition. He also turned out to be a great raconteur, familiar with many limericks, jokes and folk songs.
- Harry McCartney, Ontario Field Commissioner of the Boy Scouts of Canada. When I asked him

if he'd like to nominate someone from his staff to go on the expedition, he replied, "No. I'm keeping this job for myself!"

- The sixth walker was Chuck Harris, Executive Secretary of the Canadian Youth Hostels Association.

I was the seventh walker. Beginning in October of 1961, I started going on long weekend hikes with my young son and daughter to get in shape for the following spring.

For transport, I made sure we were well equipped. From my three years in the Canadian Army in World War II, I remembered carrying a huge pack and a rifle on 25-mile (40-km) route marches, and I didn't want anyone to have to carry anything on this expedition. We got the loan of two sizeable trucks from two major motor companies. Tiny Bennett drove one, loaded with all the camp gear. Bob Shannon had the other one rigged up as a field kitchen.

Preparations cost The Telegram surprisingly little. Many suppliers gave us free loans of camp equipment when I explained the purpose of the expedition and the publicity that would surround it. I especially remember one new business called Complete Rent-alls Limited. They charged us practically nothing for a whole camp outfit. I made sure they were mentioned often in Telegram stories about the hike. Woods Tent and Awning also loaned us their famous eiderdown sleeping bags.

Chapter 3
Ready To Go

Finally our preparations were complete. Advance stories had been featured prominently in the newspaper, and on April 21, 1962, we were ready to go. It was the Saturday at the start of the Easter holidays—a beautiful sunny day, as I recall. We collected everybody, said goodbye to families and around 9 A.M. arrived at our starting point at the parking area of a Canadian Ministry of Transport wireless station atop the Niagara Escarpment on Cedar Springs Road north of the Dundas Highway in Burlington. Here we piled out of the vehicles and, following Aubrey Diem's maps, began to head cross-country to the hamlet of Lowville for our first lunch stop on the first-ever hike on the Bruce Trail. Meanwhile, our two trucks chugged north up the road, Bob Shannon heading for Lowville Park to start cooking Irish stew and biscuits for lunch, and Tiny Bennett driving to Kelso Conservation Area, at the edge of Milton, to set up our first night's camp.

It was a long day's hike for seven people with feet not too accustomed to tramping all day. And I still remember how, as we limped into Kelso about 5:30 P.M., Ray Lowes and Bob Bateman pointed out a pileated woodpecker shrieking a welcome to us, the flaming red on its head unmistakable. We also saw turkey vultures, which in those days were rare in Ontario and were just starting to move up the Escarpment from Niagara. They are fairly common now. In forty-seven years, they have spread northward from the Niagara Peninsula to north of Parry Sound.

At Kelso, we were delighted to find a comfortable camp and a wonderful dinner waiting for us—thick steaks, mashed potatoes and gravy, and a bottle of Tiny Bennett's home-made wine. I had told Bob Shannon to get extra-good steaks, ignoring Doug MacFarlane's admonition: "Don't assume you're in the steak belt once you are west of the Humber River!"

That evening, we started what was to become a nightly routine. One of the walkers, I think it was Bob Bateman, began reading the first of Geoffrey Chaucer's *The Canterbury Tales*. I had always intended to read through this collection of ancient stories told by a group of pilgrims on a 1300s trek from London to martyred Archbishop Thomas à Becket's shrine at Canterbury. I didn't get around to it until the Bruce Trail Expedition, when I thought it would be a good idea to have each of us read one of the tales around the campfire each night. They didn't turn out to be as dull as I had expected. In fact, some of them are downright bawdy. For a laugh, you should read them sometime.

When she was reading my manuscript for this book, Kim Grove suggested that I had brushed off *The Canterbury Tales* too lightly. She felt that many readers would have never heard of Geoffrey Chaucer, and she thought that I should devote a little more space to him and his tales. So I borrowed a copy of the *Tales* from the public library and tried to re-read them. In spite of aids to translation in the margin and at the bottom of each page, it was not easy figuring out Chaucer's 1300s English. This recalled the difficulty we had had trying to read the tales by the light of lanterns and campfires on the Bruce Trail Expedition.

From the introduction to the book, we had learned that Chaucer was the son of a rich wine merchant. In 1357, young Geoffrey became a page in the household of Prince Lionel of England, and he grew up to become an important bureaucrat around the courts of King Richard II and Edward III. He also became a famous poet and has been described as the greatest figure in English literature before William Shakespeare. Aside from *The Canterbury Tales*, he is best remembered for his long poem entitled *Troilus and Criseyde*. It appears that he wrote *The Canterbury Tales* after his retirement as an official of the Royal Court of England. In retirement, one of his perks from the king was entitlement to a pitcher of wine every day for life. He died in 1400 and was the first to be buried in the Poets Corner of Westminster Abbey.

That first night at Kelso set the pattern for the delightful evenings we were to have for the next week: good food, comfortable camps and entertaining company—and tired feet.

In all, we had seven overnight stops. Our treks each day had been planned to increase in length as we got toughened up to walking. After a good breakfast and at noon a hot lunch, often beside a lonely country road, we had a midday rest to prepare us for the long afternoon walk. Some of us got blisters. Bob Shannon had been told by his doctor-father how we should soak our feet each night. There's a photo of me that ran on Page One of The Telegram. I'm shown pounding out a news story on a portable typewriter about that day's hike while sitting with my feet in a basin of warm water and Epsom salts.

Our day-long walks, aside from sore feet, were a lot of fun. To pick out our routes, we had to follow a line marked on topographical maps, mostly across open country, up and down hills, over fences and across streams (often on logs). This was escarpment country and our hike involved quite a lot of rock climbing. We helped each other frequently.

We walked in pairs, taking turns in acting as leaders. There were many pauses to consult the maps, and we wrote various notes on them to help people who would come after us to build the trail. Often we met owners of the land we were crossing. Permission for our passage had been cleared in advance, so there was no difficulty about trespassing. While walking, we talked to pass the time, bragging about our kids. I seem to remember that I asked Bob Bateman about buying one of his paintings and he told me I could get one for "a few hundred dollars". I never followed this up and missed the chance to acquire a work of art that would become very valuable in later years.

You might be interested in hearing about the seven spots where we camped on the hike. They were:

- Kelso Conservation Area near Rattlesnake Point at Milton
- A small trailer-camp site called Waterfalls Park,

halfway between Milton and Caledon and close to Terra Cotta

- William Kendall's farm west of Hwy 10 in Caledon Township. Mr. Kendall was an aerial photo expert who was praised by Winston Churchill during World War II and founded an important company called Aerial Surveys Limited
- The Goodyear Boy Scout Camp in the Hockley Valley
- Ed Huxtable's Outdoor Education Centre and farm on the Pine River near Horning's Mills
- The Devil's Glen Provincial Park on the Mad River near Singhampton
- The Canadian Youth Hostel, northwest of Collingwood at Craigleith

On the first day of our hike, The Telegram had given us a big spread on Page One. Every subsequent day, as soon as we hit camp, I had to sit down at a typewriter and write a story about that day's walking. John Sharpe, our Telegram photographer from Hamilton, acted as courier. He would meet us late in the afternoon, take pictures and drive my copy back to Bay and Melinda Streets for the next day's paper.

To brush up my memory forty-seven years after the actual first hike in 1962, I unearthed and read the seven stories I had pounded out on that portable typewriter. Here's a sample from one of them. On Monday, April 23, the story began on Page One of The Telegram and continued on Page Two. The two-column heading proclaimed: "On the Trail. Many

Blisters but it's Worth it." Underneath was the byline: "By Harvey Currell, Telegram District Editor". The story itself then followed:

"With The Telegram Bruce Trail Team—Three days and 14 sore feet after starting out to walk the proposed route of Ontario's first long-distance hiking trail, seven of us agree that the benefits are worth the blisters. We left Waterdown district Saturday morning on the first lap of our 112-mile (179-km) walk up the Niagara Escarpment to pioneer the Bruce Trail— just a line on the map so far. Up to now we have:

- Explored one of Ontario's limestone caves with its stalactites, stalagmites and two-metre deep pond, by the light of birchbark torches.
- Walked for miles along the brow of sheer limestone cliffs that are high enough to let you look down on big turkey vultures, soaring effortlessly over the valleys below. They're one of Ontario's rarest bird species and we've seen more in three days than many naturalists see in years.
- Discovered the joy of stopping, hot, tired and dusty, beside a cold spring that bubbles from limestone in a quiet valley."

After naming the walkers on the Telegram-sponsored team, the story went on:

"We explored the cave on the Mount Nemo section of the trail soon after our start Saturday morning. Bob Bateman led us to it but asked that its exact location not be revealed until the trail is actually built and arrangements made to safeguard the cave. This is because of the stalactites and stalagmites, beautiful limestone formations that are extremely rare in Ontario. Slender icicles of stone, the stalactites hang down from the vaulted ceiling to meet stalagmites—columns rising from the floor. It probably takes something like 1,000 years to form a stalactite from the continual dripping from the ceiling of water loaded with dissolved limestone. A souvenir-hunter could smash one in a second.

"....during the fuss of starting on our hike in the morning, nobody thought about getting flashlights from the Willys Jeep station wagons that a support team is using to move our camp equipment every day. When we got to the cave entrance, we had to improvise with birchbark torches. There was a steep passageway, just wide enough for one man at a time. At the bottom of it was a 30-foot (9-metre) drop to the big main chamber and the lake. There was a long pole which Bob Bateman and some of his students who've formed a speleology (cave fanciers) club use as a ladder. Since we weren't properly equipped, we decided not to go down. The cave is just one of hundreds of interest points that will dot the Bruce Trail when it's completed from Niagara to the Bruce Peninsula."

The story continued with more details about Saturday's hike and Sunday's hike and information about our campsites.

Later daily stories told about hiking across the "Cheltenham Badlands" in Caledon Township and about a civic reception at the Goodyear Boy Scout Camp in Hockley Valley.

This publicity about the Bruce Trail proved to be of enormous benefit to the eventual establishment of the Trail. Local weekly newspapers sent reporters to meet us and get interviews about the hike. Radio stations from Barrie, Orillia and Collingwood ran news reports about our progress. Local farmers and residents met us at crossroads, sometimes with gifts like cookies and maple syrup. And we had visitors at our camps each night.

Ray Lowes told me before he died in 2007 at age 96 that in his opinion the publicity developed by The Telegram Expedition was the single most important factor in making the Bruce Trail familiar to the Ontario public and in gaining acceptance for the idea of a long-distance public footpath up the length of the Niagara Escarpment.

Chapter 4

A Memorable Experience

For the walkers, it was a memorable experience. We got to know each other and exchanged ideas and life stories. In a book about his career as a wildlife artist, Bob Bateman said the hike still lives vividly in his memory. While walking, he told us about his trip to Kenya. I remember the story about an elephant that had found a stalk of bananas stashed under a Volkswagen. For months afterwards, it turned over every Volkswagen it saw, hoping to get another bunch of bananas.

For me, it was certainly the most convenient and comfortable hike I have ever experienced, thanks to the work and enthusiasm of Bob Shannon and Tiny Bennett. Tiny, I'm sad to say, died suddenly of a heart attack about 20 years ago. Bob Shannon later worked for the federal Ministry of Northern Affairs and Natural Resources. He retired a few years ago

Eventually we arrived at Craigleith, thinner and fitter than when we started, and with much more knowledge about the Niagara Escarpment. After we had been greeted by the mayor of Collingwood and other dignitaries and given commemorative gifts of Blue Mountain pottery, we held a meeting to make suggestions to the Bruce Trail Committee about how we thought the building of the trail should be organized. We suggested:

- That an overall Bruce Trail Association should be formed. This is now called the Bruce Conservancy.
- That the Trail should be divided into manageable sections, with a descriptive local name for each.
- That local Bruce Trail Clubs should be formed for each section to actually build and maintain the Trail.
- That the maps and records of our hike should be turned over to Phil Gosling to assist him in organizing the Trail.

The whole Telegram Bruce Trail Expedition forms one of those memories that last a lifetime.

There's one aspect of it, however, that still especially tugs my heart strings whenever I think about it. It concerns my son, Bob. At the start of this book, I left him clinging—with a crutch and a geologist hammer—to a cliff at Devil's Glen Provincial Park, near Singhampton. It's time now to explain what happened with Bob.

Chapter 5

What Happened To Bob

At that time, in 1962, Bob was 11 years old—just a wonderful delightful kid who had gone through a long, painful and tedious illness. It had all begun about six months earlier late one November afternoon when I had arrived home at 6 Springbook Gardens in Etobicoke to find two school friends half-carrying Bob home from Fairfield Junior School, a block away from our house. Bob was obviously in great pain. His friends explained that he had fallen while playing soccer and could not get up.

After a word to my wife Josephine, who had to stay with our daughter Judith, I got Bob into my car and drove to the Emergency Department at St. Joseph's Hospital. There they hustled Bob into X-ray, and I settled down for an anxious long wait. It proved to be unusually long until a young intern came to inform me that they were waiting for a resident doctor in bone surgery to come to talk to me about Bob's accident.

By this time, I sensed that there was something involved beyond a simple fracture, and I was becoming very tense. Finally a Dr. Dale, who had been just ready to start an off-duty weekend, walked into the waiting room and said to me, "I'm afraid I have some bad news." This almost floored me. "What is it?" I blurted. "We've found that your son has a massive bone tumour in his pelvis," Dr. Dale told me. "His fall has broken the surrounding bone and he's in a lot of pain. We've admitted him to hospital and are helping him with the pain."

The word "tumour" had of course triggered a spasm of fear. My first question was: "Is it malignant?"

"We can't tell at this stage," the doctor replied. "There's a good chance that it is not, but we'll have to do a biopsy tomorrow morning, take a bone sample and wait for the pathology lab report." He then explained that although reports on tissue samples could be made very quickly, the same was not true about bone specimens. A longer process was required for a definite finding, and it would be two or three days before we could know about Bob. A major operation would definitely be required.

With my heart in my shoes and trying desperately to keep a cheerful face, I was allowed to see Bob for a few minutes. He was drowsy from pain medication but was concerned chiefly that his mother would be worried about him.

Then I had to drive home and tell Josephine and our 13-year-old daughter, Judith, about the outlook for Bob. Josephine, bless her, was her usual strong self. I told her, "If this is cancer, it could mean Bob will die. It could also mean he won't be able to walk again." Jo replied, "Harvey, we have to be strong for Bob's sake. It will not be cancer and he will walk again. We have to trust God and pray." After a few minutes, she also added, "We should phone Dr. MacDonald."

Picture by Hugh Winsor

At age ten, Bob became the first Cub Scout in Etobicoke to win all the possible Proficiency badges. This picture was taken a few weeks before the discovery of a massive tumour in his pelvis which required a bone graft from his father.

This thought cheered me a little. Dr. John Laing MacDonald was the father of John Bruce MacDonald, one of my best friends. Dr. MacDonald was Chief Surgeon at Wellesley Hospital in Toronto and a bone surgeon at Toronto Hospital for Sick Children.

He was also personal physician to George McCullough, a mining millionaire who at that time owned The Toronto Telegram. And Dr. MacDonald had once asked McCullough to find a job at The Telegram for his son, John. McCullough obliged.

Originally, at his father's insistence, young John had started a pre-med program at the University of Toronto. But to his father's dismay, he had dropped out after a year. Then at The Telegram, John had been given a reporter's job and placed under my guidance. I found that although highly intelligent and well educated, John really did not have the aptitude for newspaper writing. He was an avid angler, however, and deeply interested in outdoor subjects. After a few fishing trips and visits to my cottage on Lake Manitouwabing near Parry Sound, I told him he should be in university, studying one of the natural sciences, probably forestry. He had the entrance qualifications and parents well able to pay his tuition fees. John finally agreed and announced to his parents that he'd decided to go back to school. Dr. MacDonald was especially happy about this and told me he felt he owed me a debt. If I or my family ever needed a bone doctor, we were to call him immediately.

So I phoned Dr. MacDonald about Bob that same Friday night. He had previously met Bob and was deeply concerned. He said he would call St. Joseph's

Hospital and arrange to attend the biopsy the next morning as a consultant and would meet me at the hospital. He had operated in many similar cases and the odds were very much in our favour. After a disturbed night, I was at the hospital next morning to meet Dr. MacDonald and Dr. George Pennall, Chief of Bone Surgery at St. Joseph's. They took Bob to an operating room, cut back tissue and obtained a bone sample.

There followed three of the most difficult days of my life. On the Sunday, I drove up to Caledon to keep an appointment to do a Trip column about a gift shop on Caledon Mountain. I had trouble concentrating but, in spite of my worries, enjoyed meeting a young couple who were struggling to build a new business for themselves in the country. I then went home and wrote the story about them. Jo gave the news about Bob to our dismayed parents and we settled down to wait.

Bob, now a professor of forestry, with his dad and
sister, Judith. With a degree from the University of
Western Ontario, Judith is a keen naturalist.

Dr. Pennall, who it turned out had been an elementary-school pupil of Josephine's Aunt Mary, an Etobicoke principal, had told us he would try to hasten the lab report. We got it from Dr. Dale on Monday, the most welcome news I've ever received. The word was "negative": the tumour was not malignant but benign!

I was also told that Dr. Pennall and Dr. MacDonald would like to see me that afternoon at St. Joseph's. I met them at the hospital and they explained the operation that would take place in two days, to be performed by Dr. Pennall. The tumour had left a large cavity in Bob's pelvis. It would be necessary to fill this with a framework of sound healthy bone. This required a fairly major bone graft. Bob didn't have enough bone mass to supply the bone from his own body. There had to be a bone donor. To ensure success of the graft, the donor should be a close family member. The obvious family member was me.

What the doctors proposed was that I would be admitted to hospital on Tuesday (the next day), submit to tests Tuesday afternoon, and on Wednesday morning bright and early be wheeled into one operating room while Bob was in one next door. Muscle and tissue would be cut back from my pelvis, and bone would then be cut away to be hurried in to Bob for the reconstruction work on his pelvis.

I was in good health. I had never had any kind of surgery and had never been in hospital except for a brief spell of pneumonia while in the Canadian Army in World War II. That afternoon, I went down to The Telegram to give the news to Doug MacFarlane that I would be off work for two weeks. An assistant was assigned to take over my job, and most of the editorial staff came to express concern about Bob and to wish me a speedy recovery.

On Tuesday, as planned, I was admitted to hospital and prepped for the next day's operation. It felt strange being a hospital patient while in perfect health. I went to the Children's Ward to see Bob and cheered him up by telling him that the doctors were sure he would make a complete recovery and be walking again by spring.

Next day, both operations took place successfully. I woke up in a recovery room at lunch time, swathed in bandages and with a drain tube in my side and a long surgical incision closed by a neat line of stitches. Because of the bone reconstruction work, Bob's operation took longer, but by mid-afternoon he was conscious. Sister Mary Louise, a nun and senior nurse who was public relations officer for the hospital, came to my room to help get me into a wheelchair to visit Bob. When I saw him, he was flat on his back in a cast from neck to ankles. As they wheeled me into his room, Bob broke into his usual wonderful smile and said, "Hi Dad. They've taken bone from you and planted it in me." Sister Mary Louise told him, "I guess that makes you a chip off the old block!" It did my heart good to hear Bob laugh at this little joke. He was to repeat it many times afterwards when friends and family asked about his operation.

I remained in hospital about two weeks until my incision was healed, then convalesced at home for a week or so until it was time to have my stitches removed. I was eager to get back to work and to resume my Trip columns. A brief note had been printed in The Telegram stating that I had been sick but would soon resume the column. We never ran any story about Bob's illness and the bone graft.

Bob stayed in hospital for most of December. On a wonderful day just before Christmas, he came home by ambulance. His grandparents were there to greet him along with a small crowd of neighbours, school friends and teachers. Josephine cried, from happiness, as the ambulance attendants carefully manoeuvred Bob into the bedroom we had prepared for him on the ground floor of our storey-and-a-half house at 6

Springbrook Gardens.

Jo and I had put a lot of thought into fitting out our bedroom for Bob, keeping in mind that he would be confined there for almost three months. We put a new mattress on the double bed. We moved our old Admiral black-and-white TV into the room. We already had a bedside telephone in the room. We rigged a big bedside table where Bob could spread his possessions, and we set up a big easel where he could draw and write with a supply of pens, coloured pencils and crayons. We both had worried about how a long confinement would affect Bob's morale and personality. It didn't bother him at all. He was chiefly concerned about the extra work it created for his mother.

The next three months proved to be a busy interval for our super son, and the weeks went by quickly. A Victorian Order nurse came regularly to change his dressing. Our family doctor, Frank McKenna, visited him. An Etobicoke Board of Education home-service teacher named Mrs. Merrithew came twice a week to keep him up to date on school work and left him assignments to keep him busy. At least once a week, Delbert Gainer, the principal of Fairfield Junior School, brought a different group of kids from Bob's class for an informal visit that always turned out to be lots of fun. Kids from along the street were always dropping in with little treats for Bob and sometimes bringing their dogs and cats. Everybody wanted to autograph Bob's plaster cast. A couple of times Bob went by ambulance to the hospital for X-rays to make sure that the bone graft was knitting properly.

Finally, in March, the great day arrived when Bob's cast was to be removed. I knew that something about this was bothering him and finally he told me: It was about the electric saw that would be used to cut off the cast. Bob dreaded the thought that it might cut into his skin. When we got to the hospital by ambulance, I hunted down the technician in the plaster lab and told him about Bob's anxiety. He said, "Leave it to me." Before the procedure began, he gave Bob a small lecture about the whole process and showed him the saw—something like a dentist's drill—and the safeguard equipment. Then he told Bob, "This is a great moment for you. Just relax and enjoy it." Bob did, and in less than a minute, after three months, the cast was off. Bob was able to stretch his legs and in a few minutes was able to sit up in a wheelchair and sit in our car for the ride home.

After a week or two in the wheelchair, Bob graduated to crutches and was soon happily cavorting up and down Springbrook Gardens and walking on crutches to and from school, toning his muscles and enjoying his freedom.

All winter, of course, I had been working on plans for the Bruce Trail Expedition and everything had been clicking into place for the opening day. We'd had many meetings with Ray Lowes, Dr. Aubrey Diem, Bob Shannon and Tiny Bennett. Some of the meetings were in Bob's bedroom and he was eager to know all the details. Eventually, he asked the question that I knew was coming: "Can I come with you?" Bob didn't need to argue the point. How could I say anything but "Yes" to a kid who had been a real hero through a frightening illness? On my own responsibility, I decided to take him along. I didn't mention it to anybody at The Telegram and never told Doug MacFarlane. I just asked Bob Shannon and Tiny Bennett if it was OK with them.

Bob obviously could not walk with the hiking group. The doctors had decreed that for the rest of his school career he was to avoid all contact sports—hockey, football, even baseball—and that he should concentrate on swimming as his main physical activity. He had to have regular X-ray checks on his bone condition and might require a second minor operation in a couple of years. Nevertheless, both Bob Shannon and Tiny said they'd be happy to have Bob along on the expedition. He could take turns riding with them in their trucks. So Bob did come along on the Bruce Trail hike and he learned a lot from it. He made friends with all the hikers and questioned them about their professions. And he quickly volunteered to help with jobs around the camp and field kitchen, even agreeing to wash dishes.

There's only one thing I regret about the whole thing. I neglected my daughter, Judith. Jo and I had arranged that she should spend the expedition week with her friend Diane Murkar, at Pickering. It wasn't until many years later that Judith told me how bitterly disappointed she had been that I had not invited her to come on the hike. I went over all the difficulties that would arise over having one 14-year-old girl with a group of men. Judith still thinks she should have come.

If Judith had been there to keep an eye on Bob, he

would not have wandered off to climb down a cliff looking for fossils. As a matter of fact, no harm came to Bob because of the fossil hunt. He did get his trilobite and it may still be part of his collection. Both Bob Shannon and Tiny Bennett, however, had missed him on that afternoon at Devil's Glen and had started looking for him. Both were horrified to find him clinging to a cliff, and they took great precautions to get him safely down. It's perhaps an exaggeration to call it a cliff. Bob himself has always insisted that it was only a steep slope with a ledge slanting down on it and that he was perfectly safe. I learned about it later that day when I arrived at camp with the walking party after a particularly long day's hike. Bob's mother did not hear about it until we got home. The whole incident has since become part of the Currell family's Bruce Trail lore.

The expedition ended successfully and the actual building of the trail got underway. There were three good results from the Telegram effort. It generated wide publicity and support for the concept of a trail up the Niagara Escarpment. It acquainted landowners with the idea of a trail so that they became ready to consider allowing it to cross their property. It made Ontario citizens generally aware of what a natural treasure the province has in the Niagara Escarpment and it eventually led to the formation of the Niagara Escarpment Commission and legislation to protect and preserve the Escarpment.

Happily, Bob made a complete recovery from his surgery and became a champion swimmer, earning the Royal Life Saving Society Bronze Medallion and the Award of Merit. On graduation from elementary school, he wrote the competitive examination for the University of Toronto Schools and was accepted. After high-school graduation from U.T.S., he entered the forestry program at U of T, earned a Bachelor of Science degree in forestry and later a Master's degree in the same science. As a young forester, he worked in northern Ontario, at Bella Coola, B.C., and on Vancouver Island. He then moved back to Ontario to take a professor's post at Sault College in Sault Ste. Marie. As I write this, he is coordinator of natural resources at his college and an officer of the Canadian Institute of Forestry, and he divides his time between teaching his students and working in the woods.

The Bruce Trail has become a reality and was officially opened during Canada's Centennial celebration in 1967. Both Josephine and I took an active part in the formation and the operations of the Toronto Bruce Trail Club, and I wrote many columns for The Toronto Telegram and Toronto Sun about various sections of the trail.

If you'd like to go for a walk on the Bruce Trail, it won't cost you anything. The trail was built by volunteers for use by citizens. You might have to pay for parking to access the trail at some provincial parks or conservation areas.

To learn about the trail, however, it's a good idea to become a member of the Bruce Trail Conservancy and to buy a copy of the excellent Bruce Trail Guidebook. This will cost you a little money. The membership fee is $50 a year. The guidebook, with detailed maps and information on each section, costs $35. Across

Ontario, the Bruce Trail Conservancy has more than 8,000 members. The Toronto Bruce Trail Club has 3,000 members.

With membership in the Bruce Trail Conservancy, you get the privilege of joining one of the nine local Bruce Trail Clubs that do the actual work of maintaining the trail. Through the year, the clubs hold organized hikes, work outings and many other events that introduce members to each other. Each of the nine clubs is responsible for one section of the trail. You can choose to join any of the nine clubs, depending chiefly on where you live.

Starting from the southeast, the local Bruce Trail Clubs are:

- The Niagara Bruce Trail Club was one of the first to be formed.
- The Iroquois Club. Its long span of the Trail circles Hamilton and the west end of Lake Ontario.
- The Toronto Club. This is the biggest of the nine, with more than 3,000 members. It's also the most active, with hundreds of hikes per year. Many hikes provide bus transport from Toronto pickup points. Besides hikes on the Bruce Trail, the Toronto Club organizes many expeditions to other scenic areas and provides lots of educational and social sessions.
- The Caledon Hills Club takes in a rugged hilly section where the Oak Ridges Interlobate Moraine meets the Niagara Escarpment.
- The Dufferin Hi-Lands Club covers Dufferin County north of Orangeville, taking in the

lovely hills and sparkling streams of Mono and Mulmur.

- The Beaver Valley Club's area covers one of Ontario's most scenic valleys, famous for its skiing and hiking.
- The Blue Mountain Club maintains the Trail section through high escarpment hills circling the southern end of Georgian Bay.
- The Sydenham Club takes in the city of Owen Sound with many waterfalls and beautiful high bluffs along the western shore of Georgian Bay.
- The Peninsula Club oversees the end of the Trail, up the limestone Bruce Peninsula to Tobermory.

For information about the Trail and the Bruce Trail Guidebook, you can call the Bruce Trail Conservancy head office at 1-800-665-4453 or go to the website at www.brucetrail.org. The office is in an historic farmhouse, called Rasberry House, on the grounds of the Royal Botanical Gardens at Hamilton.

PART TWO: TEN TRIPS

Chapter 6

An Expedition To The Top Of Ontario
Ogidaki Mountain And Its Mysterious
Artesian Well

This is the first of three sections of this book devoted to stories about some of the most interesting trips I took in the forty-nine years I wrote a weekly Trip column for The Toronto Telegram (from 1958 to 1971) and The Toronto Sun (from 1971 to 2007).

One of the trips I remember most vividly was to the top of Ogidaki Mountain (pronounced O-ji-dike-ee), about 80 km (50 miles) northwest of Sault Ste. Marie, Ontario. That was back in September 1968. If you drive some kind of rugged SUV and are attracted by challenging terrain, you might want to try to retrace my steps to this remarkable beauty spot. I think it will eventually become famous as an Ontario visitor attraction. And maybe someday, Ontario will build a special scenic highway through these impressive mountains that parallel Lake Superior between Sault Ste. Marie and Thunder Bay.

When I was there, Ogidaki Mountain at 665.4 metres (2,183 feet) above sea level had just been identified as the highest spot in all Ontario. That's what attracted me. Another nearby spot called Tiptop Mountain has since also been named as the possible highest spot.

There was a road to Ogidaki at the time, because a forest ranger named Bill Maki was stationed there from May to September as lookout man on a 30-metre (100-foot) forest-fire tower. His lonely job was to watch for smoke clouds indicating forest fires, to take a bearing on them with an alidade telescope, and to radio the angle in to a central station. Using bearings from other towers as well, the station would pinpoint the fire's location and send a crew in by canoe and on foot to suppress the fire in its early stages or radio for more help.

I haven't been back to Ogidaki since 1968, but I've talked about it with Steve Acorn, an officer of the Ontario Ministry of Natural Resources district office that is responsible for this vast area of mini-mountains between the Sault and Thunder Bay. This is one of the most rugged and scenic sections in all Ontario, full of lakes, rivers and hidden waterfalls. It is largely unknown because there are very few roads into it. Those that do exist are horrible—a challenge to all but the most rugged vehicles. Steve Acorn told me a few months ago that the road right up to Ogidaki Mountain is no longer driveable since the tower is now not maintained as a forest-fire lookout. The tower is used as a private communications facility and you are not allowed to climb it.

If you do intend to visit Ogidaki Mountain, you'll need to do some preliminary work. First you have to drive to Sault Ste. Marie, about 678 km (424 miles) northwest of Toronto. I like the Sault, mostly because my son, Bob, teaches there at Sault College, but also because I find it one of the most interesting and attractive locations in northern Ontario. Here, the waters of Lake Superior pour down the St. Mary's River into Lake Huron through a spectacular rapids bypassed by two canal systems: one on the Canadian and one on the U.S. side of the river.

Once in the Sault, go to an outdoor store called The Trading Post at 1332 Great Northern Road (telephone 705-759-4518) and ask for Mike Dowding. From him you can buy a topographic map that covers the Searchmont area. The correct map number will probably be 41 K16 or 41 N1.

Next, it's a good idea to call and arrange to visit Steve Acorn at the Ministry of Natural Resources. His phone number is 705-949-5132. He probably knows more about Ogidaki and how to get there than anybody in the Sault.

Plan a whole day for your expedition to the top of Ontario. It's only about 80 km (50 miles) but they are the kind of kilometres over which you'll need to drive slowly and carefully. Steve Acorn will probably mark the route for you on your topographic map. You'll likely have to walk the last two km or so up the mountain. At the top, you're on the roof of Ontario. At 665.4 metres (2,183 feet) above sea level, you're 123.3 metres (408 feet) higher than the highest spot in southern Ontario, which is at 541 metres (1,775 feet) on a farm beside Edwards Lake near Singhampton.

One of the first things I noticed atop Ogidaki was a beautiful ice-cold gushing spring, pouring into a stream that hurried down to Lake Superior. I asked Bill Maki, the tower jock, "Where does the water come from? This is the highest point for hundreds of miles around." He couldn't make a guess. Neither could I. The conventional explanation for springs and artesian wells is that rain falls on high ground and then percolates down through soil until it reaches an impermeable layer of clay or rock. Below ground, the water is supposed to seep on a downward slope to an opening where it pushes to the surface as a spring. But this obviously does not explain the presence of a spring on the highest point of a huge region.

Since 1968, I've been curious about the spring on Ogidaki Mountain and other springs I've seen or heard about on tops of mountains or very high hills. One of my hobbies is geology, the study of rocks and the crust of the earth. I've asked geologists about this spring. One of them suggested a dual explanation that seems reasonable. He said that in some regions—particularly in mountainous areas where there has been ancient volcanic activity or movement of the earth's crust—natural pipes, shafts or funnels have been broken very deeply into the earth's mantle. Water may have percolated far down these passages and been turned into steam by internal heat from below the surface. Alternatively, water vapour may have been formed by combustion of hydrogen and oxygen in volcanic activity. In either case, internal pressures force the H_2O vapour up toward the surface, where it cools into liquid water. The latter is then forced further upwards through cracks, shafts or pipes and emerges in the form of springs.

Chapter 7
The Shy Beauties Of Purdon's Bog

In 2007, CBC Radio sponsored a contest to name the Seven Wonders of Canada. Listeners were invited to nominate their choices for the eventual winners. I didn't submit a nomination. But if I had it would have been Purdon's Bog, a conservation area in the Ottawa Valley about 360 km (225 miles) from Toronto.

What makes this secluded wetland famous is that it's the home of Canada's biggest and most vivid display of wild orchids. Here, from mid-June to early July, up to 16,000 blooms of the showy Lady's Slipper, our most spectacular orchid, burst out in glorious display. There's a 400-metre (quarter-mile) wheelchair-accessible boardwalk through the middle of the orchids. You can admire them and photograph or draw them, but be very careful not to touch—their leaves give off a fluid similar to that exuded by poison ivy.

When I last went to Purdon's Bog in 1999, there was no admission charge or parking charge. Instead, visitors were invited to make a donation to the Mississippi Valley Conservation Authority which owns and operates the site.

Besides being home to Canada's biggest and most outstanding collection of wild orchids, Purdon's Bog is outstanding for another reason. It's the result of the determination of one farmer, named Joe Purdon, to develop a beauty spot for his neighbours and fellow citizens. Back in the 1930s, Joe found twelve orchids in his swamp. He recognized their unique beauty, identified them and set out to protect and cultivate them. From libraries and botanists he learned about their biology. Carefully thinning the swamp's cedar and tamarack trees, he worked to give the orchids the correct combination of sun and shade. He regulated water levels and worked for forty years to develop a colony of more than 40,000 specimens.

Towards the end of his life, Joe Purdon arranged to have the 24-hectare (60-acre) site turned over to the Mississippi Valley Conservation Authority in 1984. Don't be confused by the name. The Conservation Authority has nothing to do with the U.S. Mississippi River. In Ontario we have our own Mississippi, which runs into the Ottawa River near Arnprior.

The Authority is headquartered near the village of Lanark. Staff have done an admirable job of protecting Purdon's Bog and making it accessible to visitors. Guides are usually on duty in the summer months.

If you go for a visit, take insect repellent and binoculars. More than forty species of birds are seen here. There are also many other rare plants, including the pitcher plant that traps and drowns insects for food. From a lookout point, you can observe a beaver dam which helps control water flow through the fen. There are picnic tables and washrooms as well as information about the Mill of Kintail historic site near Almonte.

For information, call the Mississippi Valley Conservation Authority at 613-259-2421.

To get to Purdon's Bog, take Hwy 401 east to Hwy 37 at Belleville. Go north on 37 to Hwy 7 at Actinolite. Travel east on No. 7 for 99 km to Lanark Rd. 511 at the west end of Perth. Go left (north) up 511 through Lanark. Follow 511 from the middle of Lanark for 6.3 km to County Road 8, also called Watsons Corners Rd. Go left up this road for 7.2 km to the 8th Concession of Dalhousie, where there are Purdon's Bog direction signs. Turn right on the 8th Concession and drive for 2 km to the Purdon's Bog parking area.

Chapter 8

Visit A Sculptor Who's Becoming A Legend

I think sculptors are the kings and queens of Canadian art.

Start talking about sculpture with artists in Canada and you're certain to hear about Brenda Wainman Goulet. She's a talented mother of three who's known in art circles for three life-size figures: artist Tom Thomson, in the Town Square at Huntsville; Dr. Norman Bethune, in front of the Gravenhurst Opera House; and Nurse Rene Caisse, at Totem Pole Park in Bracebridge.

When I last talked to Brenda in 2004, at her home beside Walker Lake in Muskoka, she was working on a bronze life-size figure of Elizabeth Gwillim Simcoe intended to be placed in a parkette in front of the post office in the town of Bradford West Gwillimbury about 64 km (40 miles) north of Toronto. Elizabeth was the wife of Ontario's first Lieutenant-Governor, John Graves Simcoe. Her family name was Gwillim, and because of her 1790s diaries she's almost as well-known among historians as her Governor husband.

If you're interested in Canadian art and Canadian history, you might want to take a trip to Huntsville, Gravenhurst and Bracebridge to have a look at Brenda's three completed masterworks. You might also want to phone for an appointment to visit her small gallery to see some of her other sculpture pieces. She has become famous among Muskoka cottagers and residents since she and her husband Paul Goulet moved to Walker Lake in 1987.

During my 2004 visit, Brenda showed me items such as River Race, a bronze otter chasing a fish over a rock bottom. It was priced at $3,200. I also admired Lakeside Bather, a bronze of a woman washing her hair on a rock, priced at $3,200, and Trail's End, a pair of snowshoes beside a snow-covered spruce, $1,400. Each sculpture represents many hours of painstaking work. And one-third of the cost goes to an art foundry for casting in bronze from Brenda's moulds.

Here's a measure of how much her Muskoka fans and neighbours admire Brenda and her work. The bills for her life-size public statues have been underwritten entirely by donations from the public.

Born in Huntsville, Brenda grew up in Algonquin Provincial Park where her father, Dave Wainman, was Deputy Chief Ranger. She moved to Etobicoke, a suburb of Toronto, to attend Richview Collegiate and then the Ontario College of Art where she specialized in sculpture and won a scholarship to specialize in bronze casting. After graduation she worked five years at an art foundry.

Most days you can find her working beside Walker Lake, where she generously takes time out to show visitors her work. Before you visit, you should phone for an appointment to 705-635-1996.

To get to the studio, take Hwy 11 north to Exit 223, Highway 60 at Huntsville. Go east on Hwy 60 for 12.8

km to Muskoka Rd. 8, Limberlost Rd. Go left on this road for 2.4 km to Walker Lake Rd. and left for .8 km to No. 1071 on the left.

Chapter 9

Neustadt—Where An Ancient Brewery Came Back To Life

If you like old-fashioned European-style beer, you should take a trip to Neustadt. Tucked away in the uplands of Grey County south of Owen Sound and about 170 km (106 miles) northwest of Toronto, it's a little jewel of a community that has three claims to fame:

In a 1990s Harrowsmith magazine feature, it was judged one of the 10 prettiest villages in Canada.

It produces spring-water beer from an ancient limestone brewery that dates back to the 1850s.

It's the birthplace of John Diefenbaker, "Dief the Chief", Prime Minister of Canada in the 1950s and 60s.

Neustadt has deep German-Canadian roots. Old-timers, most of whose ancestors migrated here from Waterloo County and Kitchener, pronounce the name of the community something like "Noycchtod".

A German brewer named Henry Hugther came here in the 1850s, found cold springs gushing from limestone caves and decided he'd found the perfect location for a brewery. Local legend says he imported stonemasons from Germany to hew cellars out of the limestone and to build a massive stone building where a locally famous beer was made from 1857 to 1916.

Prohibition laws closed the brewery in 1916. Most of it then sat idle for eighty-one years until a young British couple came to Neustadt in the 1990s. Val and Andy Stimpson—she's from Sheffield and he's from Manchester—had managed pubs for 20 years in North Wales and had experience in brewing. Visits on holidays to Ontario had given them a dream— they wanted to live here and run a country pub. A search of Ontario small towns convinced them, however, that it would be almost impossible to replicate a British pub in Ontario, so they searched for a small brewery instead.

A brewery-equipment supplier told them about the derelict Neustadt brewery. Against the advice of accountants, they poured their life savings and a small-business loan into rehabilitating and equipping the ancient brewery. After nine months of work, they opened at Christmas, 1997. Local residents were so happy at seeing the old brewery come to life that they bought out the entire stock of 9,600 bottles in five hours!

Neustadt now has just under a thousand residents. I was there in 2001 and have never forgotten the place where citizens, many of them retired farmers, cling to traditions of caring for the land, keeping things neat and clean and enjoying good beer.

When I talked to the Stimpsons recently, I found that only a few things have changed since 2001. One is that economic conditions have forced them to start switching from beer bottles to cans. They're still sell-ing about half their output in bottles, but eventually it will all be in cans.

When I was there, they were making three beers: ale, pilsner and a blend of both. Now they have created a new light lager, called Bruce County Premium. (Neustadt is in Grey County but is just over the line from Bruce.) For winter they've also added Big Dog Porter. This is an English-style brew with an unusual twist. It contains a three-percent blend of Pelee Island red wine and has proved to be a favourite.

You can get visitor information in the pine-paneled sales room of the Neustadt brewery and pick up a folder about the region. If you want to visit John Diefenbaker's birthplace, go on a summer weekend. That's the only time the house is open to visitors.

Two new restaurants have been opened in town. One is the Top End which serves pub fare. The other is Noah's Inn in an 1860 tavern. It features lunch and dinner. Hats off to Harry is still famous for hearty breakfasts.

To get to Neustadt, take Hwy 10 to Orangeville. Go left on former Hwy 9, now Dufferin Road 109, through Arthur and Clifford. Just past Clifford, go right on Grey County Rd. 10 for about 11 km to Neustadt.

Chapter 10
Inn The Woods

Hidden in the hills of Oro-Medonte, about 125 km (78 miles) north of Toronto and close to the village of Coldwater, the Copeland Forest has been absorbing carbon dioxide, pumping out oxygen, preserving ground water to feed trout streams and producing timber on a sustained-yield basis for more than a century. And tucked into the edge of that forest, on the Sixth Concession line, is a very special Bed and Breakfast inn that offers bird-watchers, skiers, hikers and nature lovers a base from which to enjoy all aspects of the forest. The warm-hearted couple who run the Bed and Breakfast are Bob and Betty Shannon. Their place is called Inn the Woods, and the name fits the location perfectly.

I consider it one of the best little inns in Ontario, but I have to admit that I'm prejudiced. I've been close friends with the Shannons for more than fifty years. It began when I was Suburban and District Editor of The Toronto Telegram and hired Bob as a reporter-photographer for Simcoe County. His father was Dr. Frank Shannon, a country physician and Simcoe County coroner. Betty, the girl who became Bob's wife, worked at the lunch counter in the Barrie bus terminal where one of her customers was a young singer named Gordon Lightfoot who went on to national fame.

After their marriage, Bob and Betty lived for a while in an old mill house near Painswick, south of Barrie. A few years later, when Bob joined the suburban staff of The Telegram, they moved to North York. Later still, Bob worked in public relations for Ontario Hydro, the City of North York and the federal government. And earlier in this book, I told how he was cook for the 1962 Toronto Telegram Bruce Trail Expedition.

Betty, who loves little kids, became widely known as the operator of a day nursery at Clarkson in Mississauga.

In 1998, with Bob having taken early retirement, the Shannons moved back to Simcoe County, bought Inn the Woods and started on a new career as innkeepers. They've become highly successful, partly because of the inn's scenic location but mostly owing to the care they take to make guests feel welcome and comfortable. Their house in the forest offers two king-size upstairs rooms with ensuite bathrooms, and a ground-floor family suite with a fireplace and living room. All guests are served a gourmet breakfast that may feature kippers, scrambled eggs, eggs Benedict, pancakes, local sausage, bacon, and maple syrup from a nearby farm.

From the big decks attached to the rear of the house, there is a dramatic view out into the forest and down onto a collection of bird-feeders that attract a wide variety of bird species. In fact, many keen bird-watchers have been able to record new additions to their "life lists" here. And every spring, Betty, who is herself a highly knowledgeable bird-watcher, runs day-long birding tours through the district.

Birds know they can trust Betty Shannon.
This chickadee takes a brief rest on her finger at Tiny Marsh, close to Inn the Woods.

In addition to all the birds, sometimes deer and the occasional otter slip up from local river valleys for a snack at the feeders.

The inn is also a favourite rendezvous for wild-flower fanciers. Every year in May, millions of trilliums, Ontario's provincial flower, carpet the forest floor. Guests book ahead to be sure to get rooms in trillium time, which usually peaks around Victoria Day.

In winter, three nearby ski resorts and free cross-country trails attract skiers to Inn the Woods.

For information and room reservations, call 1-800-289-6295 or 705-834-6193 or log onto www.innthe-woods.com.

Copeland Forest was owned and cared for over more than one hundred years by the Copeland family who provided a continuous supply of timber for Simcoe County sawmills. In 1978, the Ontario Ministry of Natural Resources bought the forest and now manages it as a sustained-yield multiple-use area with a network of free walking, ski and pedal-bike trails. For information, call the MNR Midhurst district office, 705-725-7500.

Chapter 11

Where To Find Maple Syrup

In early Spring when the sun is shining warmly, snow is melting and water is flowing, I love to visit any maple-syrup bush to witness the annual pioneer rite of making incredibly sweet syrup from maple sap. Essentially the process is simple: You just boil off the water content of about 40 gallons of sap until only one gallon is left. That's maple syrup. And for more than 200 years, farmers have been improving and refining the process in order to save energy and save time.

In early days, syrup-making was a kind of spring festival. Everybody in a family would troop down to the syrup shack to help. Neighbours who didn't make syrup in their own woodlots would visit the nearest who did and offer their services in exchange for a share of the syrup.

Syrup-making was labour-intensive in pioneer years. First of all, in late February or early March, you had to go into the maple bush with a hand-powered brace and bit to tap your maple trees. This consisted of boring a half-inch-diameter hole about two inches into each tree's outer bark and cambium layer and then hammering a small pipe or "spile" into it. In earliest times the spiles were wooden; later they became steel; now most of them are plastic. You hung a small pail on each spile and had to wait until spring advanced enough to stir the tree into sending sap up from the roots where it had been stored safe from freezing all winter. When the weather is right, sap flows briskly up to every living branch of the tree in order to produce new twig and leaf buds.

Sap, when you come to think of it, is actually the life fluid of a tree, analogous to the blood of a human body. Trees make huge quantities of sap and don't seem to miss the amount they give up for syrup any more than adult humans miss donations to blood banks.

A tree is actually a factory that takes water from the ground, plus dissolved minerals and chemicals from the earth, plus carbon dioxide from the air, and in a wonderful process called photosynthesis the tree uses its leaves to employ the light of the sun to make cellulose or wood for its continual growth. While doing so, trees make life possible on planet Earth by producing the oxygen we need to breathe. They absorb carbon dioxide into their leaves and break it down into carbon, which they keep for their own use, and oxygen, which they release into the air.

I see I have become sidetracked into talking about trees, which as a confirmed tree-hugger, I truly love. Now I'll get back to my main topic and tell you about Ken McCutcheon and his 6,500 beautiful maple trees on the Ninth Line North of Oro-Medonte Township, a few kilometres north of Barrie and about 125 km (78 miles) from Toronto.

Here, Ken and his wife Rene—who also makes

beautiful pottery—produce about 6,800 litres (1,500 gallons) of maple syrup every spring. The rest of the year, Ken tends to the several million bees that he keeps in about a hundred hives. The bees make honey which you can also buy in summertime, at the McCutcheon farm, along with samples of Rene's pottery.

There are several things that make the McCutcheon place outstanding. One is the fact that Ken has a habit of winning world championships for the quality of his maple syrup. In 2000 he took the top prize—the John David Eaton Award—at Toronto's Royal Winter Fair. That's the equivalent of the World Series in maple-syrup making. In 2005, he won it again and in 2007 he took the top RWF award for maple butter.

A second factor that I think makes the McCutcheon place outstanding is its warm welcoming and uncommercial atmosphere. The McCutcheons don't sell pancakes, sausages and coffee, but Rene and Ken have put a lot of work into making their syrup house attractive and interesting. Grouped around an old-time wood stove are charts, pictures and implements telling about maple trees and their wonderful life cycle.

The McCutcheon syrup process is an ultra-modern one. Early in February, Ken starts tapping some 6,500 trees and preparing the plastic pipes that carry sap from the trees to the evaporator. Three vacuum pumps speed up the process. In the syrup house, an oil-fired steam-heated evaporator can make up to 18 gallons of syrup an hour or 1,500 gallons per season. Ken, who attended the University of Guelph, designed and built the evaporator himself.

On weekends if there's snow on the ground, Ken usually boils some syrup extra thick and then pours it on snow to give kids a sample of maple candy. That used to be a spring treat for pioneer children, as store candy was scarce and expensive in those days.

The syrup season usually runs from mid-March to mid-April, the time when nights are cold and days are warm. During that period you can visit the farm seven days a week from 1 to 5 P.M. and buy syrup in attractive jugs of varying sizes. The phone number for information is 705-835-5780. The web site address is www.mcmaple.com. In summer, to buy honey or Rene's pottery, you can visit by chance or appointment.

The farm is at 3983 Ninth Line North of Oro-Medonte. Take Hwy 400 north from Barrie to Horseshoe Valley Road. Go right on this road for 14 km to Ninth Line North. Turn left and go 2.8 km to the McCutcheon farm on the right.

Chapter 12
Britt—The Hidden Pearl Of Georgian Bay

L ook at the top-left corner of a southern Ontario road map. You'll find very few roads leading off Highways 69 and 400 into the lonely northeast shore of Georgian Bay. The people who live, cottage and boat there like it that way. They love the solitude afforded by thousands of islands and long deep lonely fiords.

One of the fiords, about 70 km (44 miles) north of Parry Sound, is called Byng Inlet. On the south side of the inlet is a tiny community that is also named Byng Inlet. On the north side, about 5 km (3 miles) off the highway, is the village of Britt, also known as the "Hidden Pearl of Georgian Bay".

Britt is still a pearl, but now it's not quite so hidden, largely owing to the increasing popularity of the Little Britt Inn. In a region not particularly known for gourmet restaurants, word about the inn's reputation has been spreading up and down the shores of the bay. I have written about it twice, in 1999 and 2005, and I always time trips from Parry Sound to Sudbury so I can detour into the Little Britt Inn for lunch.

Anne Hardy has included the inn—and given it a star—in her book *Where to Eat in Canada*. Travellers on cross-Canada car trips have been discovering the inn and detouring there for dinner or for an overnight stop in one of the inn's four suites which rent at $125 per couple per night in summer or $105 off season.

The innkeepers are Jim Sorrenti and his partner chef, Teri McLean. Jim has been at Britt about 17 years. Born to a restaurant family in Port Stanley, he grew up on the shore of Lake Erie and in London and Windsor, spending childhood summers at Tobermory. He has managed Ontario restaurants nearly all his adult life. Teri learned cooking from her family and at the Stratford Chef School.

The Little Britt Inn has two main dining areas: the Lower Deck and the Upper Deck. The Lower Deck is a snug ship-like cabin, open all year. The Upper Deck, open in summer only, is a spacious screened area with a spectacular view across the inlet where the Still River and the Magnetawan River merge to flow into Georgian Bay. Oil tankers still call occasionally at the once-huge sawmill community to deliver fuel for CPR diesel locomotives.

Cuisine at the inn is Regional Ontario with emphasis on fresh fish: pan-fried pickerel, a famous Georgian Bay chowder and perch burgers. The last time I ate there, prices went from $8 for pork tenderloin schnitzel on a bun to $23 for a six-ounce well-aged beef tenderloin. A sign on the Lower Deck sets the tone of the place, describing it as "a little bit off the highway, a little bit off the bay, a little bit off the wall". A special kids' menu describes juvenile treats but warns "For noisy kids we have fried liver, fried onions, broccoli – no ketchup – priced according to noise level. For polite kids– free ice cream."

To get there, take Hwy 69, now being transformed into Hwy 400, for about 65 km (41 miles) north from Parry Sound. Exit at Hwy 526. Go right here following signs to Britt. Loop back west under Hwy 69 and go about 5 km (3 miles) to Britt and the inn.

Chapter 13

A Natural Air Show At Hawk Cliff

Around the end of September and the begin-ning of October every autumn, many thou-sands of big hawks put on an informal air show over a high bluff on the north shore of Lake Erie near Port Stanley. The place is known as Hawk Cliff. Hundreds of naturalists gather here in the fall with binoculars, telescopes and field guides to watch and try to count the hawks in their annual southward migration.

Hawks are superb flyers. From far across northern Canada, they start gathering in big flocks, evidently because they like lots of company in their long jour-ney to escape the rigours of winter. As they migrate, the hawks are joined by other hawks to form larger and larger groups. And Hawk Cliff has become one of their major rallying points.

People who study birds—like Jim Woodford, re-tired from the Federation of Ontario Naturalists—tell me that big hawks do not like to waste energy when flying, so they seek out warm air currents for propul-sion. Certain migration routes provide the strongest and most dependable booster currents. One main route lies along the north shoreline of Lake Erie, and one or more feeder routes seem to converge here from the north. This brings hawks and hawk-watchers to this Lake Erie headland which has become famous as the best place in Ontario to observe the spectacular mass migration.

To give ordinary families a chance to see the hawks, southwestern Ontario naturalist groups such as the St. Thomas Field Naturalist Club usually sponsor one weekend gathering every fall at Hawk Cliff. Naturalists are on hand to welcome visitors, identify hawks and explain the migration patterns.

For rugged charm, this is one of the most spectacular spots along the Lake Erie shore. A giant clay and shale headland, backed by woods and fields, towers 45 metres (150 feet) above the lake.

I still remember vividly my last visit to Hawk Cliff at the end of September, 1964, and the thrill of seeing thousands of the big birds. When I arrived with Bill Girling, a London naturalist, and Jim Woodford, a few hundred hawks were lazily circling overhead like jetliners waiting to land at Pearson International Airport. "Just wait and see what happens," Jim Woodford told me. For nearly an hour, other groups of hawks appeared from north and east to join the orbiting flock which kept getting bigger and bigger. When we weren't watching soaring and wheeling hawks that spiralled upwards like columns of smoke, we observed fishing boats hauling their nets out on Lake Erie. Finally Bill Girling observed, "They're almost ready to go!"

Sure enough, a few minutes after one last arriving group had hurried to get into the formation, the whole huge flock took off, as though on some command, and headed towards the southwest across Lake

Erie. This left the sky above Hawk Cliff empty—but only for a few minutes. New groups began appearing from the northeast, and another big flock began to form. This went on all afternoon. On some autumn days, as many as 50,000 Broad-winged Hawks have been counted gathering at Hawk Cliff. Many species of smaller hawks are also seen, along with Bald Eagles and Golden Eagles.

The best time to enjoy a visit to Hawk Cliff is on the weekend of the annual gathering of naturalists, when you can get lots of information and friendly help in identifying hawks. For the exact dates, call Bird Studies Canada at Port Rowan, 519-586-3531.

To get to Hawk Cliff, take Hwy 401 to Hwy 4 just west of London. Go south on Hwy 4 towards St. Thomas. Just before St. Thomas, Hwy 4 branches right to Port Stanley. Continue on 4 but instead of going to Port Stanley, watch for the village of Union and County Road 27, also called the Sparta Line. At Union, go left on the Sparta Line about 3 km to County Road 22, Fairview Rd. Turn right on Fairview Rd. and go about 5 km to where the road ends at Hawk Cliff.

I got these directions recently from Cyril Crocker, of Sparta, who helps organize a public outing to Hawk Cliff every September. His phone number is 519-775-2253.

Chapter 14

The Monster Rock That Hitched A Ride

If the present global warming turns to global cooling, as has often happened in the distant past, Planet Earth could again see monster ice sheets advancing from the poles.

In the last ice age, which finally ended less than 10,000 years ago, continental glaciers covered Ontario and nearly all of Canada. They were incredibly big, incredibly powerful and incredibly slow-moving. One of them left a souvenir at the hamlet of Glen Miller beside the Trent River, about 175 km (109 miles) east of Toronto. It's a limestone boulder, as big as a house and some 7.6 metres (25 feet) high. By far, it's the biggest rock in Ontario. The Lower Trent Conservation Authority has established a small park around it so visitors can get some idea as to what the last ice age, called the Wisconsin Glaciation, must have been like.

I went to see the Glen Miller boulder in 1961 when it was surrounded by a farm field owned by Gerald Long. I chipped a sample off the rock and took it to Dr. Walter Tovell, then Curator of Geology at the Royal Ontario Museum. He and his staff determined that the Glen Miller boulder consists of a kind of limestone that occurs more than 160 km (100 miles) northeast of Trenton.

Geologists believe that an ice sheet, several kilometres thick and advancing from the east side of Hudson Bay, picked up the boulder and moved it an average of perhaps 10 centimetres a year, finally leaving it at Glen Miller when global warming occurred and the ice melted back. Convert 160 km into centimetres and you'll get some idea of how long it took the boulder to ride to its present location.

Close to the boulder, you'll see a streamlined little hill called a drumlin. There are scores of such hills in the area, all pointing from northeast to southwest, the direction in which the glacier advanced. They're believed to have been formed by clay moulded by the ice sheets onto rocky obstructions.

Local folklore around Trenton is that a group of U.S. citizens in the 1950s negotiated to buy the Glenn Miller boulder and take it to New York State as a tourist attraction. They gave up the idea when nobody could be found to move it.

The giant rock became public property and officially accessible to visitors after public-spirited citizens acquired the land where it sits and arranged to have it deeded to the Lower Trent Conservation Authority which now operates it as a small conservation area with a parking area. The rock is now known as the Bleasdell Boulder.

To get to it, take Hwy 401 east from Toronto to Exit 526 at Trenton. Go north here on Glen Miller Road for 1.4 km to an orange flashing light at Johnstown Road. Turn left onto Johnston Rd and cross a bridge over the Trent River. At the far end of the bridge you'll see a church. Turn left at the church and next to it see

Bleasdell Boulder Road. Go right on this road to a parking lot and a walking trail to the boulder, a beaver dam and a lookout site.

For information, you could call the Lower Trent Conservation Authority at 613-394-4829. When I phoned, I was delighted to be answered by a helpful live human voice on the first ring.

Here's an interesting question that Dr. Tovell posed about continental glaciers. How would you know that a new ice age had started? The answer is: When you get a winter in which there's so much snow in the north that it doesn't all melt during the next summer. As a result, snow keeps piling up year after year. Eventually it becomes so deep that its great weight turns it to ice. This ice then begins to act like a thick kilometres-deep liquid, slowly flowing outward, and reshaping, crushing and moving everything in its path.

Chapter 15

Killarney—A Jewel Between The Islands And The Mountains

From Toronto to Killarney by road, it's about 450 km (281 miles) and takes nearly six hours to drive. When you get there, I think you'll feel it's been worth every kilometre.

Located at the northern tip of Georgian Bay amid the most beautiful of the Thirty Thousand Islands, this tiny community ranks as one of Ontario's rare finds. Among its assets are:

- Killarney Provincial Park, 48,500 hectares (120,000 acres) of clear lakes, rivers and forests overlooked by the Cloche Mountains, not really mountains but majestic hills of sparkling crystalline quartzite, rimmed by wind-swept Georgian Bay.
- Baie Fine, Ontario's most famous fiord that winds back some 20 km (12.5 miles) into the hills of Killarney Park and to a lake that has been painted so many times by famous artists that it's named O.S.A. The O.S.A. stands for Ontario Society of Artists.
- The waterfront of Killarney village (population 500) facing George Island across a narrow channel. This is the closest you'll find in Ontario to a

Newfoundland outport village. It has as many boats as the village has houses. Until the 1960s, there was no road into Killarney. You had to get there by boat, by float plane or across the Georgian Bay ice in winter. Killarney owes its name to Lord Dufferin, an early Governor General of Canada. He and his wife came for a visit, fell in love with the place and named it for Killarney, Ireland.

- Herbert's Fish and Chip Bus at the town dock. When I was last there, they were calling it the only place in Canada where you could lunch on whitefish or lake trout caught that morning.

- Last but not least, Killarney Mountain Lodge and its owners, Maury and Annabelle East. This place is close to my ideal of the perfect Ontario vacation resort because it's lovingly maintained by the East family and they have poured a great deal of imagination into it. Built in the 1930s by Detroit truck and trailer king August Fruehauf, the lodge served for more than 30 years as a palatial getaway spot for Fruehauf's capitalist friends, customers and labour union barons, including Jimmy Hoffa. Maury East bought the place around 1962 and has since made it famous for the wide variety of wilderness experiences and learning activities it offers to guests. With certified recreation directors, you can learn to sail, canoe and kayak.

When I was last there in 2006, you could hike to a luxurious outpost camp or to Baie Fine, lunch in style with a white tablecloth on the rocks, and then sail back to Killarney in a 14-metre (46-foot) sailing yacht with a captain who had sailed twice across the Atlantic.

For more information, call 1-800-461-1117 or log on to escape.killarney.com.

To get there, take Hwy 400 to Parry Sound and continue north on Hwy 69 for about 125 km to Hwy 637. Turn left (west) on 637 and drive another 67 km to Killarney. When I last drove this road, I spotted a beaver snoozing atop his lodge beside the road and I met a young black bear walking on the road shoulder.

PART THREE: A BIT OF BIOGRAPHY

Chapter 16
Exiled From England

Most Canadians know little about their ancestors. Country people, farmers, generally know more than city dwellers. I suppose that's because farm families tend to stay longer in the same areas and acquire more knowledge about when and how their grandparents and great-grandparents came to their present farm locations. Most of us, though, are pretty vague about anyone farther back than grandparents. If you're lucky enough to have grandparents, ask them when and where they were born and when and where their parents were born. Write it down somewhere and pass it on to *your* kids. Write your own personal history to give to your children. They'll find it useful in composing your obituary!

For interested readers and my own family, I'm going to write a little about myself and my immediate ancestors. Skip this if it bores you.

My mother was Annie Louise Smith, born in Liverpool, England. Her father was Walter Smith, believed born in Bradford, England. Her mother was Florence Overton, born in Kenilworth, Warwickshire, England, not too far from Coventry. I still have second and third cousins in Kenilworth. They tend to be short, blond people who look like me.

According to oral information I received from my mother and from my cousins in Kenilworth, my mother's father, Walter Smith, was a teacher and musician who worked at a Church of England parish school in Liverpool. Both Walter and his wife, Florence, died prematurely, probably in an epidemic of cholera or typhoid fever, leaving six children as orphans, including my mother. The boys were sent to live with relatives at Kenilworth or other Midlands communities. Nobody, evidently, wanted the girls. So Anglican Church authorities shipped the girls off to Church of England rectories in Canada. My mother was thus uprooted from her native England as a little girl and sent to live with total strangers: an Anglican rector and his wife whose home was in a rural parish near Howick, in Quebec's Eastern Townships.

My mother would never talk much about her childhood experiences. From what she did say, however, I gathered that she was treated more as a servant than as a family member. I remember her telling me about one childhood incident in particular. She was sent out one day with a tin pail to pick wild blueberries. When the pail was partially full, she met a black bear. Terrified, she dropped berries and pail and ran home. The bear, not interested in my mother, finished off the berries in the pail and went about his business. Back at the rectory, my mother told her story. The reaction of the preacher and his wife was to send her back to recover the pail.

I think she must have attended a good rural school and had some high school education because she spoke excellent correct English. She must also have acquired a taste for reading, because I grew up surrounded by good books which my mother read not just for her own enjoyment but also to my brother, my two sisters and me.

She did not acquire a liking for Anglican Church ritual. Although she could quote long sections of the Book of Common Prayer by memory, she never, so far as I know, attended an Anglican Church after she left Quebec. That happened after my mother "came of age". Her foster parent, the rector, had been transferred by his bishop to Ste-Anne-de-Bellevue, at the western end of Montreal Island. As soon as she became a legal adult, my mother boarded a St. Lawrence River steamer for Toronto and a job as a seamstress, making shirts in an Eaton's Toronto factory. She had evidently learned to sew.

My father was born in Canada at London, Ontario, on February 7, 1881 and his name was registered as Alfred George Ridd, son of William Atkin Ridd and Martha Ann Lusbury. His father evidently died when my dad was very young, and his mother was married again to a George Currell who adopted my father and changed my father's name to Alfred George Currell. I have never been able to learn anything about William Atkin Ridd. He may really have died prematurely or he may have just disappeared into the United States, as happened frequently in early Ontario. I never knew any of my grandparents. All had died before I was born in 1922.

In any case, my father grew up as Alfred Currell in "London in the Bush". That's what they called London, Ontario, in the 19th century. By contrast,

London, England, was "London in the Smoke" because of its reputation for polluted air.

Childhood was interesting in the Canadian London, judging from what my father told me. His parents ran a small hotel or theatrical boardinghouse close to the Grand Trunk Railway station. Because the shortest distance between New York and Chicago is through southern Ontario, several U.S. railways had been built through Ontario, passing close to London. For theatrical vaudeville troupes and other groups, this made London a convenient stop for one-night performances. Many of the show companies, everything from Shakespearian troupes to magic shows to comedians, stopped over at the Currells' place. It was called the American House. My dad got to meet quite a few show-business types and got to like them, although they were generally bad credit risks. Some guests left fake stage jewellery behind when they left, perhaps as part-payment of bills or just through carelessness.

My grandmother evidently allowed young Alfie to collect some of this jewellery. When I was a small kid, he would sometimes show me his assortment of diamond tie pins, brooches, rings and bracelets, all glass or "paste", of course, and big and showy so they could be seen easily by audiences.

Several U.S. circuses always came to London every summer and set up tents on the edge of town while parking their brightly painted boxcars and sleeping cars at railway yards close to the station. These circuses offered a variety of jobs to small boys. Carrying pails of water to the elephants was one of them.

My dad must have finished both elementary school and high school. His mother was determined that he should become a doctor. On completion of high school, he was enrolled at the Western Medical College, then an independent medical school in London. It later was to become part of the University of Western Ontario.

He had completed only one or two years at this institution when his mother died suddenly and the American House was found to be deeply in debt. Somewhere along the way, his adoptive father, George Currell, had dropped out of the picture. I don't know whether he died or just disappeared. In any case, there was no more money to pay medical college fees. My dad quit. He once intimated to me that he had found medical school very difficult and he hadn't really wanted to be a doctor.

An aunt, Emma, came to the rescue. She had married John M. Taylor who had started a foundry business in Guelph and prospered at it. Aunt Emma, a sister of my father's mother, persuaded J.M. Taylor to give my dad a job at the Toronto branch of Taylor-Forbes Ltd. So my father migrated to Toronto where he met my mother.

My parents married in Toronto—they never told me how they met—and started building a home and family in the early 1900s. Eventually, they had four children: two boys and two girls. I was the youngest, born in 1922 on Harvie Avenue in the northwest corner of Toronto.

Chapter 17

Times Were Changing

The 1920s were interesting times to enter life in Toronto. Canada and North America were recovering from the terrible human costs of World War I, the Great War, as it was called during my childhood. Huge numbers of young and middle-aged Canadians had been sacrificed on the battle-fields of France and Belgium. Nearly every family on Harvie Avenue, the street where I was born, had lost a father, a brother or an uncle, and many young men were left to get through life minus an arm or leg. In spite of all this, the 20s were happy times. The war was over, business was booming, jobs were plentiful, food was cheap and everybody was looking forward to everlasting prosperity. Nobody guessed what lay ahead in the 1930s and 40s.

On the streets there were still plenty of horses, pulling Eaton's red delivery carts, bread and milk wagons and even tea-delivery vans. But model-T Fords, Chevvies, Whippets, Willys-Knights and a host of other cars were starting to crowd horses off the pavements and out of city life.

One of my earliest memories—I think I was about three years old at the time—is of hearing and seeing a fire-wagon, pulled by two big brown horses, racing down our street, on the way to a house fire a block or two away. I later learned that our neighbourhood Earlscourt fire hall had owned and used the last horse-drawn fire-rig in Toronto.

Another childhood memory is of waking up in my bed with a huge lump on my head and my worried anxious family gathered around. I was told I had ridden my new tricycle down the front veranda steps, only to land on my head on the concrete sidewalk! Since I showed no obvious ill-effects from the accident, my parents didn't even call the doctor.

Until age 5, I enjoyed a benevolent imprisonment in our backyard amid flowers, fruit trees, a grape arbour and an area where I was free to dig a hole to China. This became my pre-school project with a couple of little kids who lived next door.

When I was five years old, school came as a shock. I just couldn't believe I was going to leave home for half a day, five days a week, to be imprisoned in a huge brick building that looked like a castle. My mother took me to kindergarten the first day for registration. After that, it was my older sister's duty to see that I got to school. Toronto public schools had a good reputation, but in the 1920s and 30s they still combined the qualities of army battalions and jails. The buildings were tall and forbidding. Except in classrooms, boys and girls were strictly separated. There were boys' entrances and girls' entrances, and woe betide any kid who went through the wrong door. Mornings and afternoons and after recess, boys and girls were marshalled into platoons and then marched into classrooms up iron stairs; military music thumped out on a piano hurried everyone along.

Starting in Grade One, discipline was strict. Every teacher's word or whim was the law and there was no appeal. Boys who gave trouble were strapped on the hands by the principal or a male teacher using a black leather strap, and it really hurt.

Because I came from a literate family where reading and books were considered important, I did well in elementary school except for one subject – arithmetic. I had what later came to be called "math phobia". I was confused and frightened by masses of numbers. This was to plague me for many years.

Reading and writing, spelling, history, geography and related subjects were pieces of cake to me and I quickly developed a wide vocabulary. My handwriting was poor because I was left-handed. For a few months at the start of Grade One, a teacher tried to force me to use my right hand. I tried but just couldn't do it. Relief came in the form on an edict that was circulated to all Toronto public schools. It informed school staff that research had proved that emotional harm could be done to left-handed children who were forced to switch. After that, I was left alone to write as best I could with my left hand. I never won any prizes for handwriting.

I was very lucky in getting an exceptionally good Grade One teacher, a Miss White. She was an expert in teaching kids to read and in helping them to develop an enthusiasm for reading. I was to learn much later in life that some teachers have this ability and that they are highly prized by principals, school boards and parents.

Whether written material comes to us by e-mail, junk mail or snail mail, it still plays an important role in our lives. The ability to read and to express ideas correctly and clearly in all forms of writing is vital to success in life.

Miss White soon had her whole class reading, and she also read aloud to us. I can still remember how one day I suddenly realized that my mother was right. She had told me that learning to read would open up a whole new and wonderful world to me. I was hooked on reading for life and I quickly tried to read every bit of print that came before my eyes. My mother and my two sisters helped me decode difficult words and also read me stories from books that I couldn't wait to read for myself. And by the time I was in Grade Two, I had discovered the Earlscourt Branch of the Toronto Public Library and was walking over to it at least once a week.

I got through public school with a minimum of trouble, doing very well in the subjects that I liked and struggling with mathematics. I was an undersized kid; like most small people, I compensated for it by being noisy and aggressive with my peers. I think most of my teachers considered me a smart-ass, but a few took extra trouble to introduce me to books that broadened my reading.

I still recall a couple of incidents that happened when I was in Grade Four. It was called Senior Second in those days. During a history lesson, the teacher mentioned a King Lear and asked if anyone had ever heard of him. My hand shot up. I proceeded to inform the class that William Shakespeare had written a play about how King Lear had handed over power to his nasty daughters and had been double-crossed by them. The teacher asked, "How do you know about this?" I replied, "I read about it and a lot of other Shakespeare plays as well."

She immediately concluded that, at age 8, I had been reading Shakespeare's plays in their original 16th or 17th century form. She reported this to the principal, who in turn told my parents. The latter were not impressed. My mother knew that I had read a book entitled *Tales from Shakespeare* by Charles and Mary Lamb. She told me, "You should tell your teacher you got your information from that book." Little fink that I was, I never told the teachers but let them believe they had a potential young genius on their hands.

Two other public school experiences made an impression on me. One was my first sight of the Niagara Escarpment. When I was in Grade Seven, our teacher, a Miss Carbin, called the class one day over to the big west-facing windows on the third floor of Hughes Public School which was located on top of a high hill south of Eglinton Avenue on Caledonia Road. She said, "Do you see that long dark line on the horizon? That's called the Niagara Escarpment." She went on to give us an interesting, clear and accurate account of this important geographical feature of southern Ontario and how it ran from Queenston Heights at Niagara up through Ontario to a place called Tobermory at the tip of the Bruce Peninsula. Years later I learned that what we had seen was Rattlesnake Point, near Milton.

I never forgot that experience and made up my

mind that when I became an adult, I would explore the escarpment. In 1962, I did walk it as part of The Toronto Telegram's Bruce Trail Expedition.

I am grateful for one other experience from my public school days. I was selected to sing for three years in Miss Emily Tedd's Toronto Public Schools massed choir. This involved weeks of rehearsals at Harbord Collegiate and a spring concert each May in Massey Hall. I learned a lot about classical music and I remember all the songs we sang for Miss Tedd. I still sing some of them for my kids and grandkids.

It was also while I was in public school, at age 8, that I sold my first story for publication. My mother, who had left the Anglican Church when she became legally an adult, had insisted that all her children go to a Baptist Sunday School. At Sunday School we were all given a mini-newspaper each week. I, of course, read it voraciously, as in those days I read every book and other piece of print that came to my attention. One Sunday, I noticed a little item soliciting stories from young readers and promising a payment of 50 cents for every story accepted and printed. I told my mother, "I'm going to write about Winker." She said, "They'll never be able to read your awful writing." I begged her, "If I write it, will you copy it for me and send it in?" She agreed to do this for me. All our family were proud of my mother's excellent handwriting, which looked as though it had been engraved by a master craftsperson.

So I wrote the saga of Winker. She was my tiny toy-spaniel dog. A few weeks earlier, our family had been on our first-ever summer holiday. My father had been able to rent a summer cottage on Georgian Bay near Wasaga Beach at a place then called New Wasaga. We journeyed there in our first-ever car, a 1922 model-T Ford. (I could write a whole book about that car.) We spent a heavenly two weeks at New Wasaga. For shopping, we would drive a few miles along the wide beach to Wasaga Beach proper, which had hot-dog stands, stores and amusements. Winker, of course, would go with us, perched as high as possible on the car, her silky tail and spaniel ears streaming in the breeze.

On the way back from one of these trips, Winker somehow got bumped out of the car and nobody noticed until we arrived home. We drove back right away and searched for her until after dark. No trace of Winker. Nobody had seen her. I went to bed crying. At dawn next day I awoke determined to search on my own. I opened the front door and there was Winker, curled up on the step. Her feet were bleeding from the long walk back.

I wrote my story about that incident, a real tear-jerker. My mother faithfully copied it out, not changing one word, and she enclosed a certificate that it was indeed my work. It was accepted and I received a money-order for 50 cents, which I deposited in my Penny Bank account at school. I became a nine-day wonder and was told by doting aunts and uncles that I should become an author when I grew up.

That holiday at Wasaga was one of the last carefree times we had as a family. Shortly afterwards, my father became ill with a disease called pernicious anaemia, in which bone marrow loses the ability to produce red blood cells. Up until that time, the disease had usually proved fatal.

My dad spent weeks in hospital and could not work. He had volunteered for service overseas with the Royal Canadian Army Medical Corps in World War I and had served on French and Belgium battlefields where he had been gassed by chlorine released by the Germans. He applied for a disability pension but it took years of argument and hearings before a pension was forthcoming.

In the meantime, the Great Depression engulfed Canada and the world. My father's Uncle John lost control of Taylor-Forbes, the company he had founded in Guelph. The Toronto branch was closed. My father lost his job. Like almost every other family on our street, we became poor.

My two older sisters, Gladys and Wanda, saved us from the abject disgrace of having to "go on relief," in other words having to apply for welfare aid in the form of food vouchers. Gladys, who was married when I was five years old, somehow got a job at minimum wage in the office of a dry-cleaning company. This supported Gladys, her husband Herb and their small son. Herb, an accountant, had been laid off by his employer. He worked part-time, when he could, as a truck driver.

My other sister, Wanda, left school and, after months of searching, got a job as a cook at Canada Packers. Her minimum-wage pay envelope supported my mother, father and me through the grim years of the 1930s. When I got old enough, I began delivering newspapers for The Toronto Evening Telegram and

The Toronto Star. This brought in another few cents a week. Later in life, Wanda went back to high school, just to prove she could do it, and earned an Honours Graduation Diploma.

My older brother, Jack, enlisted in the Toronto Scottish Regiment the week that World War II broke out in August 1939, and he was overseas before the end of October. He did not get back to Canada until 1945.

Chapter 18
Surviving The Depression

The Great Depression of the 1930s was a terrible prolonged ordeal that should never have occurred. Oddly, however, the longer it went on, the less horrible it seemed. I suppose we all just learned to live with it and to get along with less and less.

For my family, a bright spot appeared in the mid-1930s when researchers developed an effective treatment for pernicious anaemia, the blood disease that we feared would kill my father. It was discovered that the juice or extract from a pound of beef liver per day could supply enough haemoglobin to keep an anaemia sufferer alive. This meant that my mother had to partially cook a pound of liver every day, grind it, strain it and cool it. My father then had to drink this concoction. He hated the taste, but it worked. His skin colour improved, his strength gradually returned and he started looking for work.

Then another miracle occurred. Researchers were able to synthesize the active agent in the beef liver and produce an injectable vaccine. This meant that my dad could stop taking the hated liver extract and just go to Toronto Western Hospital once a month for an intra-muscular injection.

My valiant sister Wanda, who was supporting the family with her wages from Canada Packers, got a very small raise and was even able to buy an old car for "a dollar down and a dollar a week." Gasoline was very cheap. For 25 cents we could get enough for a short family trip into the countryside once in a while. Meanwhile, my mother learned that one of her long-lost sisters was married and had a family in Montreal, and that another was living in London, Ontario. We all saved enough money for gas to drive to visit them. I learned that I had three beautiful blonde girl cousins in Montreal and three more in London. Some of them eventually taught me how to kiss a lady in a gentleman-like manner; I remember one of them telling me, "I wouldn't let just any boy kiss me like this, but we *are* cousins and cousins are supposed to kiss and show affection for each other."

For me, the major event of the depression years was starting high school. At that period, you did not just walk into a high school and register. To be admitted, you had to "Pass your Entrance." This meant you had to write at elementary school a special set of high-school entrance exams. If you failed, you could spend an extra year at elementary or "public" school and try again next year. Or, you could apply to a technical or commercial school. Collegiates, or academic high schools, were reserved for the elite who intended to go on to university.

I "passed my entrance", barely scraping through in mathematics, and the following September I enrolled at Oakwood Collegiate Institute where I was to endure a chequered career.

Looking back on the childhood years I was leaving, I have to say they had been reasonably happy. My main recreation had been reading. I had soon read every book in our house and had discovered the joys of Toronto's excellent public library system.

I had a few good friends—one of them a Jewish boy and another a Catholic. We spent much of our time trying to organize other kids into groups or gangs that were intended to protect us from bullying by bigger kids.

One thing that kids of the 1930s did not get, either at school or home, was a good self-image or a sense of self-worth. Kids in those religion-ridden days were all considered to be little sinners. We were being constantly preached at, usually at church three times on Sunday: morning, evening and at Sunday school in the afternoon. We were not encouraged to think well of ourselves—that was conceit, a sin. There was much emphasis on punishment. I resolved that if I ever became a father, I would give my kids lots of love and always treat them as valuable persons, destined for success.

I had grown up in a predominantly white Anglo-Saxon Protestant (WASP) neighbourhood and, I'm now sorry to admit, had absorbed many of the WASP prejudices with my oatmeal breakfast porridge. Along with other kids from Hughes Public School, I had fought with boys from St. Clare's Catholic Separate School. We had to pass each other going to and from school, and there was much name-calling and the odd skirmish although only a few real fights. I can't recall anybody getting seriously hurt.

Strangely enough, it was a few dozen nails—builder's nails—that taught me that Catholics were nice people, just like my own family. A man named Joe Dorion, who ran the hardware store at the corner of our street and St. Clair Avenue, provided both the lesson and the nails. It happened this way. As young kids, the boys of Harvie Avenue were obsessive builders. Everybody wanted to have a "fort" or private shack in his backyard. Parents tolerated these and there was usually a lot of scrap lumber lying around. Nails to hold the boards together, however, were in short supply—very short supply. They cost money, which was also in very short supply. Fathers straightened out and saved any available second-hand nails, kept them in old coffee cans and counted them carefully.

The only supplier of precious shiny new nails was the hardware store. The hardware-store owner had a son, Jackie Dorion. He was not a member of our gang because he was a shy kid—and he was a Catholic. We figured that, treated correctly, he could become a supplier of nails.

Carl Herman, our lone Jewish member, who was known to be a smooth talker—he was to become a lawyer and later a teacher—was assigned to approach Jackie. So Carl invited young Mr. Dorion to join our gang, and very diplomatically brought up the delicate matter of nails. Jackie, bless his honest heart, said he was *not* going to steal nails for us from his father's store. He had enough sins to confess every week without adding theft to the list. He did say, though, that he would take the matter up with his dad and thought that maybe something could be arranged. His father turned out to be sympathetic and agreed to let Jackie have a few nails once in a while, provided our requests were reasonable. That's how Jackie Dorion became a member of our gang and came to explain the mysteries of Catholicism to a bunch of WASP kids.

As for Jackie's father, he attained almost sainthood among the little hoodlums of Harvie Avenue. He never had to worry about shoplifting. No kid on our street would ever dream of stealing from Mr. Dorion. When my big brother, Jack, was much later able to buy an old car for $25, Joe Dorion once trusted him for 50 cents' worth of gas so he could take a girlfriend out on a date. You could go a long way in the 1930s on four bits' worth of gas!

Sometimes, as an old-timer, I have been asked whether I think kids were better off in the olden days than kids are today. My answer always is that I would much rather be a child today than go back to my early years. Kids today are loved, cherished and encouraged. They are treated fairly and protected—perhaps over-protected. In my childhood, kids were subjected to rigid and sometimes harsh discipline both at home and at school.

Outside of home and school, however, we had much more freedom than modern kids. Everybody, even kindergarten pupils, walked long distances to school in all weather. No school was ever closed by a snowstorm. There were no school buses. Saturdays, late afternoons, summers and holidays were freedom times for kids. We were outdoors for hours, organizing our own activities, often hiking for miles out into the woods and valleys that still surrounded Toronto.

Today's kids are highly programmed with supervised activities planned for every day and every hour. They don't have time just to be kids. A teacher friend told me a few weeks ago, "All parents seem to feel that they're entitled to have state-of-the-art children. They refuse to accept the fact that not everybody has the potential to be a leader in every field. Some of us are content just to be average, decent and kindly people."

Chapter 19
High School Headaches

At age 13, I wasn't ready for high school. I was just an immature kid on the verge of adolescence, bothered by a sense of guilt over what I later learned to recognize as natural sexual urges. I had breezed through elementary school—except for mathematics—without any real effort and had never learned to study or keep notes systematically.

Once thing I had learned, however, was how to run a small business—my daily newspaper route. For nearly a year, I had been delivering about 100 newspapers six days a week, keeping customer accounts, settling up once a week with district agents for The Toronto Telegram and Daily Star, and calling back to request payment from "slow pay" households. A customer's failure to pay did not constitute a loss for the newspaper company. It was a loss to me. I had to pay, at a wholesale rate, every Monday for every newspaper I had delivered in the previous week.

I think the retail price of a daily newspaper in those days was three cents. I can't remember the price I had to pay, but I remember that my net profit per week was less than $4, if every customer paid up promptly every week. Half of this went to help my mother buy groceries. The rest went to buy books for high-school, clothes and lunches. There was very little left for things like soft drinks and movies. I also earned a little as a part-time delivery boy for the neighbourhood drug store.

There were several advantages from this part-time employment. It gave me a sense of responsibility. I learned how to run a small business. I became intensely interested in newspapers and their contents, often reading while pedaling my bike, loaded with papers in a carrier basket.

There were also disadvantages. The paper route stole away time that should have been devoted to school. My chief worry every day was to get away as early as possible to pick up my newspapers and get them delivered. I spent no time in extra-curricular activities. I made no friends at school. I sought no extra help from teachers in mathematics, my worst subject. As a result, I fell behind the class in algebra and never did catch up

When I finally did grow up and become a parent, I remembered all this and I discouraged my own son and daughter from seeking any kind of work that would steal time from school. I used to tell them, "Enjoy your school years. Get involved in things that interest you. Learn to study and do your own research. Your business—your job—is your education."

My high-school years were not really happy ones. I did well enough in the subjects I liked: English, history, languages, botany, zoology, chemistry. In anything involving math, I was a miserable failure.

In all my high-school years, I had only one notable success. I became the only First Form student to get an article or story into the *Oakwood Oracle*, the school year book. Mine was entitled *"The Golden Thread"*, a somewhat self-important essay in which I argued that the British Commonwealth of Nations was successful because all the heterogeneous peoples who make it up had one thing in common: a sense of loyalty to the British monarchy. A kindly English teacher, Red Gilmour, congratulated me on the article and told me he thought I had the potential to become a writer.

I struggled through four unhappy years of high school at Oakwood Collegiate Institute. I now suppose that my troubles were largely my own fault. I should have worked harder at my studies. I should have been more outgoing and tried to contribute something to school spirit. I should have made an effort to take part in some sport. But I felt like an outsider. I just looked forward to getting out of the place and finding some job where I could have some experience of success.

It seemed that university was far beyond my reach; I just didn't have the brains for it. You had to have mathematics to get into any kind of university program and I was hopeless in all kinds of math. University tuition fees were much lower in those days but still far beyond my reach. I believed I was not bright enough to get any kind of scholarship. After I turned 16, an age when I could legally leave school, I began to think seriously of finding a job, any kind of job, but preferably one connected in some way with a newspaper.

By 1938, the likelihood of war had begun to loom on the horizon. Rearmament was being talked about and things were looking a little better on the business front. I told my parents I thought it was time for me to leave school and find employment. They reluctantly agreed and gave up their dream that I would become the first in the family to graduate from a university.

I privately dreamed of becoming a newspaper reporter. For years, I had been avidly reading the by-line stories of reporters in The Telegram but felt that my lack of formal education would bar me from any chance of getting into that field. One day I did mention my impossible dream to Frank Taylor, the District Circulation Manager from whom I received my papers each day. He was kind and interested. "It doesn't have to be impossible," he said. "Most of the top writers on The Telegram started at the bottom. You might get in at the back door and work your way up. Leave it with me to think about it for a while."

A few days later he told me, "I think there's a chance for you. You're an honest, bright, hard-working kid. I mentioned you to George Moir, the Business Office Manager. He has an opening for an office boy. Put on a shirt and tie and your best suit if you have one. Go down and see him tomorrow morning. He'll be expecting you. Take the Bay streetcar, get off at King Street and walk one block south. Ask for Mr. Moir on the ground floor of the Telegram building at Bay and Melinda Streets."

Chapter 20

A Real Job—And Ninety Cents For Supper

Seventy years later, I still remember how happy I was, and a little bit frightened, as I rode that June morning on a Bay streetcar for my first job interview—with a very good chance of actually getting the job. For 1939, the last year of the Great Depression, this amounted almost to a miracle. Trying to look confident, I found the six-floor, red-brick, old Evening Telegram building and approached a counter on the main floor and said, "I'm looking for Mr. Moir."

"See that big desk and that big man at the far left corner of this office," a middle-aged gentleman told me. "That's Mr. Moir. Just go and introduce yourself." I went up to the big desk and the big man who sported a big grey moustache and I said, "Sir, are you Mr. Moir?"

"I certainly am," he replied. "And who might you be?" I immediately liked his Scots accent and told him my name and the fact that Frank Taylor had sent me. "Yes," he replied. "Mr. Taylor told me about you. Come in here."

He got up from his desk to open a gate in the walnut-wood fence that separated him from the rest of the office, and seated me in a comfortable swivel chair in front of his desk. Without asking for any kind of résumé or application form, he proceeded to put me through a brief but complete interview about my family, my school career and why I would like to work for The Telegram. His kindly attitude gave me confidence and I answered truthfully and completely.

Finally, after 10 or 15 minutes, Mr. Moir said the magic words that were to launch me on a lifetime career: "I think you will do. You have the job. You will start next Monday morning at 7:30 as an office boy. Your starting salary will be $8 a week. If you are satisfactory, that will be raised to $9 after six months and up to $10 after a year. Come with me and I'll introduce you to George Woods, who is in charge of office boys." For his part, Mr. Woods told me to be sure to show up on time next Monday, to be dressed neatly with a tie, and to bring a lunch.

Shortly afterwards, I left for home, walking on air, with the news that I was now working, that somebody wanted me and that I would really be able to contribute something to our family.

After I had given the good news to my mother, I went to school to clean out my locker and tell the principal. That year Oakwood had a new principal, a Mr. Hannah, who, for a change, really seemed to like kids. He seated me in his office, gave me a sympathetic hearing and told me, "I am glad for you in a way, although I'm sorry you will not be graduating. I think you will do well as an adult. Never miss a chance to continue your education. When you leave school, you are just beginning your real education." I remembered those words and paid attention to them.

I found many ways to continue learning in the years ahead.

The next Monday morning, I entered a new world and became a different person. At age 17, I was treated as a young adult by people who seemed really glad to welcome me and who wanted to help me do well.

In those days, the position of office boy was a well-established institution in Canadian business. Every big firm had office boys. The job was what now would be called an "entry position". Working as an office boy was the first step in a training process. Since there were no community colleges, all kinds of business establishments from banks to automobile builders had to train their own office employees. And many big businesses had presidents who were proud of the fact that they had started as office boys.

Office boys, I soon learned, were young persons who began by learning the basics. On my first day at The Telegram, I was introduced to Harry Norman and Howard Heyes. The three of us staffed what was called the Mailing Desk. We were responsible for— among a thousand other things—getting out the mail every day. The mail consisted mostly of many hundreds of bills for classified ads that had appeared in the newspaper.

One of my other jobs, and mine alone, was washing and filling about two hundred small glass jars containing library paste and long-handled brushes. "This place runs on paste," Howard Heyes told me. "People are always clipping something out of the paper and pasting it on sheets of paper. Every one of them needs a jar full of paste and a brush. It is now your job to collect all the jars every Monday morning, wash them out and refill them with fresh paste." That was perhaps why Howard seemed happy to welcome me. Until I arrived, he had been bottom man on the Mailing Desk, responsible for the paste pots. I was now to take it over until somebody was promoted and I moved up a notch to make way for a new paste-pot minion.

My first immediate responsibility was to find my way around the six-floor Telegram building that John Ross Robertson, the paper's founder, had built around 1896. With a pile of inter-office mail to distribute, I went with Howard Heyes from the Press Room, two floors below street level, to the photographic dark-room on the sixth floor. I was introduced to department heads and other personages with a few private words from Howard about each. I was agreeably surprised at how kindly they all welcomed me and I began to think to myself, "I'm going to like this place."

One area I especially wanted to see was the Editorial Department which occupied all of the fourth floor. I had not mentioned to anyone my secret ambition to become a reporter. "Editorial" turned out to be a huge noisy place with sixty or more people, mostly men, seated at rows of old wooden desks and hammering away on typewriters. In the middle of the room was one long desk with four busy-looking people seated at it, surrounded by telephones and wire baskets into which teen-age boys were constantly pouring sheets of typewritten copy. "That's the City Desk," Howard told me. "The little guy in the middle is Major Wemp. He's the City Editor. We'd better not bother him now.

They're right on a deadline."

Towards one end of the big "City Room", I noticed a huge horseshoe-shaped desk. I was told it was the Copy Desk or "Rim". Seated around the outside of the Rim were twelve or fourteen older-looking men busily working on sheets of typed material which they kept passing to one man seated at the inner side of the horseshoe or the "slot". I learned that the men on the Rim were copy editors, important people who did the final editing on every story that went into the newspaper. They also wrote the headings or headlines for the stories. The man in the middle was "Slot man" or Copy Chief. He approved every story and heading before they were set in type. And two copy boys were kept busy neatly stuffing stories into cylinders that were placed into pneumatic tubes and shot up to the Composing Room on the fifth floor.

"The Editorial people are a little stand-offish," Howard said, "but they sometimes ask us to do favours for them and they're nice people when you get to know them."

In the two years or so that I was an office boy, I got to know every corner of that handsome old building and the departments and people who kept it running and who put out a 52-page broadsheet six days a week.

Until the end of World War II, everybody in Toronto except school teachers worked until noon on Saturdays. Saturday afternoon was free time when most families did their grocery shopping. By then, Loblaws and A and P supermarkets were replacing corner grocery stores. There were a few smaller chain stores as well. One of them, called The Stop and Shop, was the subject of what was then considered a dirty joke that nasty little boys used to laugh at loudly. It went like this: "Have you heard that A and P has bought the Stop and Shop? They're going to unite all their stores and call them The Stop and Pee."

Among the people and departments I got to know at the old Tely building was—starting at the bottom, two floors below street level—the Press Room. This was a huge place where daylight was never seen and where monster Hoe rotary presses poured out four editions of the daily paper. When the presses were running, you literally could not hear yourself speak. The pressmen who tended these monsters all wore neat little round hats made of newsprint. They were forbidden by union tradition from showing any outsider how the hats were made.

Another interesting place below ground level was the den of Ben Henry, the Chief Engineer. He had earlier served as an engineer aboard an ocean steamship, and he ran his department like the engine room of a ship. The first time I went down there to deliver inter-office mail, he showed me the big coal-fired steam boilers that heated the building and the huge steam turbines that could supply electric power to the presses and all other departments in the event of a failure by Toronto Hydro. Mr. Henry, a big Scot, should have been addicted to Scotch whisky but he was not. His dietary passion was chocolate milkshakes from Rutherford's Drug Store in the Toronto Stock Exchange building, across Bay Street from The Telegram. He used to ask me to run over and get one for him every once in a while.

Just above Ben Henry's domain, occupying nearly all of the ground floor, was the Business Office, ruled by Mr. Moir. It was high-ceilinged, and its marble walls were adorned with paintings commissioned by John Ross Robertson from noted Toronto artists. Many of the paintings were by Owen Staples, who had worked for The Telegram as a staff artist.

This big business office looked like something out of a novel by Charles Dickens. Important gentlemen, wearing green eyeshades and sleeve protectors, worked at huge ledger books with old-fashioned steel pens and black and red ink. They sat on high stools with footrests, and the ledgers reclined on big high sloping desks. The head Ledger-Keeper, also known as the Cashier, was a thin Scotsman named James Forrest. I got to know him in later life when his son married one of my wife's cousins. Mr. Forrest was a kind helpful person who dispensed streetcar tickets and 90 cents of "supper money" to office boys when they had to work late to get the mail out.

On the first floor (named in the British manner and hence designating the floor immediately above the ground floor) were the two Advertising Departments: Display and Classified. People who worked in them were fond of proclaiming that these departments were the real revenue producers that paid the salaries of the rest of us. This was true. The three-cent price of the newspaper barely paid the cost of newsprint.

Of interest to us office boys was the Classified Advertising Phone Room. This was a big long room with a huge telephone switchboard staffed by thirty or more young ladies wearing headsets. They sat all day plugging into red lights and taking classified ads telephoned in by customers. At that time, The Telegram boasted of having the largest classified-advertising lineage of any newspaper in North America.

As office boys, we were interested in the Phone Room for two reasons. It was staffed by a lot of good-looking girls who used to flirt with us and ask us to get them sandwiches and other treats from Rutherford's Drug Store and the Hole in the Wall restaurant on Melinda Street. And secondly, we were also called there frequently to chase mice. Because the building was old and because there was no rule against eating on the job, the old Tely building was inhabited by many small rodents. Mice would frequently run around the feet of the classified ad takers, leading to screams and panic. This infuriated Miss Piper, a big and somewhat domineering woman who ruled the Phone Room. She used to shout at the girls to get on with their work and ignore the mice. It never happened, of course. Miss Piper would finally phone the Business Office to send up a "boy to chase the mice." One of us then had to take an office broom and go to the Phone Room where we crawled under long desks amid a forest of silk-stockinged legs and were thanked profusely by the girls when we announced that the mice were gone.

I could write many pages about my work in the Business Office, how it added to my self-esteem and helped me grow from a discouraged kid into a confident young adult.

For one thing, it taught me to dress well. I was introduced by Harry Norman to Claytons Men's Wear on Yonge Street. Here, for a few dollars down and a dollar a week, I got a couple of tailor-made suits and some shirts and ties. The manager, a gentleman named Izzie King, gave good advice to his many teen-age customers. He steered us away from jazzy "zoot suits", which were all the rage then, in favour of quiet tasteful clothes. I look back on my dollar-a-week payments to Claytons as being among the best money I ever spent.

A couple of other parts of my office-boy days also frequently pop back into my mind. One involves my daily visits to John Ross Robertson's house at Sherbourne and Gerrard Streets.

When John Ross Robertson, founder of The Telegram, died in 1918, he left a will ordering that as long as his wife, Jessie, remained alive, the news-paper should be managed by trustees and that after monthly payments for the maintenance of his wife and his house, profits from the newspaper should go to the Toronto Hospital for Sick Children. He had been a founder of the hospital. On the death of his wife, the will directed that the newspaper should be sold to the highest bidder and that proceeds of the sale should go to the hospital.

J.R.R.'s widow survived him by more than thirty years. She lived in the mansion he had built at Sherbourne and Gerrard Streets, which had been a very upscale part of Toronto during J.R.R.'s lifetime but had declined sadly by 1939. When I went to work for The Telegram, Mrs. Cameron, who had remar-ried, was still living there, cared for by a butler, several maids, a cook and a chauffeur. The house always looked spiffy and prosperous. One of my jobs was to go there every day carrying two copies of that day's Telegram and any documents that required Mrs. Cameron's attention. She evidently was the chair of the trustee board that managed the estate and The Telegram.

From Mr. Forrest, I received two TTC tickets as streetcar fare for the journey. There was an unspoken understanding that if I went briskly and returned promptly, I was free to walk to the Robertson house and could keep the streetcar tickets for my own use.

Visiting the house was like stepping back into old Toronto. A maid would greet me at the door and conduct me to the formally dressed butler. He would receive me cordially and ask if I had any documents for Mrs. Cameron. If I had any, I was to hand them to her personally. She would usually be seated in her library reading or listening to CFRB on the radio. She always received me courteously, asked me a couple of questions about my work and then instructed the maid to "get the boy some cookies and a glass of milk." I remember that the oatmeal cookies were always delicious and full of raisins. I would politely devour them, thank Mrs. Cameron and take off at a very brisk walk back to The Telegram.

The other regular routine I remember from those years was getting 90 cents for supper money when we had to work an hour or two past the usual 5 P.M. quitting time. There was a rule that all the mail should go out the same day it was received at the Mailing Desk. Quite frequently, we would receive late in the afternoon hundreds of classified-advertising bills. These had to be folded, stuffed into window envelopes, run through a postage meter machine, packed into post-office bags and carried to Postal Terminal A at Bay and Front Streets. When this kept us an hour or more after 5 P.M., we were each given 90 cents to buy supper. At Wallers Restaurant on King Street East you could get a good dinner for 25 cents. For 35 cents, you could get the Blue Plate special, leaving 55 cents for an evening's entertainment. This usually consisted of attending the nightly vaudeville show at the Casino theatre where the main attraction was not the Grade B movie and not the awful comedians or the tinny pit band but a succession of strippers who took off practically everything to a strident trombone serenade.

There was a feeling of permanence and security about working for the Tely. Old-timers used to tell us frequently that the paper never laid off anybody during the Great Depression. It was a paternalistic place. There was no pension plan, but when any employee became too old to work, he or she was "looked after" by the newspaper.

In my two years as an office boy I learned a lot, including how to type and how to clear shipments through the Customs House at Front and Bay Streets. I also made a number of lifelong friends, among them Miss Maude Stickells, the chief switchboard operator. She liked me because often I cheerfully volunteered to go to Simpson's Arcadian Court takeout counter and pick up gourmet lunch orders for the Tely's three Main Switchboard ladies. I had to go to Eaton's cash office at noon every day anyway to take $25 or $35 in one-cent coins that had been collected in downtown corner Telegram newspaper boxes. Eaton's exchanged the coins for paper money which I took back to Mr. Forrest. As a highly experienced telephone operator with the uncanny ability to track people down and get them on a phone line, Miss Stickells was a wonderful asset to the Telegram news department. Her switchboard was in one corner of the newsroom. She did not realize it, but she was soon to welcome me to that sacred domain as the Tely's newest and greenest reporter.

My last notable accomplishment as an office boy was to win the Toronto YMCA's city-wide public-speaking contest. I had joined the Oratorical Club at Central YMCA and when I won the contest was awarded the Basil Tippett Trophy. I was supposed to keep the trophy for only one year, but I still have it. The Oratorical Club disbanded the next year from lack of members.

Chapter 21
A Dream Come True

Towards the end of 1940, my parents, having given up the struggle to meet mortgage payments on our Harvie Avenue home, moved to a rented brick bungalow on Queens Avenue in the suburban lakeshore town of Mimico. I, of course, moved with them.

The move to Mimico proved to be very lucky for me for two reasons. Because of it, I met a man named Hugh M. Griggs who helped me realize my dream of becoming a Telegram reporter. And through Hugh, indirectly, I met Josephine Harlock, the girl who became my lifelong love.

Born in Amaranth Township, up west of Orangeville, Hugh Griggs had been a country school teacher. Then, attracted to Toronto, he became a suburban reporter on The Telegram. I met him at The Telegram one day when he came to the Mail Desk to post a personal package. I weighed it for him and sold him stamps. He asked me about my work and wanted to know where I lived. Mimico, I told him. He said, "I live in Mimico. I'm a politician there."

It turned out that Hugh had just been elected a member of the Mimico Town Council. As a good politician, he set out to make a friend and gain a vote.

Always on the lookout for a bargain, I asked him if there was any chance I could get a ride to work with him. He said he'd be happy to give me a ride every day and could introduce me to some Mimico people. He was an Elder of Wesley United Church and invited me to Friday night meetings of the United Church Young People's Society.

Eager to meet people my own age, particularly girls, I went to a Y.P.S. Halloween party and was paired up on a scavenger hunt with a shy dark-eyed little girl named Josephine. We set out to look for a list of things required for the scavenger hunt. One of them was a Coca Cola bottle cap. Another was a black hair from a dog. For the Coke cap, we naturally went to Harold Parr's drug store on Mimico Avenue. Outside, tied on a leash, was a nice black and white dog who immediately greeted me with delighted barks. He was my dog, Danny. I pretended I didn't know him and went into the drug store where I met my big sister, Wanda. She had been taking Danny for a walk and had left him outside while she bought some cough drops.

I told Wanda about the scavenger hunt and asked her to pull some black hairs from Danny and give them to the nice girl who was outside petting him. I got the Coca Cola cap, Josephine displayed the dog hairs she had obtained, we found some other items on our list and we went back to the church basement to enjoy the rest of the party. I took her home to 148 Queens Avenue but didn't try to kiss her goodnight. I remembered one of my Montreal girl cousins telling me, "Don't try to kiss a nice girl on a first date. You'll just scare her off." Josephine did agree to go to the movies with me, gave me her telephone number and told me I could call her the next night. I still remember the phone number. It was 621-W. Before I left I said, "That was my dog you got the hair from." She said, "I know. I've seen you walking him on Queens Avenue."

So began a life-long love affair. We were married May 5, 1945, had a wonderful daughter and son and stayed happily married for fifty-seven years until Josephine died in 2003.

A few paragraphs earlier, I described how I met Hugh Griggs and arranged to get a ride to work with him every day. This turned out to be one of those great strokes of luck that were to come my way a few times during a long and happy lifetime. Hugh Griggs became my mentor, an experienced and trusted advisor—someone I needed at that particular period of my life.

On the half-hour drives to work, I told him about my aborted education and my secret desire to become a newspaper writer. I confessed my fear that it was an impossible dream. He told me, "It isn't impossible. The way to become a writer is to start writing. That's what you should be doing now." Hugh went on to tell me that because of the war—this was in the spring of 1940—many experienced reporters were leaving their jobs to join the Canadian Army, Navy and Air Force. Openings were being created for new young reporters, and The Telegram's editors were organized to train "cubs" or beginners. He said, "I'll help you. You can start the way I started at Orangeville."

So every day, on the way to work, Hugh Griggs

gave me a brief lesson on how to construct a newspaper story: how I should set my story up on newsprint copy paper with a "slug" or title in the top left corner and my name at the top right, and how I should type a brief "lead" or opening paragraph that summarized the most important fact of the story, a second paragraph explaining the lead and then a few other paragraphs, using short sentences and plain clear language. And I was to leave plenty of blank space at the top of the page and wide margins.

He told me how to cover a news event, citing a few ironclad rules. The first was to make sure to spell names correctly and to double-check things like ages and addresses. He told me to start covering minor news events in the town where I lived. How would I learn about such events? "Read the local weekly newspaper, the Lakeshore Advertiser," he said. "Clip announcements about things about to take place. Go to them. Make notes, ask questions, write a story, type it on a Business Office typewriter. Give it to me and I'll hand it in to the Suburban Editor and tell him who you are."

I did everything my mentor told me, and it worked!

I remember now my first story in The Telegram. I had clipped from the local weekly an announcement that the Home and School Society was organizing a graduation dinner for Grade Eight students of John English Public School. The dinner was to be held at Connaught Hall on a Friday night, and the guest speaker was to be Zach Phimister, Assistant Superintendent of Schools for the City of Toronto.

Armed with a reporter's pad and a half-dozen pencils, I turned up at Connaught Hall and introduced myself as being "from The Telegram". I didn't mention that I was just an office boy. I was received enthusiastically and took notes on Mr. Phimister's speech. He appealed to the Grade Eight grads to go on and graduate from high school, not to be lured by wartime jobs but to set worthwhile goals for themselves and keep working towards them.

From a public school vice-principal, I obtained a list of Grade Eight prize winners, being very careful to spell names correctly.

All that weekend, I worked at writing a news story on the event. First thing Monday morning, I typed it out on a Business Office typewriter and took it up to Hugh Griggs on the fourth floor. He looked it over and dropped it into a copy basket on the Suburban Editor's desk. I went back down to work. When that Monday's first edition of The Telegram arrived at the Mail Desk, I turned to the suburban page to behold a miracle—there were my words in print with a two-column heading.

I told nobody what I had done, but went to work every evening to seek out Mimico news stories, to cover local events, write them up and hand them in to Hugh Griggs. I carefully clipped every story that appeared in the paper, until after a month I had a file of eight or ten items. I then asked Mr. Griggs, "What should I do now?" He told me he thought I should go to see Jerry Snider.

Jerry Snider was C.H.J. Snider, Managing Editor of The Telegram. He was known as a sailing enthusiast who had written several books about the history of sailing on the Great Lakes and he was also the author of a weekly column entitled "Schooner Days". I knew where his office was, on the second floor. It was fitted out like a ship's cabin. Finally one morning, gathering up my courage and clutching my file of story clippings, I knocked on the door of "the Skipper's" office. A voice shouted, "Come in!" and I walked in to explain who I was and what I wanted.

Mr. Snider seemed happy to see me. He said, "I've seen you around the building and Major Wemp has mentioned you to me." This was a big surprise to me. I had never met Major Bert Wemp. He was the City Editor and a former mayor of Toronto and had been an air force fighter pilot in World War I. I later learned that the Suburban Editor had mentioned my stories to Major Wemp. Mr. Snider looked over my clippings, made no comment about them, but told me, "I'll see if we can find a spot for you. Go back to your job, you will hear from me." This filled me with joy. I thanked him and left the office walking on air.

I did not have long to wait. The very next morning, I received a hand-written memo signed C.H.J.S. telling me to report to Les Ward, Suburban and Community Editor, to commence work as a community reporter at $14 per week!

Chapter 22
The Start Of A Lifetime Career

That morning, when I reported for work to Les Ward, Suburban and Community Editor of The Telegram, I felt on top of the world. I was taking the first step in what was to be my lifetime career. Through a series of lucky breaks and with the help of a generous and unselfish man named Hugh Griggs, I was joining the ranks of the ancient and honourable craft of journalism. It was to provide me with a good living and fascinating work for the rest of my life. It was also to work wonders for my morale and my self-image, which had been rather low up to that time.

Try to imagine how I felt on that first day when my boss told me, "The first thing we have to do is get you some business cards. Take this voucher up to Vern Houston in the Job Room and he'll print you some cards." I knew where the Job Printing Department was on the top floor, because two days earlier I had delivered inter-office mail to Vern Houston, head of the department. When I now handed him my voucher, he read it and shook my hand. "You've made it, Harvey," he told me. "It will be a pleasure to print some cards for you." The next day he gave me a box of official-looking cards bearing my name, address and home and business phone numbers. They described me as a "Press Representative" of The Telegram. I was now entitled to call myself a reporter, but I knew that I was really just an apprentice at the bottom of the ladder, with a lot to learn.

My first teacher at the Tely was George Kidd, who was about to be promoted to the Entertainment and Music section of the newspaper. Les Ward had informed me that my "beat" for community news was to be the whole of East Toronto, an area stretching east from the Don River to Scarborough and from Lake Ontario north to the city limits. This had been George Kidd's beat, and George would spend a couple of days showing me around and introducing me to his contacts—people whom he called or visited regularly for news stories.

One of the first things George did was to show me how to keep track of my expenses and how to make out an expense account. This, I learned, was a wonderful device that would help stretch my $14-a-week salary to wider limits. I would travel by streetcar to cover my beat, George explained, but The Telegram, recognizing that it paid low wages, was generous with its allowances for streetcar tickets. For every four car tickets used, we charged 25 cents. It was permissible to charge a car ticket even to go a couple of blocks along the Danforth. Over a week, a hard-working reporter could charge for as many as 48 car tickets and claim $3. If you owned a car, you could do even better, charging 10 cents a mile (6.25 cents per kilometre) for business travel.

For two days, George Kidd and I wore out our shoes trekking along the Danforth, Gerrard Street,

Queen Street and many north-south arteries, calling on presidents of Rotary Clubs, Kiwanis Clubs, Canadian Legion branches, businessmen's associations and YMCAs. I handed out dozens of my shiny new business cards and took notes on upcoming activities that would make stories for The Telegram's community page.

George also told me what my daily routine would involve, and it soon became very familiar to me. I would turn up at the office at 7:30 every morning, claim one of the twelve or so Underwood typewriters allotted to our department and write stories for that day's paper using information I had gathered the previous day. Roughly one hour a morning was allotted for writing.

Next, at about 8:30 A.M., having dropped our copy into the Editor's basket, the other community reporters and I would gather around the Suburban and Community Copy Desk. This was a smaller version of the Universal Copy Desk, or "Rim". Our editor would sit in the centre or "slot", quickly read over each story and mark the size of heading he wanted for it. He would then hand the stories out to the staff members present, who immediately became copy editors. Les Ward and George Kidd had shown me how to edit copy, checking for spelling, grammar, clarity of meaning and striking out needless words and repetitive phrases.

After editing a story, each of us had to write a heading for it. Writing headings, I learned, was an art in itself. It took years to become expert at it, and highly skilled headline writers were always in demand and able to pick up jobs easily. Headings were designated by numbers. Each line of a given heading number had to be limited to a rigid number of letters or spaces between words. We edited copy and wrote headings for about ninety minutes, always watching the clock and mindful of our department's deadline which was 10 A.M. All our copy had to be in the composing room by that time, carried in cylinders up pneumatic tubes to a printer foreman known as the "copy cutter". He then distributed the copy out to the linotype operators.

Working on our departmental copy desk was an important learning experience. We learned from each other's mistakes. Senior reporters did not hesitate to read out examples of errors in spelling or grammar or awkward writing. Beginner reporters soon stopped being embarrassed about having their errors advertised, and we were expected to make notes to avoid similar blunders in future.

At that time, as I recall, the suburban, community and regional staff numbered about sixteen. Some were veterans who had been on the Tely for many years. A lot were kids like me. There was a helpful atmosphere in which older writers helped beginners. Together, we had to produce enough news copy every day to fill three newspaper pages: the Suburban page, the Toronto Community page and an Ontario page.

People who weren't writing their own copy early in the morning were kept busy taking stories over telephone headsets from correspondents or "stringers", calling in from places like Oshawa, Barrie, Orangeville or Caledon. Some experienced stringers—often editors on local newspapers—would dictate well-written stories. Others would just give facts, and one of our staffers would write the stories for them.

There were no bylines. Telegram policy at that time was to put writers' names only on the work of the most senior reporters.

Once we had met our deadline, we kept busy making phone calls, arranging appointments and receiving assignments from the department editor. All assignments were recorded in the assignment book. Any reporter who failed to turn in a story on an assignment was in deep trouble.

Each day of that first week—after we had waited for the first edition of The Telegram to come up from the Mailing Room, checked our own stories in the paper, and skimmed the rest of the paper—George Kidd and I headed for East Toronto. I soon got to know the area intimately and to identify locations that were likely to produce community news stories. Important among these were small neighbourhood hotels such as the Coxwell Inn where service clubs held weekly luncheon meetings, usually with guest speakers whose talks were often newsworthy. Local aldermen frequently turned up as speakers and used such occasions to announce decisions from City Hall.

A community news reporter seldom had to pay for a lunch. Kiwanis, Rotary, Optimist and other clubs were so happy to have press representatives report their meetings that they always invited us for lunch—usually chicken or overdone roast beef with pie for dessert.

The small hotels where many of these luncheon

meetings were held had sprung up like mushrooms along the Danforth and Queen Street East in the late 1930s after a decision by Ontario Premier Mitch Hepburn to legalize public beer-drinking. Ontario had been "dry" all during the 1920s following a wave of Prohibition sentiment that swept the United States and Canada (except Quebec) during World War I. Prohibition then ended in Ontario when the Liberals under an onion farmer named Mitchell F. Hepburn swept into power in 1934. Amid predictions that social disaster would soon result, Hepburn legalized "Beverage Rooms", usually called beer parlours. His government enacted legislation that allowed hotels to serve beer in two kinds of establishments: "Men's Beverage Rooms" and "Beverage Rooms for Ladies with Escorts". There were a few conditions imposed: To be allowed to open beverage rooms, hotels had also to provide guest bedrooms and full-service dining rooms. They were permitted to serve wine and beer with meals.

The beverage rooms, which usually turned out to be somewhat drab and cheerless places, proved to be gold mines for hotel owners; but not so the dining rooms, which ate up the beer profits. To keep his beer license, a hotel operator had to hire a chef and kitchen staff, waiters and cashiers. He had to run a restaurant that attracted few customers, as dining out was not a popular activity in Ontario during the 1930s and the WWII years. A result of this situation was that hotel keepers became desperate to attract dining-room business and would offer low lunch and dinner prices to regular meetings of service clubs and other groups. They were also eager to welcome reporters who might give them a few lines in the newspapers about upcoming dances or other events. An enterprising but poorly paid reporter who dropped in to visit a hotel manager around noon seldom escaped without being treated to lunch!

In the course of the first few weeks on my new beat, I got to know East Toronto and developed a daily routine. After two or three hours at the Telegram office every morning, I would head east by streetcar to gather news and usually attend some luncheon meeting which was sure to produce a story. In mid-afternoon, I would go back to the office, write stories for the next day's paper and head home to Mimico to snatch an hour's nap. After supper with Mum, Dad and my sister, I would head back east to cover evening events, such as political meetings or gatherings of local businessmen's associations.

I remember one night when I was assigned to cover an election campaign meeting of the Danforth Conservative Association at Playter's Hall. I went into the building, climbed upstairs one floor and entered a room filled with elderly people. I sat in a back row. A man at the front offered a prayer of some kind and then invited members of the audience to send messages "to the beyond". I thought this rather odd behaviour for Conservatives, and whispered to a lady sitting next to me, "Isn't this the Danforth Conservatives' meeting?" In a broad Scots accent she replied, "Dinna be daft. It's the Danforth Spiritualist Church." I crept quietly out and climbed one more flight of stairs to another auditorium where Tommy

Church, M.P., was haranguing a large crowd about the evils of the Mackenzie King government.

After such a night assignment, I would ride the streetcar back to Mimico for a good night's sleep to be ready to get to the office by 7 or 7:30 next morning.

I was so happy to have my job and to be learning how to cover assignments and write good news copy, that I worked really hard. Much of the news I wrote was concerned with Toronto's war effort. This was 1941, and many of the city's young men and a few women were overseas or training to go to England where the buildup was beginning for the D-Day landings in France.

After I had been on the job about a year, I even got a Page One headline story in the paper. I had covered a lunch meeting where a young social worker mentioned that with so many fathers and husbands overseas, social agencies were worried about deterioration of family life. He said it had been noted that young girls in Grades 7 and 8 were forming "girl gangs" and attempting to bully younger girls and even boys. I immediately seized on this as an important news story, cornered the speaker at the end of the meeting for more details and hurried back to the office as fast as the TTC could carry me. I hammered out a story which I turned in to my editor—Eddie Sprunt. He had succeeded Les Ward, called back to the Royal Navy to command a minesweeper. Eddie told me, "This is Page One. You should have phoned it in or taken a cab back to the office." My story did make Page One and was given the top headline for the last two editions of the day. The City Editor assigned one of his reporters to do a follow-up for next day. I was commended for having done a good job.

I was on the East Toronto community beat about two years. Among the stories I covered was an international YMCA conference, attended by U.S. young people on December 7, 1941. In the middle of a morning session, word came about the Japanese attack on Pearl Harbour. I wrote about the terrible sense of shock and disbelief that struck the young Americans. They were all immediately concerned about getting back home to join the U.S. forces to go to war.

Although it was wartime, those two years were a happy time for me. I became a competent junior reporter. For the first time in my life, I had a "steady" girl friend and we were on the verge of becoming engaged. I was saving money to buy Josephine a diamond ring. I had made new friends of my own age in Mimico and was beginning to have some social life.

At The Telegram, I also became friends with other junior reporters as we learned the basics of journalism together. Among them were George Kidd, George Meadows and Phil Murphy. Like me, they were all addicted to reading and were all aiming for lifelong careers on newspapers. Phil Murphy's father was Rowley Murphy, a widely known marine artist who had a commission from the Royal Canadian Navy to portray the R.C.N.'s role in World War II. Phil took me a few times to meet his parents at their cottage on Toronto's Centre Island. There was always a partly finished oil painting on an easel in the middle of the living room.

At this period of my life, my best friend was Harry

Smith, who had joined the Telegram staff as an office boy a few weeks after I arrived. Harry did not stay long at The Telegram, however. After a year or so, he obtained a better-paying job at Elias Rogers, a major coal company. Toronto at that time was almost entirely heated by coal. Harry and I remained friends. He had a good-natured older brother named Russell. One of Russell's prized possessions was a fairly new red Chrysler car which he loaned to Harry once a week for a Saturday-night date. Harry's girl friend was Joyce Cross. They both lived in Toronto's Parkdale section and had attended high school together. Harry was the soul of generosity and usually invited Josephine and me along on a double date, which was always extra special because we had the use of Russell's car. We would first go to a movie, then buy club sandwiches and French fries for ourselves at a lakeshore restaurant that had a parking lot where we could cuddle up while gazing across Lake Ontario.

Much of our conversation on these Saturday nights was about what was going to happen to Harry and me when we both turned twenty in the summer of 1942. Every young Canadian male at that time knew what his 20th birthday meant. It was the date when young men became subject to the draft—to conscription into the Canadian armed forces. At age twenty, you had a choice: to volunteer or not to volunteer. If you wished to do so, you could volunteer for active service in the Canadian Army, or in the Navy, or in the Royal Canadian Air Force. If you chose not to volunteer, you would be drafted into the Canadian Army but, at that time, you could not be compelled to serve outside Canada. (Later in the war, this was changed so that draftees could be forced to serve anywhere.) For WASPS like Harry and myself in Toronto, there was really no choice. We had to volunteer. Our families, our friends and our employers expected it.

Draftees, universally known as "zombies", were objects of ridicule and contempt. I knew that if I volunteered for active service, my reporter's job at The Telegram would be waiting for me at the end of the war—if I survived. If I waited to be drafted, the newspaper might be legally compelled to give me a job on my return, but my status would be lower than low. After much discussion, Harry and I decided we would both go to enlist at the end of August—he in the Royal Canadian Army Service Corps and I in the R.C.C.S., the Royal Canadian Corps of Signals.

But first, we would grant ourselves a two-week holiday at a Muskoka resort—Clevelands House—where they offered a special package to young men about to go off to war. We saved our money, reluctantly bade farewell to our girl friends (Joyce and Josephine), and took off for a memorable farewell binge. On our return, we went together to a recruiting office and signed up for three years of military slavery.

Chapter 23
My Military Experience

My older brother, Jack, greeted World War II with enthusiasm. It represented to him an opportunity for employment and for travel to distant places. On the day in 1939 that Canada declared war on Hitler's Germany, Jack enlisted in the Toronto Scottish Regiment. Two months later he was in England, at Aldershot, and by the end of 1939 he was in France with the Canadian First Division, part of the British Expeditionary Force that was to be evacuated at the time of Dunkirk after Hitler's forces conquered France in the Blitzkrieg of May 1940. Subsequently, Jack trained for years in England, fought in Italy, fought in France after D-Day in 1944, and took park in the liberation of Holland. He served six years, from 1939 to 1945.

By contrast, I was a reluctant warrior. To me, the war represented years out of my life. I had just become established at the beginning of what looked like a promising career. Now I was rudely plucked away. The war did, however, provide a few small benefits which I did not recognize until later. It improved my education, it added to my self-esteem, and it gave me an opportunity to leave home and to mature in a strange and demanding environment.

After a complete medical examination that placed me in a B-1 medical category—not a top physical specimen but fit enough for service anywhere—I was subjected to what the army called the M-Test. This proved to be a lengthy series of intelligence and aptitude examinations. Following that, I was subjected to a kind of job interview with a captain who began the procedure by telling me, "With your I.Q. score, you should be sent for officer training, but it's not going to happen. You are too immature. You're just a kid and need some time to grow up. We will give you technical training where you can use your brain. We will have another look at you in two or three years."

This was news to me—the fact that I was considered to be of superior intelligence. It was confirmed a week or two later when I met a friend from The Telegram who had become a clerk in the personnel selection branch of the Army's No. 2 District Depot. He had filed my M-Test results and he told me, in violation of all the rules, that I had a remarkably high score. I had always considered myself to be below average mentally, in view of my difficulty with mathematics. To be told that I was above average made me feel a little better about myself, although I doubted that it would do me any good in the Canadian Army.

My first two weeks as a soldier at the C.N.E. Horse Palace, which housed the District Depot in Toronto, were among the most miserable of my life. I came to realize that military service was slavery and I was one of the slaves. To begin with, the food was terrible—unbelievably bad. I lived mostly on hot dogs, bought at the Salvation Army canteen. During my three years in the army, I developed an affection for the "Sally Ann" and in later life supported it with donations.

After surviving two weeks at the Horse Palace, I was shipped by train to the Newmarket basic training centre for eight weeks of square-bashing and other elementary activity. During this period, the Army decided that I should have two wisdom teeth extracted. As a result, I developed a serious jaw infection, could not open my jaw to eat and was taken to Chorley Park Military Hospital in Toronto. Here I spent Christmas (1942) and New Year's (1943) in surroundings that had been enjoyed by Lieutenant-Governors of Ontario; in the late 1930s, Mitch Hepburn, premier of Ontario, had evicted the Lieutenant-Governor and turned the Rosedale mansion over to the Feds as a military hospital.

By the time I got back to Newmarket, my group of basic trainees had departed for distant fields, so I was sent on my own to the Kingston, Ontario, training centre of the army Signal Corps. The Signal Corps didn't seem to know what to do with me, so I was started on a radio operator course which consisted mostly of learning to send and receive Morse code. I enjoyed this and did well at it. After the Morse code course, I began a radio mechanic course but soon developed a severe cold that turned into pneumonia, the result of standing for hours in freezing weather on a parade square every day.

The pneumonia put me into Kingston Military Hospital for a couple of weeks. It was the only serious illness I was to experience in my whole lifetime. Because so many soldiers were felled by pneumonia that winter, the Army Medical Corps had organized a convalescent camp on the outskirts of Barriefield. I was sent there to recover for a few days, but I ended up staying for four weeks because of a comic foul-up that was typical of army life.

When the day arrived for my discharge from hospital, the convalescent centre could not discharge me because my entire document file had been lost. A strange hiatus ensued. At first, I enjoyed doing nothing but reading in a well-stocked library that had somehow been provided for the convalescent patients. But this soon became boring, so I took to bugging the clerks at the hospital office for news of my fate. Unbelievably, this went on for four weeks until, after a grand search, my documents were finally found. They were located on the chair of a little Canadian Women's Army Corp (CWAC) typist. To raise herself closer to her typewriter, she had grabbed four thick document envelopes and stashed them under her chair cushion!

As soon as the Signal Corps got me back to Vimy Barracks, I was informed that a terrible flap had taken place over my prolonged stay in the convalescent centre. Special orders had come from National Defence Headquarters in Ottawa about a new top-secret course that was supposed to have started two weeks previously, and I was one of the soldiers listed as students on the course. Nobody could tell me anything about the course. I was ordered to get my gear together immediately and to be transferred across the road to the Royal Canadian Ordinance Corps Armament School at Barriefield Camp.

Here things became somewhat clearer. Eight of us,

all lowly privates, were crowded into a small office amid an atmosphere of mystery and secrecy and were addressed by a captain. He began by warning us that what we were about to hear was "Top Secret" and we were not to talk about it to anyone, not even to our parents when we were on leave. We had been selected because of our M-Test scores, he said, to become the first Canadian soldiers to be trained as technicians for the maintenance of a device called the Kerrison Predictor. The purpose of the Predictor—actually it was a primitive mechanical computer—was to solve problems in the aiming of Bofors 40mm anti-aircraft guns that were used mostly against dive bombers.

The captain went on to explain that data about the speed and range of approaching bombers would be fed into the Predictor. Using a series of mechanical and electrical systems, it would solve problems to determine how and where the Bofors guns would be aimed so that explosive shells would hit the bombers. The Kerrison Predictor, he said, had been invented in England and had proven to be very successful in the Battle of Britain against Luftwaffe dive bombers. A staff sergeant from Britain had been sent to Kingston to act as instructor for the three-month course.

We then were introduced to our teacher and to each other. So began the most intensive period of work and study that I had ever experienced. The eight of us were a heterogeneous group from all over Canada. I was the only one from Toronto. There was Private Bereskin, I remember, a "zombie" from Winnipeg and proud of it. He had been part of a U.S. and Canadian force sent to dislodge a Japanese group from one of the Aleutian Islands, near Alaska. When they arrived, they found that the Japanese had gone. There was also Silvio Lebrun, a big good-natured bulldozer driver from northern Manitoba. There was Harry Judge, recently married, from Vancouver. I have forgotten the names of the others. They all turned out to be highly intelligent good-natured guys and we soon learned to get along well together. I've also forgotten the name of our teacher. He turned out to be the best teacher I ever had. He began by telling us to stop worrying. This was a difficult course, he said, but we were all going to pass it. If one or more of us failed, it would be bad news for him and he was not going to let it happen.

It was a difficult three months during which I learned trigonometry, algebra and physics, all of which had confounded me in high school. Because there were only eight of us, our staff sergeant was able to give each of us individual attention. He used little rhyming verses to help us remember key formulae, and many acronyms.

A big high-ceilinged bay of the Armament School had been designated as a classroom for the Predictor course. Here we had one of the Predictors, a huge box on a sturdy tripod with two telescopes mounted on it, one for elevation and one for bearing or azimuth. There was also a gasoline-powered generator to power the equipment and an actual 40mm Bofors light anti-aircraft gun. The latter was fitted with hydraulic oil motors to move the gun barrel for bearing and elevation. The whole idea was that two operators on the Predictor would sight on target aircraft with their telescopes and would adjust hand wheels to stay on target; the Predictor would quickly solve the ballistics problems and aim four guns. All the gunners had to do was feed clips of shells into their gun and depress a firing pedal.

Throughout the course, we were to strip the covering plates on the Predictor, take the whole thing apart and memorize the geometric theorems and physical laws on the basis of which dozens of electrical and mechanical assemblies operated.

There were weekly tests and we wrote full examinations once a month. All eight of us were bunked together so we could study as a group in the evenings. We all felt it important that we should score well on the big final examination coming up in June. We helped each other and our sergeant was always available to give assistance. Finally the course ended. We all passed with high marks and I led the class, much to my amazement. I had really become interested and worked harder than I had ever worked in my life. At the end of the course, we were each given a week's embarkation leave while we awaited orders as to whether we would be posted overseas to England or to units in Canada.

When word came through, we learned that we would all be staying in Canada for the time being. I was to go to the Royal Canadian Ordnance Corps Depot at Saint John, New Brunswick. I would be in the Ordnance Corps only a short time. A new Canadian arms section was being formed to be called the Royal Canadian Electrical and Mechanical Engineers or RCEMEs. I would be a member of this, with the rank of Craftsman.

Chapter 24

A Vacation From The War

When I left the Armament School at Kingston in the spring of 1943, I had been in the army about 10 months, living in Spartan conditions, eating unappetizing food and resigned to the fact that this could go on for years.

I had never been farther from Toronto than Montreal and really knew little about Canada beyond southern Ontario. Travelling alone with special orders, I boarded an east-bound CNR train at Kingston and in three hours was in Montreal. Here, after a wait of four hours, I got aboard an overnight CPR train for Saint John, New Brunswick. As a mere private, I was expected to sleep sitting up in a day coach for the 16-hour journey. However, luck was with me. A porter from the sleeping car ahead noticed me when I tried to rent a pillow from him. "Have you got two dollars?" he asked me. "For two dollars, I can give you an upper berth." I paid him two dollars and was introduced to the luxurious world of a CPR sleeping car where I enjoyed a comfortable and warm night's sleep, arriving in Saint John on a Sunday morning.

Here my army life was to change very much for the better.

At the CPR station in the middle of what looked

like a somewhat rundown city, I was met by a lieutenant not much older than myself. He explained that
I had been posted to the Fort Howe Army Instrument
Shop and that the shop was not open on Sunday. He
also informed me that there were no army barracks
or camps at Saint John. Because the city had been
very hard hit by the Depression, the Canadian government had decided that the troops of the Saint John
Fortress Area would all be billeted in private homes.
Large numbers of private boarding houses had been
opened and approved by Saint John city officials and
the army. They provided rooms and meals for the
several thousand soldiers and sailors who made up
the Saint John garrisons.

With dry docks, a ship-building yard, the CPR
winter port and railway freight yards, the city was a
vital transportation hub for shipment of war supplies
to Britain. It was heavily defended with anti-aircraft
batteries and coast-defence guns.

In place of barracks and army food, troops stationed here were paid a "subsistence allowance". I
faintly remember now that it was about $1.60 a day.
Using this, I was to find my own living accommodation and three meals per day. I remember that the
young lieutenant's name was Walter Shane and that
he was from Winnipeg. In a friendly way, he suggested—without making it an order—that he could
take me to the Saint John YMCA to get a room for
that Sunday night and that he would send a driver to
pick me up Monday morning at 8 o'clock and take me
to the Fort Howe shop where I would be working.

I was then left alone for the rest of Sunday to explore Saint John. I soon learned that the citizens were friendly and took a kindly parental interest in soldiers who had been sent here from all over Canada. They insisted on one thing, however. They liked people to pronounce the name of their city correctly. It was SAINT JOHN, not Sin John or St. John's. "Please remember that!" they all emphasized.

I had never seen the ocean, so the first thing I did in Saint John was to take a walk down to the docks where I found the harbour full to the brim with bright green water. A few hours later, I walked back to find the harbour empty, just a mass of mud. The tide had gone out. In future weeks, many Saint Johners were to tell me that Saint John and the Bay of Fundy have the highest and lowest tides in the world and that the area is home to the world-famous Reversing Falls at the mouth of the Saint John River.

Next morning, I was taken to Fort Howe and introduced to the twelve or so people with whom I would work for the next year or more. They were under the command of Lieut. Shane whom I had already met. He, however, spent most of his time at the big Ordnance Depot at Coldbrook, a few miles from the city.

In actual charge of the Fort Howe Instrument Shop was a W.O.1 (Warrant Officer First Class) Regimental Sergeant Major named Ernie Woods. He was a watchmaker by trade and a most unmilitary sergeant major. He told me that all the people at the shop were skilled craftsmen. They adjusted and repaired all kinds of precision instruments: binoculars, telescopes, range finders, dial sights, clinometers, speedometers, calculators, and even typewriters. Predictors, which aimed anti-aircraft guns, were new to them. I and a private from Quebec named Clovis Gravel had been posted to the shop to look after these mysterious new machines.

I was introduced to Private Gravel and we became immediate friends, although he spoke little English and I spoke even less French. With Sergeant Major Woods acting as interpreter, Gravel proposed that we should become roommates so he could learn English and I could learn French. He had found an excellent boarding house within walking distance of the shop, and his landlady, a Miss Mary Lamb, had a vacancy. We could share a room with two twin beds and get excellent meals. That's how I became acquainted with 26 Dorchester Street, where I was to spend more than a year in what was virtually a second home.

After work that first day, Gravel took me to meet Miss Lamb, who introduced herself by stating that she was a hard-shell Baptist Christian. She did not force religion upon her boarders, but she did insist that they refrain from use of bad language in her house and smoke cigarettes only in their own rooms. Neither Gravel nor I smoked, so this was no problem for us. Miss Lamb evidently decided that I was half-civilized even though I did come from "Upper Canada". (That's what Saint Johners always called Ontario.) She accepted me as a boarder at what I recall was the standard rate of about $9 per week. For this I would get lodging and supper six days a week and a box lunch. She didn't do breakfast. Gravel and I would have to get that at the nearby Empire Café, a

Chinese restaurant.

Gravel and I were assigned a big double room on the second floor at the front of the house. With two comfortable beds, it seemed palatial compared to army huts which were heated by coal stoves and housed thirty or more men. Miss Lamb explained that she had six boarders. Besides Gravel and I, there were two sailors, both of whom were night radio operators at the Royal Canadian Navy wireless station, located on the top floor of the Customs House at Saint John Harbour. They slept in the daytime and we saw little of them in the first few weeks. There were also two civilian boarders: Fred Butt, a bachelor bank teller too old for military service, and a Miss Harrowsmith. She was a descendant of a Loyalist family that had left New England after the American Revolution and been given a large land grant in New Brunswick. Miss Harrowsmith was the last survivor of the family and lived on the income from a trust fund left by her parents. She told us that the Great Depression had been no hardship for her. I later learned that she had, in fact, helped Miss Lamb to weather that difficult period. She was a real lady who acted as a kind of maiden aunt to the other boarders and added an atmosphere of courtesy and good manners to the establishment.

After having lived ten months in the rough ambiance of army camps, I thought Miss Lamb's establishment was wonderful. One of the first things I did was to locate the Saint John Public Library and get a library card and become friends with a nice lady librarian. After I told her a little about myself and my civilian job as a reporter, she said to me, "You should use your time here to broaden your education. I have the English book list for the University of New Brunswick undergraduate B.A. program. Would you like to start reading through it?" I thought this was an excellent idea and went right through the list during my time in Saint John. I particularly remember how I enjoyed *Tom Jones*, by Henry Fielding, and how I read much of it to Clovis Gravel who made far better progress in learning English than I did in learning French.

My work at the Instrument Shop was not very challenging. I reported for work at 8 A.M. every day and had a half-day off on Saturdays and all day off on Sundays. I was responsible for maintaining, testing and calibrating the Kerrison Predictors at six light anti-aircraft batteries, each of them armed with four Bofors 40mm semi-automatic guns. No enemy aircraft carriers had ever approached the Canadian coast. The only times the guns were ever fired was during practise shoots when the RCAF would have a light bomber tow a drogue (a long cloth bag) at the end of a long cable past the gun sites. The gunners, guided by the Predictor, were supposed to try to hit the drogue. What they would actually do was try to hit the cable, often close to the plane. This would infuriate the plane crew and lead to a barrage of official complaints to the Saint John Fortress headquarters. The gun crews would invariably blame the Predictor, arguing that they did not aim the guns; this was done by the Predictor. Following every shoot, I had to go out to check the Predictor's settings and report that everything was satisfactory.

The first day that I reported for work at the Instrument Shop, a crisis arose over transportation. After Sergeant Major Woods had shown me the locations of the anti-aircraft batteries and told me I should visit each of them twice a month, I asked him, "How do I get there?" He replied, "You drive our jeep out to them." I had to reply, "Er, I don't have a driver's license." This led to a stunned silence, then the question: "Not any kind of license, civilian or Army?" There followed a tirade against the higher-up army command responsible for sending a highly trained technician who couldn't drive a jeep.

Eventually, after a lot of discussion and phone calls to the office of the brigadier at Fortress headquarters, it was decided that Private Polly Pickles, a C.W.A.C. member in charge of the tool crib at Fort Howe, should drive me to the gun sites. This led to something close to mutiny on the part of Private Pickles. I should explain that on my arrival in Saint John, I had been promoted to the rank of lance corporal. Lieutenant Shane had almost apologized about this, explaining that I really should be at least a full corporal or even a sergeant like all the other Fort Howe technicians, but authorization for the necessary establishment change had been delayed in Ottawa. It never did come through.

Private Pickles was infuriated by the news that she was going to be driver to a lowly lance corporal—the lowest form of non-commissioned army life. "All my friends," she said, "are driving captains and majors and colonels. What do I get to drive?—A blank blank

Lance Jack." Eventually she was subdued with the threat that if she didn't obey, she would lose her cozy job in the tool crib and probably end up peeling potatoes for some officers' mess. That's how I became the only lance corporal in the Canadian Army with his own driver! My own little vacation from the war!

So began what was to become a real friendship between Polly and me. She often gave me advice on how to please "that poor little girl in Upper Canada," as she called Josephine. And she told me about her own girlhood in Sydney, Nova Scotia, on Glace Bay.

It soon became evident to me that the staff of the Fort Howe Instrument Shop was a most unmilitary bunch although everybody did place great importance on excellence of work.

I became very happy at Saint John. The relationship between citizens and soldiers was warm and cordial. Local churches and service clubs organized many activities for members of the forces. Our officers impressed on their troops that we should always be polite and helpful in our relations with civilians. For example, young men boarding with local families were encouraged to help with small chores such as shovelling snow.

At Christmas time we were welcomed to many parties and carol services. That's how I became acquainted with the Anglican Church. I went to a Christmas party at Trinity Anglican Church and was invited to attend the regular Sunday service of Evensong by Canon Lawrence, the venerable rector. I started attending, and was impressed by the dignity and beauty of the English language as written by Thomas Cranmer in the 1500s for the Book of Common Prayer. To this day, my association with the Church of England continues.

Life was pleasant at Saint John for nearly a year and a half. Every two months, I got a five-day pass to go home to Toronto. I carefully saved my money so I could afford a first-class rail ticket and an upper berth. CPR porters and sleeping-car conductors seemed to enjoy welcoming a lance corporal to their accommodation, and I developed a real liking for delicious CPR dining-car food, particularly the wonderful coffee.

After I had been in Saint John for nearly a year, our routine at the secluded instrument shop atop its harbour-side hill was rudely ended when the instrument shop caught fire one night and burned to the ground. A huge investigation took place and a court of inquiry was held but, as far as I know, the real cause of the fire was never determined. In any case, all the military staff of the shop were immediately transferred to a shop in the RCEME ordnance depot at Coldbrook, about 10 miles north of Saint John. We were transported back and forth from town in army buses every day.

Life at Coldbrook was much more regimented than at Fort Howe. For me, it came to an end after several months when I was informed that I was being sent back to Kingston for more courses. With a heavy heart, I packed my kit bag for the journey back to Ontario. I hated to leave Miss Lamb's boarding house, her good food and my many friends in Saint John, but at least it would mean I would get to see Josephine and my family every two weeks. Kingston is much closer to Toronto than is Saint John, N.B.

Arriving back at the Armament School at Barriefield, I was informed that I had been assigned to take two courses, each four months in length.

Chapter 25
Back To School And The End Of My War

The first course I was to take at the Armament School was Machine Shop, virtually an elementary education in tool and die making. It was useless to point out that I had no experience and no aptitude in this field. That didn't matter. I was hustled down to a machine shop two miles away in what had been the peacetime stables of the Royal Military College, just across the Cataraqui River from Kingston. Here a Major Murphy from Sudbury informed six other new arrivals and myself that in four months we were to learn machine-shop skills that in civilian life normally required four years of apprenticeship.

It was back to school again. Having no choice in the matter, I settled down to learn a new skill. I concluded that I just had to work as hard as possible. The unspoken threat was that anybody who flunked out on these courses would be transferred to the infantry and sent overseas in a reinforcement draft.

The machine-shop work proved to be not too difficult. We had good-natured sergeants as teachers, many of whom had learned their trades in northern Ontario mines around Sudbury. I wasn't noted for good hand-eye skills, but I learned to rely on precision machines and micrometers to meet tolerances of one-thousandth of an inch. (One inch equals 2.54 centimetres.) Beginning in November, we marched every day all winter from Barriefield down to R.M.C. As a lance corporal, I commanded the mini-parade. When the course came to an end in February, I learned that I had headed the class in spite of my ineptitude.

Then I began my second course. This one took place right at the Armament School, without the two-mile march to R.M.C. every day. The course title was Optical Instrument Mechanics. I was given three months to learn how to maintain, clean and repair telescopes, binoculars, range finders, clinometers, dial sights and all the other small instruments, including compasses, that an army uses in the field. The theory behind all these gadgets had to be mastered as well. Nobody explained why I was required to study and learn all this. I concluded that the real reason was just to keep warm bodies moving through the classrooms of the RCEME Armament School so that the teachers' and officers' jobs would be secure.

The course dragged on through winter. The war in France and Belgium had intensified and so had the Canadian Army's need for reinforcements. It began to look as though I might finally be sent overseas and be thrust into the real war. On my weekend leaves to Toronto, Josephine and I talked about this and we decided to be married in the spring of 1945. I had an interview with her parents, who gave us their blessing. I had developed a real affection for Jo's mother and father. They were to become a much-loved second set of parents to me.

I obtained Army permission to marry, and the date

was set for Saturday, May 5, 1945. We arranged a two-day honeymoon to Buffalo. The wedding took place at Wesley United Church, Mimico, with Harry Smith being my best man. When Jo and I subsequently arrived in Buffalo, we heard wonderful news: the war in Europe had ended!

Jo had earlier insisted that she was coming with me to Kingston to live. I had been able to rent a two-room flat there as our first married home. We moved in, and I was able to get overnight passes every day to spend the night with Jo.

Back at the camp, where I had finished my instrument-mechanic course, I was now taking a sergeant's course, just to keep the instructors busy. I declined the invitation to volunteer for service in the Pacific. No pressure was applied for this.

There ensued a delightful summer. Jo, bless her heart, had obtained a secretary job at the C.I.L. plant in Kingston. This was the same company for which she had worked in New Toronto. As part of her Kingston job, she was given a pair of nylon stockings to test-wear every week. This was a delightful perq since stockings had been almost impossible to get during the war.

We had a wonderful real honeymoon together that summer in our little two-room home in the house of a spinster named Miss Canning. And on August 14, 1945, I had an equally wonderful birthday present: the war with Japan ended. It was V-J Day.

Harvey and Josephine happily walked the middle
aisle at Wesley United Church, Mimico, on Saturday,
May 5, the weekend World War II ended in Europe.
It was the start of 57 years of happy marriage.

One week later, we went to Toronto for a weekend. On Saturday morning I went, in uniform, to the Telegram office and once again knocked on C.H.J. Snider's door—with a little more confidence this time. He welcomed me and asked what I was doing in the army. Just putting in time, I told him. Priority for discharge was being given to long-service men who had served overseas, I explained. Long-term leave, however, was being given to soldiers whose employers urgently needed them back. "That sounds interesting," Mr. Snider said. "Write down your service number and unit name for me. I'll make a phone call to Ottawa."

We went back to Kingston, and I went back to camp on Monday morning. About 10 A.M. a runner arrived at my classroom with a message that the Colonel wanted to see me at Camp Headquarters. I hurried over. The O.C., whom I had never even seen before, said to me, "Are you Currell, B132059?" I said, "Yes, Sir." He said, "I don't know why you're so important, but I've got an order from Ottawa that you are to be on the train to Toronto this afternoon on six months' leave to resume your civilian occupation. The staff sergeant here will hurry you through the routine. Congratulations."

"Thank you, Sir," I said and saluted.

A frantic morning and afternoon followed. I turned in all my kit except one uniform, collected my pay, and managed to get a phone call through to Jo at her workplace. We met at our flat, paid up our rent, made a long-distance call to Jo's mother to give her the news, and called a taxi to take us to the Kingston

Outer Station. By 6 P.M. we were on our way, out of the Army, and headed back to our own lives.

Six months later, when I had to spend a day being formally discharged from the Canadian Army, an officer told me I was in line for officer training if I elected to join the Canadian Army Permanent Force. I said, "Thanks but No Thanks." I wanted to have nothing to do with any military organization for the rest of my life.

Chapter 26
Living Again

Ireturned to the Telegram suburban staff the day after I was released from the Canadian Army, and it was wonderful—I felt that I had started living again.

The atmosphere at the Tely was much different, I soon found. The entire editorial staff had changed. In charge were many former editors who had been re-called from retirement to take the place of people who had gone into the armed services. Filling reporter jobs were many kids younger than I was—I was twenty-three by this time. Copy boys had been trained and promoted. Most of them were doing very well. And it was a pleasant surprise to me to learn that I was now considered an experienced reporter, capable of filling in for the Suburban Editor on his day off.

In charge of the department was Herb Berkley, who was looking forward to resuming his retirement. He immediately informed me that my salary would be $20 per week and that I was assigned to cover Scarborough and East York. When I protested that I was living in Mimico on the opposite side of Toronto, he commented that this was "too bad" but I would just have to put up with it. He didn't intend to re-arrange suburban beats to suit me. I would have to wait until a permanent Suburban Editor was appointed.

I should tell you that Josephine's parents had offered to take us in temporarily until we could find rental accommodation. Housing had become extremely scarce during the war. Returning veterans were finding it almost impossible to find affordable apartments or flats. So while I was getting used to covering Scarborough and East York by streetcar, Jo and her mother were reading classified ads and searching for accommodation for us.

After several weeks, they found a basement apartment for $40 a month in the cellar of a big old house on the corner of Jameson Avenue and King Street West in Parkdale. It was rather dismal with a makeshift kitchen and bathroom, a shared refrigerator one flight upstairs, a brick-walled bedroom, and a tiny living room with bars on the small windows. Jo immediately took an office job to help us pay the exorbitant rent. Using a Re-establishment Credit provided by the Canadian government, we managed to furnish the place, and we settled down to enjoy marital bliss. We were very happy just to be together and stayed at that address for one year.

For me, it was a new experience to be turned loose to cover two large municipalities. My previous experience had involved coverage of community affairs only. But now I had been given the job of reporting everything that went on in two big townships. That included everything relating to police and fire departments, township council meetings, boards of education, public utility commissions, magistrates courts, high schools and neighbourhood affairs. I was also expected to be on standby duty to be sent out on major stories in the outer suburbs.

After I had been back only a couple of weeks, Herb Berkley called me early one Sunday morning to meet photographer Madison Sale and head out to Ajax to cover a murder case. The young wife of an RCAF officer had been found raped and strangled in her home after an all-night party; her husband was still overseas. Covering an important story like this one was another new experience for me. Fortunately, Mad Sale, the photographer assigned with me, was very familiar with newspaper reporting and gave me considerable help. In addition, the senior cop on the case, an Inspector Gurnett of the O.P.P. C.I.D., could see that I was a green crime reporter and took time to explain the case to me. I was able to write a presentable story, and although it was no prize winner, it appeared on Monday's Page One.

A teenager named Lorne Harris was charged with the murder. I covered the trial at Whitby. He was convicted, but on appeal he was granted a new trial at which he was found not guilty.

Happily for me, I was on the Scarborough-East York beat for only about three months. Here's how the change occurred. One day, around December 1st, the members of the suburban staff were all informed that we had a new boss. Major Bert Wemp had returned from a stint as a war correspondent in Europe and had been given an appointment to take over and revive the Suburban and Regional Department. I admired "the Major" as he was called. He had been a fighter pilot in World War I, had been elected mayor of Toronto in the 1930s and had had a distinguished newspaper career.

On the first day of his new job, Major Wemp called me over and asked me what beat I was covering. I told him Scarborough and East York, and that I was living in Parkdale. He then asked, "Who is covering the Lakeshore (Mimico, New Toronto and Long Branch)?" I said, "Ed Monteith is, and he lives in Scarborough." The Major replied, "We can soon fix that." He called Ed Monteith over and asked if he would like to take over the eastern area. Monteith said, "I sure would." So that was arranged on the spot.

Major Wemp then asked what I was being paid. When I told him $20 per week, he said, "You can't live on that as a married man. I'll try to get you $30." He went to bat for me with the Managing Editor, and a week later I got a $10 raise.

PART FOUR: TEN MORE TRIPS

Chapter 27
Where Are We Going This Weekend?

This section of the book contains updated versions of another ten trips that I remember well. But first, I would like to provide some additional background.

From the day Laurie McKechnie talked me into starting the "Town and Country Trips" column in March 1958, those trips became part of my life and part of my family's life.

Because I was being paid extra for the trips—$15 a column and 10 cents a mile (6.25 cents a kilometre) for travel—I was supposed to do the trips on my own time. Sunday seemed to be the best day for most of them. My two kids gave me their own very good reason for this. They wanted to go with me on most of the trips but did not want to go out of town on Saturdays.

Here is why. Saturday morning was Kids' Club Time at the Royal Ontario Museum. It probably had a more formal name and it may still be operating at the R.O.M. I hope it is. In any case, it was a stimulating program which the museum had started at the suggestion, I think, of leaders of the Toronto Field Naturalist Club, many of whom were staff members at the museum. My kids, Judith and Bob, had become enthusiastic members. There was no way they wanted to miss either the Saturday morning sessions or my trips, so they always urged me to do my trips on Sundays. And I remember how, at Friday night suppers, they would eagerly ask, "Where are we going this weekend, Dad?"

Josephine, their mother, would sometimes come along as well, but because many of the winter trips involved plowing through snow, sometimes on skis or snowshoes, she preferred to miss the more rugged ones.

Whenever possible, I would make advance appointments to meet somebody who could give me information about the destination I had in mind. My contact was often a provincial park superintendent or a conservation officer or a museum curator.

Once, Bob and I (he was about 16 at the time) were stranded on a trip in a wilderness area north of Coldwater in a real howling blizzard. We had been taken into the area by a Lands and Forests officer on a snowmobile. Part way along the route, the storm got so bad that the snow machine could not carry three people any longer. The conservation officer had to take the machine and leave the two of us while he went for help. Bob and I waited for more than an hour in very heavy blowing snow. Bob still says it was the worst snowstorm he has ever experienced. Finally we were rescued by six or eight members of a snowmobile safari. The conservation officer had luckily met them on the trail and brought them to our rescue. It was scary, waiting there alone in the middle of the Torrance Barrens, although we were warmly dressed and prepared for bad weather.

We did not have many experiences like that, but over the next few years we did see hundreds of fascinating spots and meet many interesting experts in many fields. And for forty-nine years, my spare time was organized every week around some kind of trip to be researched, undertaken and then written up. If we were on holidays at our Parry Sound cottage in summer, I would seek nearby spots to write about. I personally went to every destination, with a very few exceptions. These were book reviews. Around Christmas every year, I would usually devote one column to reviews of natural science books that I had especially enjoyed.

The trips I wrote about were not always within Ontario. As a family, we usually took a week-long car trip to the southern United States in the school Easter holidays. I would find some spot to explore, like Hawk's Bill Mountain, on the Appalachian Trail, or an oyster dealer at Murrell's Inlet in South Carolina. The kids learned a lot from these expeditions. Sometimes we would get permission from their principals to keep them out of school for a couple of extra days. One of their principals, George Petrie at Fairfield Junior School, once told me, "They'll learn more from being with Josephine and you than they would in two days at school."

As I climbed the editorial ladder at The Telegram and was given more important jobs, it became easier for me to get time off to go on more extended trips, often for three or four days or a whole week. I would suggest an interesting expedition to Doug MacFarlane or to the current Managing Editor. I would then usually get an OK to be away from the office for a few days and sometimes to take a photographer or a staff artist along with me to provide illustrations for a feature story and Trip columns.

Early in the 1960s, for example, Jo and I became almost the first travellers to drive the newly opened stretch of Highway 17, the Trans-Canada route between Sault Ste. Marie and Thunder Bay. We drove right around Lake Superior. It was quite an adventure. There were no motels or inns on most of the route, very few gas stations in isolated hamlets, and we met very few cars. Between the Sault and Thunder Bay we made one overnight stop. It was at Terrace Bay in a combination inn and boarding house opened by the Kimberly Clarke paper company to house employees and visitors to a KC pulp mill. We visited Kakabeka Falls west of Thunder Bay, and stopped briefly at the Pigeon River site where fur-trade canoe brigades from Montreal and the far northwest used to meet at an annual summer rendezvous. Josephine and I crossed into the U.S. at Pigeon River, then followed the northwest shore of Lake Superior past a spectacular cliff-top lighthouse at Grand Marais, and finally rounded the tip of Lake Superior at Duluth, Minnesota, across what seemed like dozens of railway crossings. The south shore of Lake Superior seemed flat and uninteresting compared to the high cliffs and endless vistas on the Canadian side.

I took many such trips in the next few years. One of them was with Telegram artist Hugh McClelland on the CPR steamship Keewatin from Sault Ste. Marie to Port McNicol, near Midland. This was during the last season that the Keewatin and her sister ship Assiniboia operated on the Great Lakes.

A few years later, Hugh McClelland and I took another memorable voyage, this time aboard a coal carrier named "Ontario Power". We sailed from a coal-fired electric power plant at Mississauga, just west of Toronto, all the way to Sydney, Nova Scotia. To keep coal mines at Sydney in operation, the Canadian government was at that time subsidizing the cost of hauling coal from Sydney to two huge Ontario Hydro power plants at Toronto and Mississauga. Hugh and I were given a suite of rooms provided for steam-ship company guests aboard the ship. Cruising down Lake Ontario and the St. Lawrence past the Thousand Islands and through the Seaway locks in late September, we enjoyed the scenery and the memorable sight of whales spouting in the Gulf of St. Lawrence off the North Cape of Nova Scotia. I wrote a Saturday Section Page feature story about the trip, and Hugh provided drawings to illustrate it, as he did for many of my travel stories and Trip columns.

It was on one such expedition that I enjoyed the most exciting fishing of my lifetime. One spring day, while I was still Suburban Editor, I began wondering how far north it was possible to drive in Ontario. I knew that three-quarters of the province was situated north of Lake Superior but had no idea how far it was possible to take a car into this vast hinterland. I called a friend in the Public Relations section of the Ontario Transport Ministry and asked him. He didn't know either but started to ask. He called me a day or so later with the information that the most northerly motoring destination was a community called Pickle Lake and a gold mine named Pickle Crow. They were, by road, almost 2,500 km (nearly 1,600 miles) from Toronto. These two hinterland outposts, far to the northwest of Lake Superior, had just become accessible by car because the Ministry had concluded an arrangement with a logging and paper-mill company to open to public travel a private company road that linked up to an existing road to the mine.

I took this interesting information into Doug MacFarlane's office. He asked, "What's all this in aid of? I suppose you want to go there."

"Er, yes, sort of," I replied. "It would make a good story for the start of the spring travel season."

"What do you want?" the Editor-in-Chief asked.

"Bob Shannon, one of our Barrie reporters, has a new van and a small house trailer. I could get Bob to take us in his van and pull his trailer behind. Instead of 10 cents a mile, The Telegram could just pay for the gas plus a small rental fee for the trailer. I have an aluminum boat we could take on the van roof as well."

"Who do you mean by 'us'?" MacFarlane asked. "Who else are you including in this conspiracy?"

"I'd like to take Tiny Bennett to write fishing columns," I replied.

"It's crazy," MacFarlane said after a moment of thought, "but go ahead. It should provide some good copy and pictures. I know I can trust you not to let expenses get out of hand. But no diving suits!!" (I knew that this last reference was to reporter John MacLean's recent attempt to put the purchase of a diving suit onto his expense account for a feature story on ship-wrecks in Georgian Bay.)

So a week or two later, Bob Shannon, Tiny Bennett and I took off on a June day for the far northwest. It was a memorable expedition to the headwaters of the Albany River which runs down into Hudson Bay. On the way, we stopped at Michipicoten on Lake Superior where the stone chimneys and fireplaces of rival Hudson's Bay Company and Northwest Company trading posts still faced each other and where steel rails had been unloaded from ships for the building of the Canadian Pacific Railway in the 1880s.

We also visited a First Nations community called Doghole Bay. Here Roy Skunk, the mayor, took us on a boat ride into an active Hudson's Bay Company post called Osnaburgh House, where a young factor from northern Scotland named Charles Livingston made us welcome. Charles had been recruited in the Orkneys, flown to Montreal, then to Winnipeg and finally by small aircraft to Osnaburgh House, where he fell in love with a First Nations woman and they were married. All he had seen of Canada so far was Dorval Airport at Montreal, a bit of Winnipeg, and miles and miles of lakes and forest. But he was look-ing to the future. And when he'd heard that the region was about to be opened up by a road, he had ordered a shiny British sports car and had driven it in over the new road from the railway station at Savant Lake. He was driving this car on the few miles of miserable road around Osnaburgh House and Doghole Bay. I later heard that he had left the H.B.C. when it closed Osnaburgh House and he had become a community development officer at Fort Albany, employed by the federal government.

I still remember that trip for three things: the terrible roads, the black flies and the fishing. Using my aluminum boat, we fished many of the lakes and rivers we encountered on the way. In every one of them, we met voracious pike and pickerel. In fact, Tiny Bennett nearly lost some fingers to a monster pike. He had hooked a small pickerel, and while he was reeling it in, the unfortunate fish was torn in half by a big pike. Tiny, leaning over the side of the boat, was attempting to unhook the remains of the pickerel when a monster pike leaped from the water and grabbed the fish out of Tiny's hand, just missing two fingers!

This was just one of many spectacular trips I enjoyed while working for The Telegram.

In the 1950s and 1960s under the governments of Premier Leslie Frost and Premier John Robarts, Queen's Park had some excellent public relations programs. Frank McDougall, the Deputy Minister of Lands and Forests, was noted in those years for his particularly good relations with the press. Reporters from The Telegram, The Toronto Star and The Globe and Mail were always welcome in his office. Editors knew that when they needed advice on getting reporters to remote northern Ontario locations, Frank McDougall or his Director of Operations, Phil Rhyness, were the people to call.

I recall that one afternoon when I was acting City Editor, a small Canadian Press item came in about a First Nations teenage girl at a place called Shining Tree. The girl's family was distressed because their daughter was being denied high-school education in their remote home district. The only way she could attend high school was by boarding with a family in Sudbury, more than 160 km (100 miles) to the south. There was no way her parents could afford this. The Tely education reporter at this time was Isobel Gordon, who later married the paper's publisher, John Basset. I called Isobel over and showed her the CP item. "Sounds like a good story," she said. "Would you like to go there?" I asked. She replied that she surely would, so I phoned Phil Rhyness at Lands and Forests and asked him how we would get our reporter to Shining Tree. Without hesitation he replied, "Fly her by Air Canada to Sudbury and I'll have our district man get her to Shining Tree, wherever it is."

Isobel left immediately and by next day filed a first-rate human interest story that led to an Ontario Ministry of Education program to assist poor students from remote areas in obtaining high-school education. I later heard from Phil Rhyness that the arrival of beautiful Isobel Gordon had created quite a stir in Shining Tree.

In 1969, officials of the Lands and Forests Department—sometime around 1970 it became the Ministry of Natural Resources—helped me go on an unforgettable canoe trip down the Abitibi River and Moose River in northern Ontario. They arranged for a University of Windsor graduate student named Terry Damm and myself to begin this adventure at the Onakawana River north of Cochrane and to paddle downstream to Moosonee on James Bay. Terry's job was to gather material for a government booklet about canoeing to James Bay. Mine was to write a Saturday Section Page feature about the trip. I still shudder when I re-read my story about shooting the horrific Allon rapids where the Abitibi River runs into the Moose.

One other trip I should mention is a canoe trip that I took through Quetico Provincial Park with Park Superintendent Ross Williams. It had importance for my son, Bob, because it led to his getting summer jobs as a member of the "portage crew" (maintaining portage trails, etc.) at Quetico Park during his U.T.S. high-school years. I think those wilderness summers also had something to do with his choice of profession. He later earned B.Sc. and M.Sc. degrees in forestry at the University of Toronto and became a professor at Sault College in Sault Ste. Marie.

Chapter 28
Confessions Of A Raw Oyster Addict

I love raw oysters on the half shell with a drop of vinegar and a few grains of freshly ground black pepper. Only once in my life have I had all the oysters I could eat, and that was nearly 1,600 km (1,000 miles) from home.

It happened in November, 1973, during a nine-day holiday that Josephine and I took with Peter Brewster and his then wife, a nurse named Ellie. The four of us had gone to Myrtle Beach on the Grand Strand of South Carolina for some surf-fishing and had rented an apartment in a quiet part of town.

At that time, Peter, just back from a home-sickness cure in Britain, was an editor on The Toronto Sun. Besides being an avid and expert fisherman, he was—and still is—an oyster addict. The day after our arrival at Myrtle Beach, I mentioned to Peter that this was oyster country and we should look for some. After making some inquiries, we drove in Tokyo Rose, my Toyota Celica, about 24 km (15 miles) south of Myrtle Beach to what in those days was a quiet fishing village called Murrell's Inlet. A clerk in a grocery store directed us to a wholesale oyster establishment. I approached a couple of workmen standing beside a mountain of oyster shells and asked if I could buy oysters in the shell. "Y'all sho' came to the right place," one of them replied. "Y'all see that man in the red suit?"

I looked around and there was a man in a red suit—not a coverall or a track suit but a perfectly cut suit of jacket and trousers, bright red and topped with a red cowboy hat. He allowed that it was a nice day, guessed that we were from Canada "because y'all talk so funny," shook hands with us and asked how many oysters we'd like. Maybe eight or ten bushel? I mentioned two or three dozen. He looked incredulous and finally muttered, "Don't y'all talk foolish. I'll give y'all half a bushel." He turned to an assistant who dragged an empty bushel basket to a mighty pile of oysters just unloaded off a nearby barge; they'd been gathered from oyster beds that morning at low tide. The assistant picked up a shovel and filled the bushel three-quarters full, then dumped them into a beat-up cardboard carton for me. I asked about the price. The red-suited boss said, "Oh, give me two dollah," and added with a grin, "but not one of them phony two dollah Canadian bills."

Peter and I couldn't get the oysters back to our ocean-side apartment fast enough, delaying only to pick up a case of beer and some brown bread and seafood sauce. I'm afraid we made an awful mess of the kitchen sink, sluicing off the black mud that covered the oysters, all wonderfully fresh. I had earlier learned the knack of opening oyster shells. We sat on the porch, surrounded by rapidly growing piles of oyster shells. Nobody kept count, but I must have eaten more than three dozen before Peter gashed his thumb opening a shell and begged for first aid. (He can't stand the sight of blood.) With nurse-like efficiency, Ellie quickly slapped on a band-aid so she could get back to her own oyster lunch.

It took us two days to eat through the pile of oysters!

As we were opening and eating, I recalled an earlier South Carolina visit when our landlord, Nathan Lewis, took me out fishing for sea trout. At lunch time, he drifted the boat onto an oyster bed and, wearing hip rubber boots, gathered a couple of dozen oysters which we opened and ate with brown bread. He explained to me that any South Carolina taxpayer was allowed—for his own use—to gather two bushels a season from public oyster beds along the coast.

I now get my oysters from an establishment called the All Seas Fishery in Etobicoke. Last time I was there, the price was $1 per oyster.

I haven't been back to Murrell's Inlet for many years. It has probably changed greatly and the oyster beds may have even disappeared. If you happen to go there, look for a seafood spot called Lee's Inlet Kitchen. I remember having a good seafood lunch there with a fresh oyster cocktail.

Chapter 29
See Canada's Oldest Living Emblem

Canada's national tree is undoubtedly the sugar maple (*Acer saccharum*). Both its English name and its botanical Latin name remind us that every spring the sap of this tree is sweet enough to be boiled down into incomparably delicious maple syrup. But there is more to sugar maples than just maple syrup. Every fall, they decorate the landscapes of eastern Canada (and the U.S. northeast) with magnificent displays of crimson colour around our Thanksgiving Day, the second Monday in October. And, most important of all, the maple tree has given us our national emblem, a crimson maple leaf for our national flag.

Where, in Canada, is the biggest and oldest specimen of our national tree to be found?

In 1966, I set out to answer this question for one of my Trip columns. My quest led me to a community called North Pelham in the grape-growing country of the Niagara Peninsula, between Lake Erie and Lake Ontario. North Pelham is about 112 km (70 miles) from Toronto and close to Fonthill.

Here, in a delightful little park, I found the Comfort Maple. At that time, this biggest and oldest sugar maple tree in Canada was believed to be more than 450 years old. That would make its age about 500 at the present time.

Try to think what Canada and North America were like in the year 1509 when one autumn a maple key spiralled to the fertile soil of North Pelham and took a precarious hold on life by sinking a couple of tiny hair-like roots into the ground beneath a parent maple grove. (Sugar maples are shade-tolerant. They always grow best under the canopy of parent trees.) When the Comfort Maple took root, Samuel de Champlain, Canada's first permanent European settler, hadn't even been born. He didn't get to Quebec until 1603. By that time, our maple tree was nearly 100 years old.

By 1816, when a family of United Empire Loyalists named Comfort arrived here as refugees from the American Revolution, the tree was already more than 300 years old. The Comforts recognized it as a venerable giant. They cleared the forest around it to plant an orchard but protected "Old Glory" from encroachment. That was the family nickname for their much-loved tree.

More than a century later, in 1946 to be exact, Miss Edna Comfort and her brother, Earl Hampden Comfort, found themselves sole owners of the Comfort farm and orchard; being elderly, they decided they had to sell, but they retained ownership of the field where the Comfort Maple stands, along with a laneway leading to it. The tree was at that time estimated to be 438 years old.

Edna Comfort, in 1960 after her brother's death, honoured his memory by donating the tree, its surrounding field of .2 hectares (half an acre), and the laneway, to the Niagara Peninsula Conservation Authority.

These days the Comfort Maple, probably more than 500 years old, flaunts its autumn colour high over the surrounding pear and cherry orchard. The tree is recognized as a Canadian national treasure. It's about 27 metres (90 feet) tall and has a crown diameter of about 21 metres (70 feet). Tree surgeons keep a close eye on it. After it was hit by lightning in the 1960s, they braced many of its huge branches, sealed its cavities with bricks and concrete, and fertilized its huge root systems. It is now enjoying a healthy old age.

You can visit Canada's oldest maple any day of the week, any month of the year. There is no admission charge or parking charge. To get there from Toronto, take the Queen Elizabeth Way across the Burlington Skyway to Exit 57 at Victoria Avenue. Go right on Victoria to Metler Rd. Turn left onto Metler. Past Balfour Street, you'll see a sign on the right to the Comfort Maple.

For information about the tree, call Kim Frohlich at the Niagara Peninsula Conservation Authority. Her number is 905-788-3135, Extension 241.

My family and I especially love trees. My son, Bob, is a professional forester and my daughter, Judith, is a keen naturalist. We own 270 acres of managed forest near Parry Sound and Bob has a woodlot of his own at Echo Bay near Sault Ste. Marie. Because of this, I did a little research on trees and came up with a few interesting facts:

- Trees are the tallest and oldest living organisms

on planet Earth.

- Trees continue to grow all their lives in two directions, upward and outward, adding to their height and diameter every year.
- The oldest trees in the world are bristlecone pines in the Inyo National Forest in central California. They are more than 4,600 years old.
- Trees need light, water, soil and air to survive. They absorb incredible amounts of carbon dioxide and give us huge volumes of oxygen to breathe.
- Trees are among our oldest friends, and the maple tree is close to the hearts of my generation of Canadians. When I was a child, every kid knew the words of a Canadian patriotic anthem entitled "The Maple Leaf Forever". It was written in 1867 by a Toronto teacher named Alexander Muir to celebrate Canada's birth. There is still a Toronto school named for him.

Chapter 30

Trout Leap Over The Nicolston Dam

For 156 years, five generations of Nicols have been running the Nicolston Mill on the Nottawasaga River just east of Alliston, about 70 km (44 miles) north of Toronto. Today, Frank and Charmon Nicol and three of their four sons still keep the old mill running. But instead of making flour from local wheat, the Nicols now grind bird seed for suburbanites. They also provide riverside campsites for vacationers, rent canoes and kayaks for river trips, invite visitors to enjoy views of rainbow trout leaping up a fish ladder, and conduct walks through their antique mill. Families are invited to visit the dam and mill without charge. There are ducks, chickens, horses and pigs for kids to admire and pet. The whole place is a fascinating, low-key, little oasis of history.

The first Nicol came to Canada from Scotland in the early 1800s and settled at Hoggs Hollow, just north of Toronto. His son, John, migrated north to the banks of the Nottawasaga in 1853, and built a dam, flour mill, sawmill and woollen mill. A village sprouted soon around the mills and was called Nicolston. The original 1850s wooden flour mill burned down in 1900 and was replaced by the present sturdy brick structure in 1907. Powered by the river, the mill kept grinding until 1967. The waterwheel turbine has since been removed, but nearly all the intricate old mill machinery is still in place.

Now on a weekday about once a month, Frank Nicol connects the old machinery to a tractor engine in order to grind out a supply of bird seed. With a great clattering, shaking and roaring, the old mill comes to life to show how grain was ground in the old days. If you'd like to get a date and time to see and photograph the old mill in action, you can phone the Nicols at 705-435-7946.

Early every spring, thousands of rainbow trout migrate from Georgian Bay up the Nottawasaga to spawn. Only the strongest managed to leap over the 2.7-metre (9-foot) Nicolston dam until 1961 when the Ontario government chose this location for the province's first fish ladder. In the 1950s, I remember as Regional Editor of The Telegram sending Bill Foote to get pictures at Nicolston of the leaping trout. He got a prize-winning shot which we displayed prominently in the newspaper.

Introduced to Ontario from the Pacific coast, the rainbow trout still fight their way upstream but now have a much easier route getting above the dam. The run usually extends from mid-March to mid-April.

If you like to go canoeing, you might enjoy a trip down the Nottawasaga to Wasaga Beach from Nicolston. The Nicols rent canoes by the hour or day. You can ask them about guided trips downstream and rides back up to the starting point. The river runs briskly between Nicolston and Georgian Bay.

I have fondly remembered this place and the Nicol

family and their animals since my last visit in April 2001.

When I telephoned recently, Charmon Nicol told me that one of the family's main businesses is operating a campground where families bring trailers and tents for vacations of a week or two beside the river and millpond. Lots of families also come to get bird seed for their feeders.

To get to the Nicolston Mill and the campground, take Hwy 400 or Hwy 27 north to Hwy 89. Go west on No. 89 for 10 km from Cookstown. Turn right to the millpond just before the Nottawasaga River bridge.

Chapter 31
Visit The Tropics

Doug Wilson likes to offer what he calls "a cheap trip to the tropics". He is president and CEO of the "Wings of Paradise" butterfly conservatory on the edge of Cambridge, about 85 km (53 miles) west of Toronto. For $9.50 adult admission and $5 for kids, he gives you a half-day or more in a lush indoor garden where 2,000 to 3,000 butterflies, big and small, fly free over waterfalls and streams, stopping to nibble at dishes of fruit or even to perch on visitors' shoulders. College-trained guides explain the life cycles of butterflies and moths. Occasionally, you may even experience the wonderful sight of an emerging butterfly unfolding itself carefully from a chrysalis or cocoon.

Besides the big tropical house (temperature 25-30°C), you'll visit the insect gallery where a big tarantula named Rosie lives along with giant hissing cockroaches, assassin beetles and big African millipedes. If you have patience and time, try counting to see if the millipedes really do have 1,000 feet.

In the same section, there's a glass-enclosed working colony of honey bees. In winter they snuggle up in a great ball of warmth, but on a warm spring day they send scouts out through a private hole in the building wall to search nearby fields for flowers where nectar can be collected to make honey.

As well as providing a fascinating short escape from winter, Wings of Paradise is a place where kids and parents painlessly pick up a lot of education about the butterfly, plant and moth worlds. On weekdays, some 15,000 school kids a year visit here with teachers. Scouts, Cubs, Guides and other groups book visits all year. You can also plan a birthday party at the conservatory or even arrange to be married beside the waterfall in the tropical garden. It's a friendly intimate kind of place where visitors are encouraged to feel they are part of nature. Doug Wilson told me that one of his favourite memories is of seeing a tiny boy, his nose almost at ground level, gently petting a hairy caterpillar on a rock.

Opened five years ago by a small group of district businessmen, Wings of Paradise has ties with the University of Guelph. As for the butterflies themselves, they nearly all come from butterfly farms in the Philippines, Malaysia and Costa Rica. They travel to Ontario by air and courier in the pupa stage

It's a good idea to plan your visit to Wings of Paradise for a sunny day because that's when the butterflies are most active.

When I was last at the conservatory in 2006, a café offered lunch to visitors—soups, salads, sandwiches, wraps and pizzas. A big mural by Brenda Veerman depicted the annual migration of monarch butterflies to Mexico.

For information, the phone number is 519-653-1234. The place is open every day from 10 A.M. to 5 P.M.

To get there from Toronto, take Hwy 401 west to Exit 282, Regional Road 24 at Cambridge. Go right (north) on this road for 7.3 km to Kossoth Road (Regional Road 31). Go left on Kossoth Road for 5.4 km to No. 2500 on the left.

Chapter 32

Over The Hills And Through The Woods To Esther's Hidden Doll House

Despite the lure of computers, cell phones and TV, little girls still love dolls. Many grown-up girls also have a passion for dressed-up imaginary models and collect them by the hundreds as a hobby. These are the kinds of people who find their way to Esther Stover's doll factory. It's tucked away on a back road in forested hills some 300 km (188 miles) north of Toronto, 96 km (60 miles) from Huntsville and 24 km (15 miles) from the nearest highway. Here, with the help of her husband Fred, her daughter Pearl, friends, neighbours and students, Esther makes dolls, dresses dolls, repairs dolls and teaches the ancient art of doll creation.

If you have a child in your life, get some coloured photos of your little darling, take them up to Esther and she'll turn them into an almost perfect doll replica, from about 7 cm (about 3 inches) to 80 cm (about 30 inches) tall, beautifully dressed in clothes of your choice. The cost could be somewhere around $400.

Stover dolls are all porcelain. Esther casts them first in moulds, delicately sculpts the features, fires them in an electric kiln and paints them. When I went to visit, she and Fred—a converted carpenter—

were delicately shaping the face of a Rhett Butler doll. In her doll gallery, she showed me many movie-star dolls as well as Royal Family personages. Two of her favourites are tiny replicas of Katherine Hepburn and Humphrey Bogart, made to fit into a model of the African Queen movie steamship.

How did the Stovers, a family of musicians from Ontario tobacco country near Tillsonburg, end up making dolls in the Almaguin Highlands? Well, Esther, who was never able to keep dolls as a child because her nine siblings kept breaking or appropriating them, found herself developing a belated longing for dolls at around age 50. She began collecting dolls and painting them. This interest grew into a passion and led to trial-and-error efforts at making dolls, Then she took some Canadian courses on the subject. Finally, she got serious and went to Pigeon Forge, Tennessee, for some real education about dolls. To doll fanciers, Pigeon Forge is what Nashville is to country-music enthusiasts.

Around 1975, because their daughter had moved north, the Stovers bought a former fire-ranger cabin in the bush west of South River. In 1990, they moved there full-time and built a garage for Fred's car. The car got to spend only one night in its new home before the garage was requisitioned as a doll workshop! The garage has since been enlarged to accommodate a doll museum cum showroom.

Now, doll fanciers and bus-tour groups find their way through the woods to buy dolls, take lessons and admire the 400 to 500 dolls that are always on display. There's no admission charge and no pressure to buy. From March 31 to December 31, the place is open Tuesday to Saturday from 9:30 A.M. to 5:30 P.M. It's closed on Sundays and Mondays because the Stovers, all trained musicians, are often in demand to supply music at church and community events. The phone number is 705-386-0307.

If you go, be prepared for what seems like an interminable drive through the woods. The Nipissing Road, on which the Stover place is located, was built in the 1860s as a colonization road to connect the Muskoka Lakes with Lake Nipissing. To get there, take Hwy 11 north from Huntsville for about 72 km (45 miles) to South River. At Ottawa Ave. in South River, go left four blocks to Eagle Lake Road. Turn right here and follow this road for 22.7 fascinating km (14.2 miles) until you finally come to the old Nipissing Road. Go left here a short distance to Stovers Hidden Retreat on the right.

Chapter 33

A Visit To Tea Granny's

Kimberly Chant-Allin has made a career out of serving afternoon tea in her modern farm home on hilly Newtonville Rd., east of Oshawa and 54 km (34 miles) from Toronto. Her organic-farmer husband, Ivan, often acts as butler, while Kimberly, in 1800s costume, recreates the full ceremony of afternoon tea as it was performed during the reign of Queen Victoria and into the early 1900s.

Residents from Toronto to Kingston, and often visitors from Europe and the United States, come to Tea Granny's for a cup of tea and a hearty but formal mid-afternoon refreshment that consists of fruit, four kinds of dainty sandwiches, hot fresh-baked scones and homemade shortbreads. Patrons select a teapot from an assortment of fifty or more bone-china pots and find themselves taking part in an event—not just a snack—seated at a lace-covered table in a room with a year-round Christmas tree decorated with teacups.

The cost is $15.95 a person plus tax, with an extra $1.50 if you want Devonshire cream and $10 for the optional services of a walk-in teacup reader. You must make an advance reservation for tea at Tea Granny's, usually 48 hours ahead.

From early girlhood in Toronto, Kimberly has been

keenly interested in the Victorian era, particularly tea drinking and the traditions that grew around it. Information sheets at her two-person tables tell how afternoon tea was popularized by Anna, the seventh Duchess of Bedford. The Duchess evidently felt that it was a long time between meals and demanded a little something to keep up her strength until dinner. The Tea and Etiquette pamphlets also explain the difference between "afternoon tea" and "high tea", with the latter being a full meal served late in the day or early in the evening.

When not handing out delicate tea cups and three-tiered cake platters, Ivan Allin grows organic soy beans and spelt on 51 hectares (126 acres) of land. His family has been farming in the Oshawa area since 1852. He and Kimberly met at a Whitby roller-skating rink and moved to their present home in 2001.

To make a reservation, call 905-983-5816. The website is **teagrannyandfriends.com**.

To get to Tea Granny's, take Hwy 401 east from the edge of Toronto about 54 km to Exit 448 at Newtonville Rd. Go north up Newtonville Rd. for 9 km to No. 5784 on the west side.

Chapter 34
Visit HMCS Haida In Hamilton Harbour

To celebrate the fact that our country has the longest national coastline in the world, Canada has opened a glitzy new Marine Discovery Centre at the west end of Lake Ontario. Through touch screens and other electronic marvels, the huge centre in Hamilton harbour takes you into undersea caves, back to a 1500s whaling ship and through such habitats as a salt-water kelp forest.

In summer months, less than one km (half a mile) away, you can also go aboard one of the last surviving Canadian warships from World War II. She's HMCS Haida, a tribal-class destroyer, built in Britain for the Royal Canadian Navy in the 1940s, commissioned in 1943 and manned by Canadian sailors through D-Day and the Normandy invasion until the end of the war. She later served during the Korean War. Then, for nearly 30 years, Haida was moored as a museum piece at Ontario Place on Toronto's waterfront. About 2004, she was towed to Hamilton as part of a long-term Hamilton plan to "Bring Back the Bay" by cleaning up and revitalizing this historic port, the heart of Canada's steel industry.

Haida is open only during the summer, but the Marine Discovery Centre is a year-round destination for any family wishing to uncover facts about Canada's four coastlines: Atlantic, Pacific, Arctic and the Great Lakes.

When I was last there in 2006, admission was $7.25 for adults, $6 for seniors and $3.50 for kids. In winter months, the centre is open Thursdays to Sundays from 10 A.M. to 5 P.M.

On arrival, you view an introductory movie and then are turned loose to marvel at four huge interactive galleries, with helpful guides always close at hand. I noted a number of thoughtful displays depicting history, coastlines, ocean life, national parks and marine art. I still remember an attic with an antique trunk that turned out to be full of electronic marvels. And on the attic wall were old-time picture frames. When I touched one of the frames, out popped B.C. artist Emily Carr with a series of her familiar famous paintings.

In another exhibit, I saw a replica of an ancient plank, recovered from the wreck of a Basque whaler that went down off Newfoundland nearly 500 years ago. The marvel of this was that one of the crew, sometime before the disaster, had used a knife to carve a picture of his ship onto one of her planks. Cold salt water had preserved the carving until a modern diver discovered the wreck. There was no clue as to whether the carver escaped from the shipwreck.

When I was there, there was free parking at the centre and an excellent cafeteria and gift shop. Plans were underway to build a waterfront trail and a trolley line between the centre and HMCS Haida.

For information, the phone number is 905-526-0911.

Chapter 35

The Clock Doctor Who Makes House Calls

If you have a grandfather clock whose tick seems to be losing some of its tock, you should see Dan Hooper at Bowmanville. Dan is a clock doctor. He's actually a clock specialist. After six years of training as a clockmaker and watchmaker in Ontario, he took 11 months of post-grad specialty training on a scholarship at Neuchatel, Switzerland, the capital of the clockmaking world. Now he spends his days repairing, adjusting and cleaning clocks and watches from all over Ontario in his clock hospital at Hoopers family jewellery store in downtown Bowmanville.

Many of Dan's evenings are devoted to house calls, tending to big grandfather clocks in country homes from Kingston to Niagara. He even has a clock ambulance, a van with foam-rubber fittings in which he transports critically ill grandfather clocks to his shop for repairs. If he needs parts that aren't obtainable from factories, he makes them himself.

From Dan, I learned that although clock sales are booming in Canada, every year there are fewer and fewer repair technicians. The last course to train them in Canada—at George Brown College in Toronto—closed its doors a few years ago. Meanwhile the demand for clocks, particularly big grandfather clocks, is growing, as exurbanites fill up the Ontario countryside with big houses that seem to demand important-looking clocks for their front halls.

Dan Hooper grew up in a clockmaking family. His father, Art, was a watchmaker and instrument mechanic for the Canadian Army and later in private practice. Dan graduated from Bowmanville High School, served an apprenticeship with his father and took the four-year course at George Brown College. After returning from studies in Switzerland, he worked for his father and other watchmakers and for a time travelled for the Canadian government to Ontario towns where he cleaned and cared for huge old weight-driven clocks in post-office towers.

From the clock and watch corner of the Hooper jewellery store, one of the oldest in Ontario, he now sells as well as repairs many new and used clocks and watches. Television's Antiques Road Show has recently focused a lot of attention on old clocks, he says.

Every year, the store sells a dozen or more new and used grandfather clocks for $2,500 to $3,500. Most of the new ones come from factories in Waterloo, Ontario, or Zeeland, Michigan. Big ornate cuckoo clocks are also favourites, the new ones powered by batteries, the older ones by weights. For bigger clocks such as grandfathers, weights are preferred because they provide a constant power source. Spring-driven clocks tend to lose power and get slower as springs run down. That's why so-called eight-day clocks really need to be wound every four days to keep them accurate.

If you'd like to look at some clocks or consult Dan about a clock, you're welcome to drop in to the jewellery store. Dan and his brother, Ron, took it over when their dad retired in 1980. It's open every day but Sunday and employs six full-time people as well as two watch repairers, a goldsmith and designer, and an engraver.

For information, call 1-888-578-2457 or 905-623-5747. The web site is <u>hoopersjewellers.com</u>. The store is at 39 King St. West in Bowmanville. Take Hwy 401 east to Exit 431 at Waverly Road. From the exit ramp go left to traffic signals and through the signals north on Regional Road 57 for 2 km to Old Hwy 2, now Regional Rd. 2. Go right on No. 2 which becomes King St. to No. 39 on the right.

Chapter 36
Digging Deep Into Dynamic Earth

For more than a century, Ontario's Sudbury basin has been the world's major supplier of nickel and copper. Much of Canada's industrial prosperity has been centred on the City of Sudbury, about 390 km (244 miles) north of Toronto, with its two major mining companies: Vale Inco (formerly Inco) and Xstrata (formerly Falconbridge).

To give visitors an unforgettable exposure to the mining industry and how it has changed over the past hundred years, the Ontario government has dug deep into Mother Earth at Sudbury to create something called Dynamic Earth. No visit to northern Ontario is complete without a visit to Dynamic Earth, but don't go if you have a fear of enclosed spaces. This adventure takes you deep down into the Precambrian rock that forms the basement of Canada. And when you find yourself in a mine tunnel seven storeys underground, they set off a simulated blast. It's all just sound and fury. There's no real explosion, but the roar and rumble seem to go on forever.

To reach the underground exhibits, you slowly descend in a glass elevator into a deep dark chasm. Then, suddenly, the rock walls around you light up into huge screens that come alive with the birth of mountains and the shifting of continents.

In a journey through time, you walk through three re-created nickel mines. One, from the 1900s, shows how the miners hewed rock by lamplight with picks and shovels. It was brutally hard work but it paid well. In the second mine, from the 1950s, there was lots of noise because the miners used air hammers to break up the rock, but the work was somewhat easier on backs and muscles. The third mine is a tele-mine, showing partly the present and partly the future. Here the dangerous heavy work is done by robot machines controlled by remote computers.

Billed as northern Ontario's biggest new family attraction since Science North opened in Sudbury in 1984, Dynamic Earth uses a combination of authentic science and hands-on adventure to make the visit truly memorable for kids and adults alike.

Small kids like the mini-mine. Here they play with small-scale plastic machinery that scoops soft plastic rocks with a blast of air that shoots them up into toy ore carriers to be trundled to a hoist.

Older adventurers pick actual ore samples from a rock wall. They test them with real instruments for qualities such as colour, crystal shape, magnetism and electric conductivity in order to identify mineral content.

Teens and parents operate TV monitors and controls that move robots in a demonstration mine and they actually talk to visitors in other mine tunnels.

A half-hour movie presents the geology and history of the Sudbury basin. The former Inco donated $500,000 to help create Dynamic Earth, which replaced an earlier Big Nickel mine.

Nickel is widely used in coins around the world. A display shows that 175 nations use it in their coins, including Canada. Our current 5-cent piece contains about 2 percent nickel.

Dynamic Earth is open seven days a week from 9 A.M. to 5 P.M. through the summer. It closes around mid-October for the winter and re-opens in mid-March. Admission in 2008 was $18 for adults and $15 for kids. For information, call 705-522-3701 or log onto dynamicearth.ca

To get there, take Hwys 400 and 69 north. From the junction of Hwys 69 and 17 at the south end of Sudbury, follow 69 which becomes Regent St. for 6.6 km to McLeod St., just past a hospital. Go left on McLeod St. 6 km to Ontario St. Turn left on Ontario and follow signs towards Hwy 144 and Timmins. At Lorne St. take the right-hand entrance to Hwy 144, but just before the highway go right onto Big Nickel Road and follow to Dynamic Earth.

Chapter 37

Perth—A Living Sample Of Canada's Past

Built almost entirely of stone, the town of Perth probably has a greater number of picturesque historic houses and public buildings than any other town in Ontario. This makes it a delightful place to work, dine and shop. Perth citizens are proud of their town's unique atmosphere and have learned how to combine heritage and utility. They know how to house restaurants, shops, galleries and public spaces in graceful old stone buildings that invite you to stop, browse and explore.

Tourist information guides list eighty boutiques and other places worth a visit, all located in historic buildings within five blocks of the town centre. During the Christmas season, Perth is always aglow with lights and decked out in its festive best. Located on the swift-running Tay River and a branch of the Rideau Canal, it's about 75 km (47 miles) west of Ottawa and 325 km (203 miles) from Toronto, which makes it a good place for a low-pressure break in a journey between Toronto and Canada's capital.

One of my personal memories of Perth is of sitting on a folding chair on a summer evening beside the river and the handsome old Perth Town Hall while listening to a concert by the town band. What made the concert especially memorable were flocks of chimney swifts, graceful birds of the swallow family, circling the Town Hall in time to the music and periodically breaking off in small groups to dive down the building's wide stone chimneys to nesting sites.

Perth is not just preoccupied with the past. One of its many beautiful parks beside the Tay River is a fairly recent one called Big Ben Park. It's named for a famous jumper horse that lived near Perth for most of his life, made three Olympic appearances, won two gold medals at Pan American Games, won two consecutive World Cup titles and achieved more than forty Grand Prix victories. Big Ben died in 1999. The centrepiece of Big Ben Park is a striking life-size statue of Big Ben and his owner-rider, Ian Millar, taking a 1.7-metre (about 5 feet 7 inches) jump. Big Ben now has a place in Canada's Sports Hall of Fame and has been depicted on a Canadian postage stamp. Perth staged a community effort to have sculptor Stewart Smith of New Hamburg create the statue of Big Ben and his rider. It's a favourite subject for amateur photographers who visit Perth.

You can obtain a flyer about Big Ben at the Perth Chamber of Commerce, which is housed in an old fire hall at 34 Herriott Street. I picked up several other brochures there as well, when I was last in Perth in 2006; they included walking-tour maps and information on ten outstanding eating places in the town centre. With my daughter, Judith Wolfe, and son-in-law, John Braden, I then had a delicious lunch at Fiddleheads in the restored Code's Mill at Stewart Park beside the river.

Photo by Judith Wolfe

Big Ben's commanding statue is one of
Perth's outstanding landmarks.

While you're in Perth, visit the local museum in the old Matheson House. Here you can see the pistols used in Canada's last fatal duel in 1833. You may be able to buy a book called *Perth Remembered*. Published in 1967, it's one of the best Canadian local histories that I've seen.

For more on Perth, contact <u>perthchamber.com</u> or 613-267-3200.

To get to Perth, take Hwy 401 east from Toronto about 190 km to Hwy 37 at Belleville. Go north here about 36 km to Hwy 7 and east on No. 7 about 98 km to Perth.

Don't confuse the Town of Perth with Perth County. They are a long way from each other!

PART FIVE: CLIMBING THE LADDER

Chapter 38
Life As A Suburban Reporter

At the end of my last autobiography chapter, I had been released from the Canadian Army and was back to work at The Telegram.

In the late autumn of 1945, I began my real life as a suburban reporter, covering what was known to Torontonians as "the Lakeshore". This was a news-fertile suburban strip made up of three independent municipalities: Mimico, New Toronto and Long Branch.

Situated a couple of miles west of the Humber River, Mimico had started life as a railroad town. Around 1906, the Grand Trunk Railway, which covered southern Ontario like a spider web, had bought up farmland and moved its Toronto-area freight marshalling yards from East Toronto to Mimico. A hoard of freight-yard officials and workers moved with the yards. They formed the nucleus of a solid and comfortable residential district that was to become the commuter town of Mimico—the name was an Ojibwa Indian word meaning "home of the wild pigeon". In the early 1960s, I was to write a history book about Mimico. Commissioned by the town, it was entitled *The Mimico Story*. I still have a couple of copies.

Immediately west of Mimico was the rival town

of New Toronto, established as an industrial centre in the 1920s as the result of a factory-building boom following World War I. New Toronto had four major industrial firms: Goodyear Tire, Anaconda American Brass, Campbell Soup and Continental Can, plus a sprinkling of smaller companies. Most of the New Toronto north-south streets were numbered instead of named. The major east-west artery of all three communities was Lakeshore Road.

The westernmost of the three communities was the village of Long Branch. It had begun life as a summer-cottage colony named for Long Branch, New Jersey, the summer White House location of U.S. President Ulysses S. Grant.

By the time I took over its news coverage for The Telegram, the Lakeshore was not only flourishing, but was also in the middle of an acute housing shortage and was spilling over its borders northward into the market-garden and farming township of Etobicoke. From Ed Monteith, who covered the Lakeshore before me, I learned that I was responsible for covering the weekly meetings of three municipal councils, three Boards of Education and two weekly Magistrate's Courts as well as the activities of three police departments and three Ontario Provincial Police constables who patrolled the Queen Elizabeth Way, Canada's first expressway, which stretched from Toronto to Hamilton to Niagara Falls. Ed gave me a list of his Lakeshore "contacts" or news sources. I immediately set out to meet all of them, promising to mention them in news stories and to spell their names correctly.

I also soon met my two rivals: the reporters for The

Toronto Star and The Globe and Mail. The Star reporter was a very smart and formidable lady named Jean Hibbert. She was a historian as well as a news reporter. After her death in middle age from cancer, the Etobicoke Historical Society was to establish the Jean Hibbert Award, presented annually in her memory for contributions to the preservation of local history. I was to become a recipient of the award in 2001 for editing and publishing an Etobicoke history by Esther Heyes.

We three reporters usually met at least once a week, sharing the press table at council meetings and court sessions. Here we exchanged jokes, and the two ladies brought me up to date on local folklore and gossip. One of the legends they related—I can't vouch for its truth—was about a very big local cop who had passed out on his way home from a drinking session and had lain down in the snow for a short snooze. A citizen spotted the recumbent form and put in a panic call to the police station. Two constables arrived to arouse the sleeping giant and take him home. Next morning, he was paraded before the local chief and chewed out for misconduct, and that was the end of the matter.

I soon settled down to covering local routine events as well as trying to dig up interesting stories about Lakeshore schools and other organizations. The big railway yard sometimes provided a news event such as the derailment of a freight train which could block the main line and delay passenger trains. Here I sometimes got tips from Josephine's family—nearly all of them railroaders.

Another source of news stories was the Etobicoke River, at Long Branch. During the 1920s and 30s, summer cottages had sprung up along the "flats" or flood-plain of the river between Lakeshore Road and the Lake Ontario river mouth. Then in the World War II years and immediately following the war, most of these temporary dwellings had been renovated for year-round use. Almost every April, however, the Etobicoke River could be counted on to flood the flats area, isolating whole families in their somewhat flimsy homes. Two or three of my contacts on the flats would call me at home, usually in the middle of the night. The Telegram now paid for me to have a bed-side phone extension. I would phone the office for a photographer to pick me up and we would head for the flood. There we'd find local police and firemen on hand and sometimes an ambulance as well. It seemed inevitable that some unfortunate expectant mother would be scheduled to give birth just as the flood was peaking. Fire ladders would be stretched from roof to roof to reach the home of the mother, so she could be carried out on a stretcher and taken to St. Joseph's Hospital by ambulance.

I covered many floods at Long Branch. The most serious was in April 1948 when a really bad situation developed. A southeast gale was piling up water at the river mouth while ice jambs and a record spring flow had created a dangerously high flood along the flats. I remember watching all night while firemen and cops rescued dozens of people from rooftops. Two Toronto Harbour Police veterans, the Hurley brothers, brought lifesaving boats on trucks to stem the swift river current and make many rescues. I wrote a graphic story which made Page One the following day.

The four years or so that I spent on the Lakeshore beat were important in my training as a reporter. Besides covering stories in my own area, I was often sent by Major Wemp with a photographer on other regional stories as far away as Hamilton, Brantford, Kitchener and Barrie.

In 1946, Josephine and I were able to leave our cellar home at King and Jameson and move to Mimico. Once again I was indebted for this to my old mentor Hugh Griggs and his wife Greta. They had heard that a Mr. and Mrs. Armstrong had decided to help relieve the housing shortage by renting out the ground floor of their comfortable house on Hillside Avenue. The Griggs put in a good word for Jo and myself, and we were able to get the comfortable ground-floor flat for $30 a month on condition that I would shovel the snow and take out the ashes for Mr. and Mrs. Armstrong. Houses were still heated by coal in those days, and heavy cans of coal ashes were collected from the street side every week by town workers.

We spent two very happy years with the Armstrongs, who were like parents to us. They were Scottish. I picked up many Scots adages from them, such as: "Many a mickle makes a muckle" and "Ne'er cast a clout till May be out."

It was due to the Armstrongs that we bought our first home. One day, Mrs. Armstrong told us, "A young couple like you should be buying your own home, not frittering your money paying rent." She went on to tell us that her friend, Mrs. Lowe, wanted to sell her five-room brick bungalow on Station Road, next to the Mimico Library. The price was $5,500, and if we could raise $1,500 as a down payment she would take back a $4,000 mortgage at four percent. We talked to Jo's parents and my parents. We had some money saved from my salary and from what Jo had earned from a part-time job. My mother revealed to us that she had deliberately saved—for just such a purpose as this— the portion of my army pay that I had assigned to her. Jo's parents offered us a loan at no interest. Putting all these funds together, we bought the little house and we lived there for five happy years. And because the house was next door to the library, I was asked to become a member of the Mimico Public Library Board.

At ages four and two, Judith and Bob pose at their first home, 45 Station Road, Mimico, for 1953 Christmas Card.

While we lived on Station Road, I achieved another ambition. I was able to buy a car: a 1939 Chevrolet. It was really an old clunker and needed constant repair, but it produced expense-account revenue of 10 cents a mile (6.25 cents a kilometre). I practised driving on a learner's permit for three months and then got myself tested by a driver's license examiner at Port Credit who was noted for not being very strict. After a 10-minute drive, he gave me my license. I felt like phoning Polly Pickles to let her know she would no longer have to drive me!

Chapter 39

Reporter Or Editor?

As the 1940s drew to a close, I found myself working less on the street at my Lakeshore beat and more in the office on desk duty. By the end of 1948, I had become an unofficial assistant to Major Wemp, the Suburban Editor. I was also being given lots of out-of-town assignments. For many of these, I was required to write "feature" stories: longer items not of immediate news importance but concerning background developments of interest to readers in the Toronto-centred region.

In 1948, I got my first-ever byline on one such story that was printed on a Saturday Section Page with a layout of pictures by Jack Judges. It dealt with the almost unknown reforestation movement that was transforming neglected or abandoned farms from deserts of blowing sand into productive forests in the hills of northern York County around a hamlet called Vivian. Getting a first byline made me feel pretty good, but I'm afraid my family and friends barely noticed it. I had to draw their attention to the story. My loyal loving wife certainly saw it, however, and she told all her relatives.

Around this time, I had been starting to think about my future—whether I should try to concentrate on being a reporter and writer or whether I should set my sights on becoming an editor and feature writer, working mostly in the office. I was inclined towards an editor's job, but suddenly the decision was taken out of my hands.

Here's how it happened. Sometime around 1948, Mrs. Jessie Cameron died. She was the widow of John Ross Robertson, founder of The Telegram. Under the terms of his will, the newspaper was to be sold after her death and the proceeds of the sale were to be paid over to the Toronto Hospital for Sick Children. The paper was sold for $3,610,000, and the money went to build a new children's hospital on University Avenue which replaced the antiquated red-brick building next to the Toronto General Hospital on College Street.

The purchaser of The Telegram turned out to be George McCullagh, a gold-mine promoter who had struck it rich in the northern Ontario gold rush of the early 1900s. He was also the owner of The Globe and Mail, Toronto's morning newspaper. I remember well the day the purchase of The Telegram was announced. George McCullagh came over to The Telegram, gathered the whole staff on the editorial floor and told us to stop worrying. He was not going to merge The Telegram with The Globe and Mail. The Tely would continue its life as a separate paper, and he said he had a million dollars to spend to make it greater than ever. We all went back to work with happy hearts.

A few weeks later, there was another announcement from McCullagh. He was sending J. Douglas MacFarlane, who had been the controversial editor of The Maple Leaf, the Canadian Army newspaper in World War II, to take charge of The Telegram's editorial operation. A young man from Montreal named

John Bassett would have charge of Tely business departments. This second announcement was barely noticed in the furor of publicity over MacFarlane's appointment. MacFarlane had been a hot-shot City Editor on the Globe and was expected to inject new life into the somewhat stodgy WASP-oriented Telegram.

All the expectations about JDM, as he was called, turned out to be true. He blew through The Telegram like a tornado. He immediately redesigned the newspaper. He revived the "Pink Tely", printed on pink newsprint, as the last edition of each day. He handed out promotions to the most able editors. He fired C.O. Knowles, the unpopular Editor in Chief, and C.H.J. Snider, the Associate Editor, who said he was ready to retire anyway. As City Editor, MacFarlane took over the entire editorial operation from the City Desk and was in charge from early morning until late at night. He handed out pay raises to people who deserved them, and he hired new and talented reporters and columnists from across Canada. He announced that the best stories in each day's paper would always be bylined. He even noticed me and transformed my life.

One afternoon, shortly after I had written a Page One story from our Caledon correspondent, Islay Brown, about a train wreck at Forks of the Credit, JDM beckoned me over to the City Desk. The front-page headline read: "Loose Caboose Wrecks Train".

"That was a nice story you wrote about the loose caboose," he said. "I was pleased that you put Islay Brown's byline on it."

"It was her story," I replied. "I was just the rewrite

man." I didn't tell him that I was familiar with the section of CPR track where the wreck had occurred, a familiarity based on the fact that I often went trout fishing on the Credit River between Cataract and Forks of the Credit.

What had happened on this particular day was that a railway brakeman had left an empty caboose sitting on the main line while a freight locomotive was shunting boxcars onto a branch line at Cataract Junction. Too late, the brakeman noticed that the unattended caboose had started rolling downhill towards the next station at Forks of the Credit. He ran into the Cataract station and phoned down to The Forks to have the loose caboose derailed. Too late! The caboose flashed by as the station agent at Forks of the Credit answered the phone. It hit the afternoon passenger Up-Train head-on just south of a high curving bridge over the Credit River. With a terrific crash, the caboose jumped the track and rolled down a steep embankment to catch fire just a hundred yards or so from Jimmy Roberts' house.

I knew Jimmy Roberts, an old bachelor. He had often given me a cup of tea when I fished the Credit past his house. Islay Brown, who was also a telephone operator for the Caledon Municipal Telephone Company, connected me with Jimmy who gave me a graphic account of the wild empty railway car hurtling down the hill. Nobody was injured. It was a great story and a complete scoop. The Star didn't have a line on it.

After MacFarlane had congratulated me on the loose-caboose story, he launched the bomb that was to overturn my life. He said, "You're a real eager beaver. I've had my eye on you. How would you like to become Night City Editor of this newspaper?" While I sat speechless, he explained what he wanted.

Up to that point, The Telegram had had virtually no organization for night coverage of news events in the city. There was a night copy editor on duty, but all he did was edit copy turned in by reporters on daytime and evening assignments. What JDM wanted was an editor to organize a night staff and to take charge of covering news events breaking during the night. He wanted to have much of the work done and stories set in type by the time he took over at seven in the morning. I recognized this as the chance of a lifetime. Despite many fears as to whether I could hack such a job, I quickly accepted. Doug said, "Good. Start next Monday. Set your own hours. Your pay will go to $40 a week. Get yourself some business cards with your new title on them."

I hurried home to tell Jo about the promotion that was to turn our family life upside down for a year. We now had a house in Mimico, an old Chev car and a new and wonderful baby daughter named Judith, about 1½ years old. We were expecting another child in six months. We had put a down payment on a summer cottage on Lake Manitouwabing near Parry Sound, and I had reached the wonderful salary peak of $40 a week.

According to an old saw in the newspaper business, "A reporter is a person who can write but can't spell. An editor is a person who can spell but can't write." For better or worse, I was launched from that day forward as an editor.

Chapter 40

King Of The Midnight Hours

With a happy but apprehensive heart, I walked onto the editorial floor of The Telegram at 7 P.M. that first Monday night as king of the "Nightside". My only companion was Charlie Grafton, a copy editor. I could tell that he had doubts about this young whippersnapper who had been placed in charge of what until then had been Grafton's exclusive kingdom. So I began by explaining to Mr. Grafton what MacFarlane expected of me, and asking for his help. "What should be my first move?" I asked Grafton. "Get a night police reporter," he replied. "There are police stories breaking all over the city all night and we have nobody to cover them." He went on to explain that the only reporter on duty during the night was the "Bureau" man in the Press Room at police headquarters on College Street. This was a lone individual who represented both The Telegram and The Star. His duties were to monitor the police radio, to check periodically with the cop in charge of the detective office, and to phone both newspapers about anything that looked important. "He calls me, but there's nothing I can do," Charlie said. "I have no staff to send out. If something appears really important, I call the City Editor at home, wake him up and leave it up to him."

Then and there, I decided to ask MacFarlane right away to appoint not one night police reporter but two: one for the evening hours and a second one to start work at midnight. I also asked for a night photographer to work from midnight to 7 A.M. There already was an evening photographer named Ray McFadden. He worked from 5 P.M. to midnight, covering photo orders for evening events on instructions left by the day staff. If I could locate him—this was before we had a staff-car radio system—I could divert him to spot-news events, but this led to bitter complaints from the day staff whose photo assignments had consequently been left uncovered.

I soon learned that there were many spot-news events happening at night all over this busy city: fires, robberies, accidents, murders and assaults. I had to decide which of them were important enough to deserve on-the-spot coverage and which could wait until morning. For immediate coverage, I could wake up dayside reporters at home and dayside photographers. This usually led to complaints. But if a reporter refused point-blank to go out, I could tell him to wake up MacFarlane and present his complaint to the boss. This never happened. When he took over the City Desk, MacFarlane had posted a memo advising editorial staff that as a condition of employment they were to be on call 24 hours a day. When he hired new reporters, JDM also informed them of this fact.

What in fact happened was that I got to know which reporters were keen, young and enthusiastic and were willing to go out on what looked like good stories. These were the people I called first. I also learned which staff members always answered their phones and which ones just unplugged their telephones or left them off the hook when they went to bed. This led to an unfair situation. It meant that the same people were always taking the night calls, while the drones never worked at night at all.

After about a month on the job, I wrote out some recommendations to MacFarlane about this. My first main recommendation was that he appoint two night police reporters: one for the early shift and one for after midnight. These should be volunteers who liked night work and enjoyed being free all day. They should work out of the City Room and report to me.

My second main recommendation was that he begin a Night Standby system. All general-assignment reporters should be available on Night Standby duty for one week every two months. This meant that, on rotation, they should be reachable by phone at any time during the night for one week out of every eight. Reporters called out at night should have the choice of being paid overtime or accumulating credit for days off. I suggested that my proposed Night Standby system would likely prove to be only an interim measure because the editorial staff was becoming unionized by the Toronto Newspaper Guild; under a union contract there would probably be two night shifts, so that it would not be necessary to call out off-duty people except on very big stories.

MacFarlane accepted all my recommendations and quickly put them into effect.

I had just been on the night job about two

months when the Harding family fire occurred in Scarborough. It killed six children of one family. About 1 A.M. I got a call from Doris Ward, one of our suburban stringers. From the scene of the fire, she reported that bodies of six people had been removed from their old wooden home and firemen were vainly trying to revive them. Immediately recognizing this as a major story, I called out the troops. First, I told Doris to try to borrow pictures of the entire family. With her own camera, she had already taken pictures of firemen attempting to revive the children on their front lawn. A relative of the Hardings then gave her the family's photo album.

Next, I phoned two Tely staff photographers, Jack Judges and Madison Sale, who lived in the east end, to get to the fire scene. I then phoned six reporters and sent them to talk to the parents, to firemen, to neighbours, to the family's minister and school principal and teachers.

Lastly, I woke MacFarlane. He told me, "Phone Phyllis Griffiths, the Photo Editor. She'll want to get into the office extra early. Carry on with what you've been doing. I'll be in by 6 A.M."

By the time JDM walked in, everything was organized and under control. I can't remember now whether it was Alan Kent or Ron Poulton who had just finished writing the main story. Doris Ward wrote a sidebar which was used on Page One with her byline. It led to her promotion from part-time stringer to full-time suburban reporter. We all were saddened at the death of the six Harding children. I drove home to Mimico at 7 A.M., feeling guilty at the thought that my career prospects had been improved through the deaths of six innocent people.

For me, there then ensued a hectic year. I would go into work about seven o'clock every evening, looking forward to an exciting night's work. First thing on arrival, I'd read a memo from MacFarlane listing events or follow-up stories he wanted to cover that night. Then I'd quickly read the day's final editions of The Telegram and The Star. By that time, calls would start coming in from the "Bureau" reporter at police headquarters and from suburban and regional correspondents about events in the "boonies" (the suburbs and exurbs).

After the first two months, I had a fairly adequate night staff to deploy on various assignments. MacFarlane had implemented my recommendations and I now had six reporters and two photographers on night duty. One police reporter worked from 5 P.M. to midnight; a second worked from 11 P.M. to 7 A.M., their shifts overlapping by an hour. Two general assignment reporters also worked the early shift and two the graveyard shift from 11 P.M. to 7 A.M. All the night staffers were volunteers who liked working at night and being free in the daytime.

An eventful news year followed my appointment as Night City Editor. I worked five nights a week with Friday and Saturday nights off. Every night, it seemed, important news stories were breaking: murders, fires, hold-ups, floods, blizzards, train wrecks, fatal highway accidents and political meetings that turned into fights. And every night, the Tely news room was a busy place. Not only were my night staff reporters working on their stories there, but also various columnists were hammering out their copy for the next day, and the paper's entertainment reporters and music critics were working on their own stories as well.

MacFarlane had told me that the two copy editors, Charlie Grafton on the evening shift and Bill Wallis after midnight, would work under my direction. I didn't like the idea of this. Both were veteran editors and knew more about copy-editing than I did. What bothered MacFarlane, however, was the fact that columnists, particularly entertainment and music writers, tended to write very long stories which had to be drastically cut by the Copy Desk next day to fit the news space available. He had ordered the columnists to keep their work down to certain definite lengths and had told the night copy editors to cut the columns to those lengths. Nevertheless, the angry columnists would harangue the copy editors for cutting their deathless prose, and the copy editors would refer them to me. I would tell them to talk to MacFarlane and show them memos from JDM positively ordering me not to send to the Composing Room items of more than a specified length.

With soap-opera overtones, the fight with the columnists went on for several weeks until MacFarlane finally called a daytime meeting of all the columnists and the entertainment editor and laid down the law: Any writer, he said, who could not keep his or her stories down to a specified length had better look for another job; The Telegram was not going to waste money setting type that was going to end up as "over matter". "Over matter" was newspaper jargon for type that never made it into the paper. Keeping the "over matter" down to short lengths was a continual battle in those days. It probably still is on today's newspapers.

Finally, my year as Night City Editor drew to a close. I began reminding JDM that he had put a term of one year on the position. He replied that I had done a good job and he would like me to stay on for another year. In a series of heart-rending memos, I told him my health was suffering. I was just not a night person. I could not sleep in the daytime. Josephine, my wife, was vainly trying to keep our two-year-old daughter quiet in the daytime, and was expecting another baby in a couple of months. I was just living for weekends when I could get two nights' real sleep.

An essentially kind-hearted boss, Doug MacFarlane eventually agreed to let me return to daytime work. He told me to return to my position as assistant to Bert Wemp for a couple of months while he considered what I should do next. He paid me the compliment of stating that I had proved my worth as a news-coverage manager and that I had done what he had told me to do. So I returned to daytime work on the suburban staff. Josephine and I went to the Old Mill restaurant for dinner to celebrate.

Going back to the dayside, I felt that I was being "Recalled to Life", to quote a phrase from *A Tale of Two Cities* by Charles Dickens.

Chapter 41
Suburban Editor

Doug MacFarlane was not only a very talented and efficient editor but also a likeable and good-humoured person who inspired loyalty among those who worked for him. He had charisma.

Sometimes, McFarlane would announce staff changes at information meetings. In other cases, he would just post an official announcement on the editorial staff bulletin board. But about two months after I had returned to daytime duty following my year on the Night Desk, I learned unofficially about my next important appointment from Art Holland who had become interim Suburban Editor to replace Major Bert Wemp.

Major Wemp, a World War I flying ace, had enjoyed a long and distinguished career with The Telegram. He had also taken time out to serve a term as mayor of Toronto. When "the Major", as he was universally known, approached age 65, Doug MacFarlane evidently felt that it was time for him to retire and make room for a younger man as Suburban and Regional Editor.

The Telegram had no formal pension plan. The custom had been to offer older employees part-time undemanding jobs at lower salaries. The word through the grapevine was that MacFarlane had proposed that Major Wemp should vacate the suburban desk and go to Toronto City Hall to take over direction of the joint Telegram-Star Court Coverage Bureau.

The "Bureau" was a strange example of co-operation between two newspaper enemies. Toronto's 1890s gothic City Hall at Bay and Queen Streets not only was the municipal centre for the City of Toronto but also served as the York County courthouse. In a warren of courtrooms, it housed all the Magistrates' Courts for the City of Toronto and also York County Judges' Courts as well as sessions of the Supreme Court Assizes for the city and the county.

In the 1930s, in order to cover all these courts and save a few dollars, the Tely and Star, had organized "the Bureau". This hybrid was staffed by three Telegram and three Star junior reporters who covered, or at least kept an eye on, what was going on in all the City Hall courts. They typed duplicate copies of all their stories and turned both copies in to the bureau chief. He gave them a cursory scan and then sent one copy to the Tely and one to the Star through pneumatic tubes under the downtown streets.

It was to direct this organization that Major Bert Wemp was being downloaded from the Suburban Desk. To replace him, Art Holland was named Interim Suburban and Regional Editor. What made me prick up my ears was a grapevine whisper that Art Holland would fill the suburban job for only a few weeks. MacFarlane wanted Holland permanently on the City Desk staff as Assignment Editor. The buzz was that Harvey Currell was going to be the new Suburban

Editor.

MacFarlane kept me dangling for a couple of weeks and then formally announced my appointment in a memo on the bulletin board. Privately, he told me my salary would be raised to $55 a week. Under the new union contract, I would be classed as management and could not be a union member. I would be authorized to hire staff, subject to MacFarlane's approval, and would take over the next week. This was a wonderful promotion for me, to be head of my own department. I resolved to work at it as I'd never worked before.

That summer, on August 29, 1950, Josephine gave birth to Robert, a brother for Judith who was a lively two-year-old. Jo had a very difficult time. Our family physician, Dr. Gordon Ferrier of Mimico, told me he had been afraid we were going to lose her. Under no circumstances, he said, should she again become pregnant. We would have to accept two children as the limit of our family.

In later years, I was to look back on my years as Suburban and Regional Editor as the happiest period of my life. I just loved that job and looked forward every day to going to work.

These were the early 1950s when the post-war baby boom and economic good times were really getting underway for Canada and all North America. The suburban area just beyond the Toronto city limits was exploding with housing development. Until World War II, the three biggest suburban townships, Scarborough, North York and Etobicoke, had been mainly farm and market-garden land. Now they were very rapidly being transformed into suburban neighbourhoods to meet the demand for homes both for young couples who had married after the war and for waves of immigrants, mainly from Britain and Europe. Building speculation did not stop at the fringes of the immediate suburbs but poured over into Toronto Township and Trafalgar Township in Peel and Halton Counties on the west, Pickering, Ajax, Whitby and Oshawa on the east, and north to Vaughan, King, Aurora and Newmarket and right up to Lake Simcoe.

I was responsible for news coverage of this area out to almost 80 miles (128 km) from the Toronto city boundaries, and there was a high-tide of news every day and every week.

When I took over as Suburban Editor, the staff had consisted of about 10 full-time reporters in the immediate suburbs and another cadre of part-time stringers or correspondents in the outer suburbs. MacFarlane and I both foresaw that the suburban building boom would continue spreading mostly to the west. He suggested that I identify hot spots of growing news importance such as Oakville, Port Credit, Cooksville, Brampton and Newmarket and staff these with full-time reporter-photographers. The Circulation Department was planning sales campaigns to obtain new readers in these areas. It therefore made sense to provide readers with full news coverage of the districts where they were putting down roots.

I began recruiting new staff members in my first year on the job. We did not have to advertise job openings. Word spread quickly among the staff of small daily papers and country weeklies across Ontario about employment possibilities on The Telegram.

Telegram management and the officers of the newly formed Toronto Newspaper Guild Union had agreed that our suburban reporters should come under the union contract only when they left the suburban staff and were hired onto our city staff. It was understood that the suburban staff should be considered a training ground and that successful suburban staffers should be given preference for city staff jobs after a trial period of about two years.

Part of my job was selecting new suburban staff members. Doug MacFarlane received lots of job application letters, many of them from reporters on Ontario daily and weekly papers. He hired some city staffers directly; other applications he turned over to me.

By this time, I had a car and an expense account that paid me 10 cents a mile (6.25 cents per kilometre) for business travel. Often I would drive out of the city to interview job applicants in their home towns. I hired people mostly on the basis of their work for their former employers. I always asked to see their clipping albums—stories they had written for local papers. By the time I had been on the job a year or so, I had doubled the size of the suburban staff. I had also doubled or more the number of important suburban stories that appeared in the paper every day.

I became known as a tough but fair editor who expected good results. I also tried to encourage excellence in writing. I used to tell new reporters, "After two years, we'll look over your Telegram clippings. If you've done a good job, I will recommend you for promotion to the city staff. If you want to stay on the suburban staff, we'll increase your pay and I will look for opportunities for advancement for you."

I made a few mistakes in hiring. In one or two cases, I had to advise people that they just didn't have the talent or aptitude or energy for newspaper work. I suggested that they should start looking for another type of job and helped them locate suitable openings.

Gradually I gained a reputation for running a tight but happy department. I became known among politicians and civic administrators in the Toronto-centred region as a fair and unbiased editor.

In the early 1950s, it became obvious to politicians at both the municipal and provincial levels that some kind of re-organization was needed to co-ordinate planning, development and administration between the City of Toronto and its twelve immediate suburbs: Mimico, New Toronto, Long Branch, Swansea, Etobicoke, Weston, York Township, Forest Hill, North York, Leaside, East York and Scarborough. Much argument and discussion ensued. On one side were the proponents of amalgamation who favoured uniting city and suburbs into one big city. On the other side were the champions of "home-rule" who fought fiercely for maintaining the independence of small communities such as Weston, Mimico, Forest Hill and Leaside.

Ontario Premier Leslie Frost appointed a commission headed by Lorne Cumming, a deputy minister, to hold hearings and make recommendations. The Cumming report, as it came to be called, recommended formation of the Municipality of Metropolitan Toronto. After a series of debates in the Ontario Legislature, the Frost Government adopted the recommendations of the Cumming Report and passed the Municipality of Metropolitan Toronto Act. As a result, Toronto and the twelve suburbs were formed into a municipal federation which was to function successfully for forty-five years.

Under the new plan, the city and the twelve suburbs remained as independent municipalities, each with its own elected council, headed by a mayor or reeve. Each retained control over local affairs. But important major services that were used and shared by the city and suburbs were taken over by a new level of government answerable to the Metropolitan Toronto Council. The latter was made up of the elected heads and senior councillors of the city and the twelve suburbs. Metro services included arterial roads, major parks, water supply, sewage disposal and public transportation. Education remained a local responsibility. But new schools, which had been springing up like mushrooms, were henceforth to be built and financed by a new Metropolitan Toronto School Board. The plan was to make the huge tax base—of Toronto and the twelve suburbs—available to finance essential services for the whole area.

To explain the intricacies of the new system, a first for North America, Premier Frost held a press conference at Queen's Park. I attended along with other Telegram editors. No municipal politicians were invited. This constituted a major public relations goof on the government's part. The Tory politicians and the bureaucrats had evidently intended to hold a series of explanatory conferences in the weeks and months following the announcement of the Metro Toronto plan. Local politicians, however, wanted details immediately.

That's when The Telegram jumped into the gap. We knew in advance—as did everyone—the broad lines of what the government was going to announce. So at a Telegram editors' meeting held shortly before the Government press conference, I suggested that as a follow-up to Premier Frost's announcement we would want to get reaction from the people most immediately affected: the city and suburban politicians. I suggested that we should invite all the mayors, reeves and municipal councillors to an afternoon Telegram meeting at the Royal York Hotel to hear details of the Frost plan. We could get local reaction at the same time. This "press conference in reverse"—a Telegram event, not a government event—was quickly arranged. Telegram reporters got on the phones with personal invitations to more than one hundred local politicians. The Royal York staff, professional as always, immediately assigned us a large meeting room with coffee service. A Telegram team trooped directly from Queen's Park to the hotel to welcome our guests.

While we were waiting for the politicians to filter in, I brought up a question that had been bothering me all morning. "Who is going to be ringmaster of the circus?" I asked Laurie McKechnie, the City Editor. "You, of course," he replied. "It's your show. You are the Suburban Editor. You know most of these people. You've been following this debate for months.

Be ready to get up there to welcome everybody."

Shaking in my shoes, I did get up there. With all the details still fresh in my mind, I explained the new plan and the government arguments as to why it would work. I called on senior Telegram reporters from our Queen's Park bureau to answer questions, and I invited Toronto controllers and suburban mayors to give their opinions. The whole affair was considered a success. It made good balanced coverage possible in late editions that day as well as in the next day's paper. It also helped launch me on a long and satisfying stint as Suburban Editor.

When I got home that night, I told Josephine that this was my second real performance as a public speaker. My first had been ten or twelve years earlier when, as an office boy, I won the Toronto YMCA trophy for oratory.

I could write a whole volume about my years as Suburban Editor, then Regional Editor and then District Editor of The Telegram. The title changed but the job remained essentially the same.

To avoid boring you with bushels of words, I've tried to summarize some important events and accomplishments of those happy years.

In order to build morale and a spirit of teamwork among the extended staff, I started writing a monthly Suburban Staff Newsletter that went to every staff member as well as to every part-time photographer and correspondent in all the communities that we covered. Modeled after JDM's daily Assessment Notice, it handed out plaudits for good work and included ideas on how to improve news coverage.

I received an OK from Doug MacFarlane to spend money on a conference for our suburban correspondents and stringers. On a sunny spring day at a Salvation Army summer camp at Jackson's Point on Lake Simcoe, nearly all our part-time reporters and photographers gathered to get tips from a team of Telegram editors on how to write news stories, how to set up photographs, how to transmit news copy and how to dictate a story to the Rewrite Desk.

On a spring day in the early 1960's the Telegram's suburban staff, reporters and country correspondents, gathered at a Salvation Army camp beside Lake Simcoe for the first-ever suburban staff conference. Many senior Telegram editors attended to act as instructors. In attendance were twenty-three persons and one dog. Harvey is fifth from the left in the front row.

For a hectic week in October 1954, I managed suburban coverage of the devastation caused by

Hurricane Hazel, the greatest natural disaster ever to strike Toronto up to that time.

In August of 1954, I deployed suburban troops to join our city staff in coverage of Marilyn Bell's famed swim across Lake Ontario.

When Telegram management struck a deal in the early 1950s to supply news coverage to a new television station at Barrie, I was told to set up a Telegram Barrie bureau, working out of the CKVR-TV television studio. I hired three reporter-photographers who worked long hours producing what was billed as Toronto Telegram News for CKVR newscasts.

Also in the 1950s, a Telegram promotion idea involved the production of three once-a-week suburban zone editions entitled "Suburban Living". I had to appoint an editor for each of the zones and supervise production of what were essentially three separate suburban weeklies for the eastern, western and northern areas of greater Toronto. We sold display advertising in each paper at a lower lineage rate. Each paper had its own columnists and reporters. I had to write editorials for the three papers. This project lasted about three years but was then dropped because of distribution difficulties. Telegram carrier boys were supposed to insert the zone newspapers into regular copies of The Telegram. Many of them refused to do so and instead would dump the zone editions into ditches or rubbish bins.

Similar problems doomed The Sunday Telegram which Laurie McKechnie was appointed to produce in 1957. He put out a good readable paper but just couldn't get it to readers. Carrier boys weren't interested in working on Sunday mornings, and not enough adults were willing to go to newsstands at Telegram corner boxes to buy a Sunday Telegram. The new paper lasted about 20 weeks. Toronto just was not ready for a Sunday newspaper in 1957.

I was recruited—with extra pay—to write twenty fiction columns for the Sunday paper. I created a mythical suburban—actually it was exurban—subdivision named Jackpine Hills. I peopled it with a crowd of suburban stereotypes and a different situation every week. Some of the characters were based on people I knew at McKellar, where our first Parry Sound cottage was located; others were based on neighbours of ours on Springbrook Gardens in Etobicoke. It was my first and only attempt at fiction writing. I still have twenty clippings of the columns pasted up in an album. An artist named Gordon Bailey was commissioned by The Telegram to draw cartoons to illustrate the Jackpine Hills stories. As "Captain Andy", he later was the star of a children's program on a Hamilton, Ontario, television station.

In addition to a long busy day at The Telegram, I did some moonlighting, writing two books. One of them, entitled *Where the Alders Grow*, was published by the Etobicoke Mimico Conservation Authority. It was a history of the Etobicoke River with an account of the devastation caused when the small stream became a deadly torrent, fed by the rain of Hurricane Hazel in October 1954. Etobicoke Board of Education adopted the book as a local text for use in schools. The other book, entitled *The Mimico Story*, presented the history of the Town of Mimico.

While I was Suburban Editor, I was selected to go on a few interesting travel junkets or "freeloads", sponsored by airlines. One was to Vancouver on the first non-stop commercial flight from Toronto to the West Coast. The aircraft was a noisy piston-driven North Star and the trip took all day. Another was an expedition to Frobisher Bay on Baffin Island, my first visit to the Arctic. I also remember a train-and-bus trip sponsored by Bob Saunders, then Chairman of Ontario Hydro. It was a trip in a cold December to Wikwemikong Indian Reserve on Manitoulin Island to celebrate the arrival of Ontario Hydro service to that First Nations community. After a freezing weekend, we all came home with frozen turkeys, gifts from Ontario Hydro.

Many of the staffers I worked with during this period ended up having successful careers on The Telegram, on other newspapers, on television news or on government public relations services. I always tried to encourage suburban staffers to aim high. I also made sure they got credit for their work—that my bosses knew who was really responsible for good ideas and good stories.

We had a few oddballs on the suburban and regional staff. One of them was a terrific reporter and "legman" who had two wives (one legal and one common-law) and two families living in separate homes a few blocks from each other. This unstable situation ended when the mother of one of the wives arrived from Vancouver and packed her daughter and grandchild off to the West Coast.

In my old age, I now enjoy recalling the many

firm and lifelong friendships that originated during my term as Suburban, Regional and District Editor. Among them were Russell Cooper, Jim Emmerson, Barry Murkar, Sam Crystal, Tony Drew, Dave Chamberlain, Bill Dodds, Bill Foote, John Downing, Doug Creighton, Lloyd Robertson, Ray Biggart, Tiny Bennett, Bob McKittrick, Al Chandler, Marion Gillen and Jean Bolton.

While I was Suburban Editor, another change in The Telegram's ownership had taken place. In 1952, George McCullagh, owner and publisher of the paper, was found dead in his swimming pool at Thornhill. Under the terms of his will, The Telegram was to be sold to the highest bidder. This turned out to be John Bassett, who had been working for McCullagh as General Manager of The Telegram. Backed by John David Eaton, president of the famed Eaton's department store chain, Bassett got The Telegram on December 1, 1952 for $4,250,000. He took over immediately and formally appointed J.D. MacFarlane as Managing Editor and later as Editor in Chief. If you are interested in Bassett's colourful life, get a copy of Maggie Siggins' excellent book *Bassett*, published by James Lorimer and Company in 1979.

My years as Suburban, Regional and District Editor involved a lot of hard and intense work, competing every day with The Toronto Star and trying to live up to Doug MacFarlane's expectations. They also included lots of fun. I now sometimes entertain or bore my kids and grandkids with stories from my Telegram days. Many are anecdotes about things that never got into the newspaper.

On a typical working day, we used to get a lot of visitors through the big Telegram news room on the fourth floor at Bay and Melinda. Most of them came in on legitimate business to see reporters and editors. Part of the job of any reporter is to have tipsters and contacts all over the city. I remember one professional magician who regularly came in twice a year to see an entertainment writer in hope of getting a plug for himself into the paper. While talking, he would put on an impromptu magic show, which we all enjoyed. There was also a ventriloquist whose talking dummy would flirt with the girl reporters and copy girls who had begun to replace some of the boys. And there were also the "nut cases", some with inventions that were going to revolutionize the world, and others with endless stories about crime rings or conspiracies.

There was no security man at the door. Anybody could walk in. Copy boys usually met any unexpected visitors and directed them to appropriate reporters and editors. Our attitude to such visitors was ambivalent. We had no time to waste on fantasies; on the other hand, nobody wanted to turn away an informant with a legitimate story. We had all heard about the Ottawa editor who had brushed off Igor Gouzenko when he tried to give his information about a Soviet spy ring. If any visitor seemed to make sense, he or she usually got a hearing.

Then there were our regular telephone callers. I used to tell my wife and kids so much about these poor deluded people that they started to feel they almost knew them. There was one lady from Mimico who liked the sound of my voice and insisted on talking only to me. She had invented two elaborate plots to which she added new details on every call. One was about her neighbour. She believed he had a tunnel into his basement from Lake Ontario, two blocks away. It was used, she said, to infiltrate foreign spies into Mimico in mini-submarines. Her other fantasy involved the telephone company, which she believed was trying to poison her with gas transmitted through her telephone wires. She also believed that the mayor of Mimico had a moonshine still in his basement.

We had a regular list of mad callers. Everybody knew about them, including the police. Call-blocking procedures had not yet been invented. Usually we just set down the telephone and let them ramble on while we continued our work.

Once in a while, relatives or friends of habitual callers would phone to apologize and bring us up to date on psychiatric treatments. We'd thank such people and suggest they try getting the afflicted person to call The Star or The Globe for a change.

Chapter 42

Labours In A Foreign Field

After about 10 years, I was still enjoying life as Suburban Editor but my bosses were starting to hint that it was time for me to move on. A new Managing Editor, Andy MacFarlane, was particularly interested in my career. I liked and admired Andy. He was a distant relative of Doug MacFarlane and had had a brilliant newspaper career before coming to The Telegram. His father, Dr. Joseph MacFarlane, was Dean of Medicine at the University of Toronto. Once at a formal dinner, the chairman thought Dean MacFarlane was a clergyman and asked him to say Grace. Dean MacFarlane declined with the words: "Sorry, I'm not that kind of dean."

At an informal conference over coffee one morning, Andy MacFarlane said to me, "I think you need a new challenge. How about trying a spell as Foreign Editor?" I thought about it for a minute and then replied, "I'll give it a try." So began another sharp turn in my newspaper career. I took over the Foreign Desk a week later.

That turned out to be a mistake, at least as far as I was concerned. I remained on the Foreign Desk for less than a year, giving it my best effort but never really feeling at home there. I still felt happy at going to work every day, but I also looked forward to the end of the day and to the weekend when I would be driving somewhere to do a Town and Country Trip or heading to our Parry Sound cottage. The trouble with the Foreign Desk was that it involved long-distance coverage and very little human contact. I had become used to close-up coverage. It also involved a lot of eye strain.

Every morning I had to get in to the office before 6 A.M. in order to have time to read through a huge mass of wire copy before the first-edition deadline. "Wire copy" referred to all the news from around the world that had been churned out all night long on teletype machines by Canadian Press, Associated Press, United Press, Reuters, Tass and a string of other news services. It was all waiting for me every morning in a heap ten inches thick or more. I had to read it all and select which two or three percent of it was important enough and interesting enough to be included in that day's newspaper. This was about 1960, at the height of the Cold War. The Korean War had ended, but negotiations over a peace treaty had been dragging on for years. The Vietnam War was heating up, and satellites, UFOs and nuclear-warhead rockets were very much in the news.

The Foreign Desk was a one-person operation. The only human contact I had from it was in "cablese". That's the abbreviated language that editors and reporters had invented to cut down the per-word cost of undersea cable transmission. A typical resignation in cablese would read "upshove job".

There's an old story about the London, England,

editor who cabled to a Hollywood correspondent, "How old Cary Grant?" The correspondent fired back: "Old Cary Grant fine. How you?"

At this time, The Telegram had a stable of foreign correspondents around the world, some of them full-time employees like Jane Armstrong in London, many of them part-time stringers. They all cost a great deal of money and were supposed to report to the Foreign Editor. They all felt, however, that they were much too important to have anything to do with a jumped-up Suburban Editor. They insisted on talking only to JDM or at least to the Managing Editor. They all insisted on filing long dull stories every night that I was supposed to cut down and brighten up enough to make them worthy to appear in the Tely's tight news columns.

The correspondents would all whine and complain to JDM or Andy MacFarlane about having their copy cut—at a per-word cable cost. All except Peter Worthington. Peter and I never became personal friends, but I admired his writing skill, sharp mind and sense of humour. His specialty was crisis-hopping, jetting around the world to international hot spots. I enjoyed editing his copy, and he was such a tight writer that I seldom felt I needed to cut it.

Finally, after about a year of this, I confessed to Andy MacFarlane that I felt I would never be a truly great Foreign Editor and I asked for a re-assignment. He asked what job I would like. Art Cole was at that time firmly fixed as City Editor, and I did not feel I had the slightest chance at that lofty position, so I suggested that I be appointed as an Assistant City

Editor.

And that is how it was decided. Art Cole agreed to accept me on the City Desk as Afternoon City Editor, and we co-ordinated our hours. Art would start work early in the morning, about 5:30 or 6 o'clock, and would run the City Desk until the day's first editions of The Telegram and The Star had landed on our desks. I would take over the desk about 11 A.M. and work until the early Night Editor, Jim Hanney, came in around 5 P.M.

John Downing had succeeded me as Suburban Editor. He usually left his desk at about noon, so I could also manage any suburban work that came up in the afternoon. It felt like a good arrangement, and it did work out well for five years or more.

I had my business cards changed to read "Assistant City Editor".

Chapter 43
Afternoon City Editor

Frank Tumpane, an old Tely irritant columnist (one who makes readers mad at him), used to say that writing a daily column separates the men from the boys. I would agree with this but would add that running an Afternoon City Desk on a multi-edition newspaper separates the pros from the amateurs. During my five or so years on this job at the Tely, I began to feel I was earning my salary—now up to $10,000 a year. It was also in this period that Jo started to worry about my health. I was developing signs of a stomach ulcer and sometimes came home at night too tired to eat supper.

A lot had been happening at The Telegram in the first years of the 1960s. John Bassett was now firmly in control as owner and publisher of the newspaper, backed by his friend John David Eaton. The only signs of any Eaton influence at the newspaper, however, were that every Telegram staff member received an Eaton's credit card the same month that Bassett took over, and one summer young Fred Eaton, John David's son, appeared as a summer-staff reporter. He was a pleasant unpretentious young man who made a good impression.

About that time also, senior Tely editors started

to receive invitations to the annual Eaton Christmas party at the Royal York Hotel. Lady Flora Eaton—and sometimes John David Eaton himself—usually put in an appearance at this very lavish affair with its wonderful food topped off by the famous Eaton Yule Log dessert. There was one unwritten but rigid rule about the Eaton party: You did *not* get drunk at it if you wanted to continue working at the Tely.

On the other hand, it was OK to get slightly drunk at the Ontario Hydro party, an equally lavish but more hilarious affair thrown every December by Robert H. Saunders, chairman of the Hydro Electric Power Commission of Ontario. Bob Saunders, a former famous mayor of Toronto, loved to party and loved newspaper people. At the slightest provocation, he would organize junkets to remote parts of Ontario, with private railway cars to ferry newspaper people there and back. I went to a few of these events, including one celebrating the extension of Ontario Hydro power to Killarney, a remote fishing port on northern Georgian Bay.

Bob Saunders was to die a tragic death in a plane crash at London, Ontario. My friend Jim Emmerson, then head of The Telegram's Queen's Park bureau, wrote The Telegram's Page One story about it. Jim used to say how ironic it was that the czar of electric power in Ontario died because of the failure of a 25-cent fuse. His private plane was coming in for a landing in a storm when a fuse blew at a small airport and the runway lights went out. The pilot mistook car lights for runway lights and the plane crashed.

Lots of old-time newspaper people fondly remember Bob Saunders and his parties. I still treasure a Hydro barometer. It was one of the gifts handed out to the press at an Ontario Hydro party.

My afternoon shift on the City Desk began about 11 A.M. when Art Cole would leave the desk and retire to his office to handle administrative work for an hour or so. From then on, I would read, edit and sometimes make changes in copy dropped by city staffers or copy boys into the City Desk "in" basket. A few boys and later girls would be stationed around the City room to respond to yells of "Copy!" from reporters or to calls for coffee, copy paper or pencils.

I would answer telephone calls on an elaborate box and key system. These calls would usually be from reporters completing assignments. They would explain what had developed on their assignments and ask for direction: Should they dictate a story to the Rewrite Desk, come back to the office to write it, or go to lunch and writer an "overnight" later that day for the next day's paper?

All during my shift, I would be keeping an ear open for calls coming in on the police radio monitor which kept blaring all day. A reporter on the Police Desk would also be listening for dramatic calls about things like bank hold-ups. Sometimes cops would get excited and report in plain language instead of police code. I'll never forget the day during the Boyd Gang era when a Detective Perry shouted on the air words to the effect that "Tong's down and I'm hit." He was reporting the fatal shooting of Detective Sergeant Edmund Tong and his own wounding in downtown Toronto.

Whenever spot-news events erupted, I would have to get reporters and photographers to the scene in a hurry, with speed being especially important in the case of photographers. We would usually have a couple of photographers at work up in the darkroom, and they were generally available to speed off on very short notice.

Along with this, I would quickly scan every new edition of The Toronto Star as it landed on the desk and take action to check and "scalp" any local Star stories that we did not have.

Occasionally, we'd get a call from one of our reporters, stringers or contacts that a Toronto Star reporter had been seen speeding in a certain direction. I'd ask the Police Desk to check if anything had been happening.

One day a group of six suburban Tely reporters, just going off duty, decided to play a round of golf at the Cliffside Golf Course in Scarborough. They piled into two cars and headed eastward. A Star reporter spotted them speeding along Kingston Road and phoned the Star City Desk which responded by sending a Star crew in pursuit. The Star people, we later heard, got as far as Whitby before the chase was called off.

All afternoon, there would be stories to update and a constant flow of copy coming from Jim Emmerson's Rewrite Desk. I kept a running list of assignments I handed out and of follow-up action required.

Once I was accused of fomenting a strike on the Yonge Street subway construction project. It happened this way. The Ontario Editor sent me a duplicate of a Canadian Press story from Ottawa about a fatal accident on an overpass construction job in which wooden support work had collapsed, allowing newly poured concrete to bury some workmen. I called over Frank Drea, our labour reporter, and asked him, "Is there any chance of this happening on the Toronto subway project?" He said, "I'll ask Gerry Gallagher." In a few minutes he reported back, "Gallagher says he doesn't know, but he's stopping all construction work on the subway until he finds out." Gallagher was head of the main labour union involved, and he called a wildcat strike until he got an engineer's report that support work on the Yonge Street subway project was safe. Frank Drea's story about the strike made the Page One headline on our last two editions that day.

In the early 1960s, John Bassett sold the "Old Lady of Melinda Street", the original Tely building, and built a new sprawling giant of a plant at Front Street West and Spadina. Much later, I concluded this was a mistake that contributed to the Tely's demise. Bassett should have followed The Star's example, built upwards, and rented out the top fifteen floors as office space to provide revenue.

We moved into the new building in 1963. It was a model of convenience and efficiency but lacked the character of the old Tely home. It also had very few windows. In particular, the outdoors could not be seen at all from the Editorial Department. One winter afternoon when Bob Vezina had succeeded me on the City Desk, Doug MacFarlane buzzed him on the intercom. MacFarlane was buzzing from his own office, which *did* have a view of the outdoors.

"What are we doing about this blizzard?" he asked.

"What blizzard?" Vezina responded.

"Don't you ever look out the window?" MacFarlane asked.

"What window?" said Vezina.

MacFarlane clicked off. He had made his point. Vezina called the weather reporter over and instructed him to check with the weather office and traffic police and to write a storm story for the final edition of the day. Vezina then sent a photographer out to look for pictures.

I was on the desk the day the big power outage began in the 1960s. We had emergency lighting in the new building and diesel power to run the presses. It took me a long time to get home that night because the traffic signals were out. Before I left the office, we had a crew working on the story which saw a huge area blacked out.

Towards 1965 or 1966, Andy MacFarlane noticed that I was looking somewhat tired. He started pulling me off the desk for special assignments and finally told me, "I think you've been on afternoons long enough. I've got some work I want you to do for me. Come in tomorrow morning and we'll talk about it."

Chapter 44
Special Assignments

When I reported to Managing Editor Andy MacFarlane the next day, he told me what he had in mind for me. I would continue in the rank of Assistant City Editor but would be relieved of regular shifts on the City Desk. Instead, I would report directly to him for special jobs that he would dream up from time to time.

The first would be to write a style book for The Telegram. For this job, I would need an office and the help of a part-time secretary. My office would be a partitioned-off part of the reference library office in the new Telegram building. My secretary would be Bette Laderoute, a graduate nurse from the Ottawa Valley who had become bored with nursing, taken a secretarial course and ended up with a job as part-time secretary to Barry Callaghan, the Book Editor of The Telegram. She would now divide her time doing secretarial work for Callaghan and me.

The thought of having both an office and a secretary was, of course, breathtaking to me. It indicated that the Tely management valued my services, wanted to keep me on staff and had further promotions in mind for me. Right away I began tackling the special assignments that awaited me. These included, in addition to the style book assignment, the following: doing a survey of North America's best newspaper libraries and making recommendations for re-organization of the Telegram library; becoming Editorial Training Officer for The Telegram; and writing a manual for new editorial staff.

All four jobs frightened me. They all seemed beyond my capabilities. I was stuck with them, however, and could only give them my best effort, so I knuckled down first to the style book, which I considered the most difficult. "What's a style book?" Josephine and our kids wanted to know. I explained that every newspaper needed a book of rules covering things such as abbreviations, spelling, capitalization, articles, adverbs, adjectives, date lines, bylines and scores of other problems that come up in everyday writing. A style book sets down regulations to ensure standardization so that writers know which abbreviations, spellings and other forms to use when there is a choice.

It took me three months or so to come up with a new Tely style book. The newspaper had had one many years earlier but I was told to ignore it and start out afresh. I began by collecting and reading style books of major newspapers in North America and then collecting all the spelling and abbreviation lists in use by Telegram editors. I met with all Telegram editors to get their opinions on which spelling, grammar and abbreviation styles they favoured. After much sweating and frustration, I produced a 91-page guide which was submitted to all Tely editors for their comments and opinions. A committee then went over the editors' recommendations, made a few changes and approved the book for publication in loose-leaf form so future revisions could be easily made. In all, it was a trying and demanding job. I was glad to finish it and fervently hoped I would never have to repeat it. I still have a couple of copies of the book in my library.

The next special assignment I undertook consisted of a survey of newspaper libraries. I had always considered that The Telegram had a good library or "morgue" as we called it. A competent staff carefully checked and clipped hundreds of stories from our paper every day as well as from The Globe and The Star. If a reporter was writing a story on Rev. T.T. Shields, for example, he or she would ask for the Dr. Shields file. It would contain clippings of everything ever written about Shields in the Toronto press. The clippings were filed away in cardboard folders under the names of the people and the subjects involved. I often used the clipping files but had come to recognize that the number of clippings was outgrowing the filing system.

To learn about the new computerized filing systems that were just being invented, I visited five North American newspaper libraries, including those at The Christian Science Monitor in Boston, The New York Times, The Milwaukee Journal, and Newsday on Long Island.

After talking to many newspaper librarians, I made two major recommendations about the Telegram library. The first was that a professional librarian with a degree in library science should be hired. This was done within a few months and led to many improvements in the Tely library. The second was that an electronic filing and reference system should be installed. The recommendation was approved by management but never implemented because of cost.

My third special assignment involved my appointment as Editorial Training and Education Officer. Andy MacFarlane explained that he wanted me for this job because I had, as Suburban Editor, been so successful in hiring and training inexperienced kids as suburban reporters and later getting them placed on our city staff.

Some years earlier, while I was still Suburban Editor, the Tely had begun sponsoring an annual student essay contest, offering the ten top student winners summer jobs as reporters. Guess who got stuck with putting the kids to work when they arrived for their 10-week jobs? None other than good old Harve, the genial Suburban Editor. I wasn't going to have time personally to teach newspaper writing to ten novices all at once, so I devised a plan to farm them out to experienced reporters on our city staff. To do this, I had to sweet-talk ten experienced reporters into accepting student assistants. I approached ten good-natured men and women staffers and introduced them to the essay writers, all of whom proved to be intelligent, friendly kids. I explained that each student would be paired with a staff reporter for a week at a time, would accompany the reporter on assignments, would gather the same information and would write a news story on each assignment, with some help from the reporter. The student would keep one copy and give the other to me. I would edit it and review it with the students. The system worked well, so well that the City Editor hired some of the kids when they graduated from their university programs.

By the time the summer student program had been going a few years, I had carried out another of Andy MacFarlane's assignments: the preparation of a 43-page manual entitled *An Introduction to New Editorial Staff*. It was to prove useful not only to summer students but also to new full-time reporters until The Telegram ceased publication at the end of October, 1971.

On the whole, once the style book was finished, my stint doing special assignments turned out to be a pleasant and relaxing interlude for me. It encompassed the time that President Kennedy was assassinated in Dallas, Texas. I well remember what I was doing on that fateful autumn day in 1963. I was out with Josephine, closing the deal for a new house at 15 Conifer Drive in Markland Wood, Etobicoke. It proved to be our dream house in a pleasant tree-shaded neighbourhood. Jo and I lived there together until Jo died tragically of Alzheimer's Disease in 2003. I still live there alone.

Another special assignment that I vividly remember from this period required me to conduct a full review of the Fred Fawcett case. Fawcett was a farmer from Grey County. In 1856, his ancestors had obtained a farm through a Crown grant under a plan to encourage settlement in that county. From a study of the Crown grant, which was issued under the name of Queen Victoria, Fawcett eventually concluded that neither the Province of Ontario, founded in 1867, nor local municipalities had any legal right to levy taxes on his farm. In 1961, when two assessors went to the farm to update assessment data, Fawcett waved a pistol at them, fired a shot into the air and kicked one assessor to the ground. Three weeks later, five Ontario Provincial Police officers and another official went to the farm with a warrant to arrest Fawcett. Fawcett held them off with a loaded rifle for four hours before he finally surrendered peacefully.

The Crown argued in court that Fawcett suffered from paranoia and had unshakable delusions according to which the Crown grant made him exempt from provincial laws; the Crown argued further that he was likely to use violence in defence of his beliefs. The court agreed and ordered Fawcett confined to a mental hospital. Fawcett's family launched appeals to the Ontario Court of Appeal and the Supreme Court of Canada and applied for a habeas corpus writ. Many court hearings were conducted and the case attracted wide publicity. The courts finally concluded that Fawcett was mentally ill and should be confined until doctors considered him to be cured.

In accordance with Andy MacFarlane's instructions, I spent a month reading all the court transcripts of the hearings, interviewing witnesses, talking to psychiatrists and reading textbooks they loaned to me. I wrote a complete review of the case. It occupied two full pages of The Telegram on Monday, April 12, 1965. I later received a personal letter from an Ontario Supreme Court judge congratulating me for having written a fair and impartial review of the case. I don't know whether my story had anything to do with it, but a few months later Fred Fawcett was released from the mental hospital to return to his home and family.

I should also mention that, as part of my Editorial Training Officer duties, I got to know the Dean of Continuing Education at York University and arranged a series of weekend seminars for Telegram reporters at the university. I attended these myself and also took evening courses at the university.

Chapter 45
Hoist By My Own Petard

It was during my special assignments period that I spent several months at Northwestern University in Evanston, Illinois. This was a case of "The engineer hoist by his own petard".

As part of my job as Editorial Education Officer, I had read somewhere that the Ford Foundation had funds available to assist in the education of journalists. So I wrote to the foundation chairman in New York. He promptly replied, telling me to contact the Dean of Journalism at Northwestern University in Evanston. When I did this, Dean William Cole phoned me. He invited me to come for a visit to the Medill School of Journalism to learn about the school's fellowship program. I flew to Chicago, was met by a car and driver at O'Hare Airport, installed in an Evanston hotel and taken to meet Dean Cole.

Bill Cole and I liked each other immediately. I told him about my own career. He explained that his school had organized an urban journalism institute to educate reporters about the various problems being experienced by North American cities. One-year fellowships in urban journalism were being offered, and newspapers were invited to nominate reporters for these fellowships. Those accepted were enrolled for one or two semesters at the university. They were given residence and meals, their regular newspaper salaries were paid by the university and they were given the use of a car. A program of individual studies was laid out for each reporter accepted. Most of the programs involved auditing lectures in urban sociology as well as travel to meet and interview officials of U.S. cities that had devised innovative approaches to urban government problems and urban social problems.

So far, the fellowship program had included only U.S. newspapers, Bill Cole told me. The School would like to extend it to Canada and would offer the first Canadian fellowship to a staffer from The Telegram since The Telegram had been the first Canadian paper to contact him.

I collected a mass of material about the program and flew back to Toronto to report on this wonderful opportunity to extend the education of a few Telegram staffers. On the flight back, I even decided which Telegram reporter I would recommend for the first fellowship. When I presented my report to Andy MacFarlane and JDM—or "Bigdome" as we affectionately called him among ourselves—both were enthusiastic but came up with a proposal that filled me with dismay. Both instantly decided that the first Canadian fellowship should go to me!

I know I should have been filled with gratitude for this wonderful educational opportunity. I know that up until this point I had regretted bitterly my own lack of formal education and had read and worked at every opportunity to remedy this. But the thought of having to leave my loving wife, wonderful son and daughter and our happy home for six months or more was just more than I could bear.

With something less than enthusiasm, I went home to break the news to Josephine. She was not filled with joy at what she heard, but she sensibly thought for a few minutes and came up with an idea. "Maybe you could break it up into segments," she said. "Go there for two weeks at a time and come home to your job for two or three weeks."

That's the proposal that I laid before my bosses the next day and that I then had to make by phone to Bill Cole at Evanston. Eventually, everybody accepted it, mainly because it would keep me happy, allow me to keep writing my Trip column and also let me finish several assignments still uncompleted.

Arrangements were completed for my first university semester. Bob, then in an undergraduate B.Sc. program at the University of Toronto, asked me, "Dad, where are you going to stay down there?"

"I'll just ask them to give me a room in a student residence," I said.

"That won't work," he replied. "You'd just survive one night in a residence and be booking into the Hilton next morning."

When I got to Evanston, however, I found that Bill Cole and George Heitz, his assistant, had different plans for me. The university had rented a house in Evanston belonging to a math professor who was on sabbatical at Stanford University in California. I was to occupy the house and I was also to have the use of a car and a gasoline credit card. I told them the

Tely would continue paying my salary. Only travel expenses would be charged to the Ford Foundation.

Altogether, I spent about six months—in segments—away from home at Northwestern University, studying and travelling. George Heitz worked out structured and unstructured programs for me. The dullest part was reading my way through a huge tome entitled *The City* by Max Weber, the high priest of urban sociology.

The most exciting part was flying with Bill Cole in a Beechcraft Baron aircraft, chartered by the Ford Foundation. Dean Cole had a private pilot's license, but on inter-city trips he also took along as co-pilot an off-duty United Airlines captain. We flew to many American cities for conferences and interviews. Once we flew to Washington for the introduction of a computer game about city management. Taking part were mayors and city officials from across the U.S. The whole game occupied a couple of days during which I met lots of mayors and several U.S. Senators.

Years later when I was visiting Sault Ste. Marie, my grandson, Tom, asked me if I'd like to play the "City Game". On a computer disk, he had the same thing I'd encountered in Washington. Somebody had put it on the market for commercial use.

I learned a lot from my fellowship at Evanston but was glad when it was finished. I was very lonely there. Jo flew down for a couple of weekends but was reluctant to spend much time away from her job at Herb Blaikey's motor vehicle licence bureau on the Kingsway.

One part I did enjoy was conducting seminars

for graduate urban sociology students. The subject was the evolution and operation of the Metropolitan Toronto system of government. City officials in the U.S. as well as urban sociology professors often referred to Toronto as "the place where you did things right". Since I had conducted a briefing for municipal officials when I was Suburban Editor of The Telegram and had followed all the pro and con arguments about the Metro Toronto federation, I was very familiar with the subject.

Just after my period at Northwestern University, I had two other interesting experiences. One was my trip from Toronto to Sydney, N.S., by ship, and the other was my month-long stay at La Presse, the biggest French-language newspaper in Montreal.

At a managing editors' conference, Andy MacFarlane had been having a drink with his La Presse counterpart and the two of them had come up with what seemed like a great idea. They would bridge the "great solitude" between Toronto and Montreal by exchanging a couple of editors shortly before Expo 1967. I was sent to spend a winter month with the staff of La Presse, and a La Presse columnist named Raymond Grenier came to The Telegram for a month. He wrote four pieces on his impressions of Toronto, and I wrote four about my experiences in Montreal. My four ran in The Telegram in English and in La Presse in French. Raymond Grenier's were similarly translated and printed in both newspapers. I hope that the series did something to promote the spirit of amity that characterized Expo and the Canadian Centennial celebrations.

My chief memories of that month in Montreal are of the bitterly cold weather and the continual partying with the La Presse staff. Every night I was introduced to a new gourmet restaurant and to wines from the best cellars in Canada. I also learned a little more French and I began to appreciate why Canadian francophone citizens are concerned about preserving their language as a small island of French in a huge North American ocean of English. It reminded me of my friendly arguments with Clovis Gravel in Saint John, N.B.

That month in Montreal also reinforced my opinion of French Canadians as the warmest, most hospitable people in the world. Everyone I met in Montreal welcomed me. Most of them laughed at my attempts to speak French but were eager to be helpful. The visit achieved what I believe was Andrew MacFarlane's true objective: to expose a Toronto WASP to francophone culture and aspirations.

Chapter 46
My Grand Tour Of Europe

It was around this time that still another experience contributed to my cultural education. For the first time I was exposed to Europe. In co-operation with tourism promotion agencies in eastern and western Europe, Scandinavian Air Services (SAS) organized a three-week European tour by a group of eight Canadian editors. The tour was to include two east European nations behind the Iron Curtain and four countries of western Europe.

From Toronto, The Telegram and The Globe and Mail were invited to send representatives. The Globe elected to send Vince Egan, a senior writer. The Telegram sent me.

I don't know who made The Telegram's decision. I suspected it was Ernie Bartlett, the Travel Editor, who handled my weekly Trip copy. He had often advised me on travel writing and told me I should try to broaden my experience of the world. In any case, I was grateful for the chance to see both sides of Europe.

To begin the trip, I took the CN Rapido train to Montreal for a kickoff party at which I met my fellow travellers. On that same night, we took off from Dorval Airport, made a brief fuel stop at Glasgow, and then flew on to Copenhagen. It was my first trans-

Atlantic flight, my first sight of Europe, and my first experience of first class air travel, and I enjoyed it all immensely.

The three weeks that followed were hurried and confusing, as conducted multi-country tours usually are. From Copenhagen, after a one-day glimpse of Denmark, we flew to Frankfurt where we boarded an east European plane for Budapest. I think we had four days in Hungary, which was still under Communist rule. First we toured both Buda and Pest on the two sides of the Danube, and then we drove around the countryside.

I vividly remember our visit to Eger in the Matra mountains. We visited a winery deep inside one of the mountains and sampled Eger Bull's Blood, a famed Hungarian red wine. Our official Hungarian guide, a Dr. Bartos, drew our attention to a motto on the wall of a cave. It read "In Vino Veritas". Dr. Bortos then proceeded to tell us the truth about the devastation caused by the Russian-imposed communist government in Hungary. We tried to hush him up, fearing that he would be reported to the state police, but he told us not to worry. Everyone in Eger was anti-communist, he said, and eventually Hungary would be free again. Already, communist governments were starting to welcome visitors from Canada and the U.S. because they needed U.S. dollars.

From the winery, we walked half a mile (about a kilometre) in bitter cold to a huge cathedral which we entered and then stumbled onto benches. The vast building was utterly dark and very cold. As we sat, bundled in overcoats, wondering what would happen next, the darkness was split by a mighty organ thundering out the notes of J.S. Bach's Tocatta and Fugue in D Minor. From that moment on, I became a fan of Bach's music and started collecting Bach records. After half an hour of glorious music, we were led up interminable winding stairs to meet the dean of the cathedral who was also Hungary's leading organist. He was snugly ensconced in a comfortable little loft, warmed by electric heaters.

From Eger, we went to Prague for a tour of Czechoslovakia. We found the Czechs equally anti-communist and also eager to tell us jokes about the Hungarians. One was about the Greek philosopher, Diogenes, who walked around Europe with a lighted lantern "looking for an honest man." By the time he left Hungary, the Czechs said, he didn't have the lantern; it had been stolen.

From Prague, we flew to East Germany and got off our plane at the East Berlin airport long enough to eat a huge lunch with East German officials in an airport building. While we ate, the other passengers on the plane were kept waiting for two hungry hours on the tarmac.

Next, we had a very pleasant tour of West Germany, mostly by train. We visited Cologne, Dusseldorf and Rudesheim on the Rhine were I developed a liking for a wonderful white wine called Rudesheimer Rosengarten. It's named for the rose garden that covers the main street of this lovely little town.

From West Germany, Eric Kutti, our guide and the public relations chief for SAS, took us to Finland, his homeland. I found Helsinki to be quite appeal-

---

ing, particularly the nude sauna where we slid down a chute from the steam room into a shallow inlet of the Baltic Sea on a cold March night. We spent a few enjoyable days in Finland, hearing lots of jokes from Finns about their Swedish neighbours, then went to Sweden where the jokes were all about the crazy Finns. We finally crossed by boat to Norway and flew home by way of New York.

Back at Front and Spadina in Toronto, I found I had been given a new job and title. I was to be Urban Affairs Editor of The Telegram.

Chapter 47
Urban Affairs Editor

The move to make me Urban Affairs Editor was the result of another of my reports to Andy MacFarlane. He had asked me to have a look at our City Hall coverage and make recommendations. I wrote that the whole Toronto area, from Oshawa west to Burlington and north to Newmarket was becoming one big city and that politicians and newspapers should treat it as such. Using a word I had picked up in my time at Northwestern University, I called it a "megalopolis". I also made the mistake of mentioning the term "Urban Affairs Editor". Our Promotion Department liked the title and seized upon it as a new buzzword. They talked the editorial brass into appointing such an editor, and somebody concluded that the logical choice for the position should be the person who introduced the term.

I wasn't really enthusiastic about the term, because nobody had paused to think out what exactly an Urban Affairs Editor would do. Would he be a sort of super City Editor, in charge of all the reporters covering municipal affairs at Toronto City Hall and in all the giant townships and towns that were filling up the suburbs? Or would he be a columnist combining news and opinion about affairs of the megalopolis?

I didn't really have a choice as to whether I wanted the job or not. The decision was made for me. John F. Bassett, the Tely Publisher's son, was very much in favour of having me in the new position. Our Promotion Department had even prepared giant posters for display in subway cars and at bus stops announcing the appointment of a Telegram Urban Affairs Editor. Headed "Harvey Currell: City Slicker", they proclaimed: "Harvey Currell is our Urban Affairs Editor, no other newspaper in Canada has one. His job is to report on the growth of the Toronto Megalopolis, and to be its watchdog. Mr. Currell writes: 'Because of political boundaries, governments are not yet able to deal with this huge megalopolis as a unit but we hope, as a newspaper, to do so.'"

So there I was, stuck with a job I had not sought, and which had not yet been defined. Nobody every did really define it.

After discussion with Andy MacFarlane and the Editor in Chief, Doug MacFarlane, we concluded that I should begin by writing "think pieces"—really opinion columns—for Page Seven, the op-ed page, about city and regional politics and problems. I did not really want to try to be the boss of news coverage not just of Toronto City Hall but also of all the suburban city halls and of the Metropolitan Toronto Council as well. To do so, I would have had to be a sort of super City Editor.

Things jogged along fairly well. I wrote columns bylining me as Urban Affairs Editor, and I finished up my special assignments for Andy MacFarlane. After a few months, however, a new development forced an important decision upon me. I got a job offer to leave The Telegram and move to Humber College. I don't remember whether the first approach was made from me to the college or whether the college contacted me first. In any case, I received an invitation to go to meet Gordon Wragge, the president of Humber College.

This was one of the new community colleges that Bill Davis had started as Ontario Minister of Education. Officially called CATS (Colleges of Arts, Technology and Science), they were intended to provide post-secondary education for people who would not or could not go to university but wanted advanced training for the job market. Three CATS were organized for the immediate Toronto area. One of them, Humber College, had opened in northern Etobicoke and had immediately filled with students and been proclaimed a huge success.

Gordon Wragge, Humber's president, proved to be a popular choice. When I met him, he said he was being submerged with administrative details and needed somebody similar to an adjutant but much higher than a secretary to organize things for him and to do important writing assignments. After some discussion, he offered me the job at a salary somewhat higher than the $10,500 a year I was getting from the Tely. I partly accepted the offer but said I would give him a final decision by next day.

I drove back to the Tely, walked in to JDM's office and told him what I had done. He reacted immediately: "Don't be a damn fool! You don't belong in some college. You're a newspaper man. You belong here. We've put a lot of effort into educating you." He then went on to tell me that Alan Noblston, one of the Tely's four Associate Editors, was about to retire and he (JDM) intended to recommend me to John Bassett as Noblston's replacement. JDM then added, "It will take a couple of months, but you phone Gordon Wragge and tell him you've changed your mind."

I did as I was told. Gord Wragge was pleasant about it. He said, "I was afraid I really wasn't going to get you. I would have liked to work with you. Perhaps our paths will cross again." Then I had to go home and tell Josephine what I had done. She gave me no flak, supporting my decision as always.

I composed myself to wait for my new job at the Tely, and I busied myself in my spare time with doing my Trip columns, working at my cottage, and preparing geology material for the Thursday Night Society. This was a group of friends who met once a month for field trips and studies in geology and Ontario archaeology.

Chapter 48
Associate Editor

True to his word, J.D. MacFarlane did promote me to be an Associate Editor of The Telegram in 1969 and he obtained approval for the move from the Publisher, John Bassett. This was necessary because Associate Editors on The Telegram were members of the editorial board which was presided over by the Publisher. Our paper had four Associate Editors at this time: Reuben Slonim, the rabbi of a small Toronto Jewish temple, Peter Dempson, our senior federal political writer, John Harbron, a writer on world affairs, and myself.

In informing me of my appointment, JDM told me, "You will be writing editorials and Page Seven opinion pieces on city and suburban situations so that we can continue calling you Urban Affairs Editor. That will keep the Promotion Department happy." The decision also kept me happy. It relieved me of responsibility for actual City Hall coverage but gave me the job of expressing the newspaper's opinions on local politics.

According to a well-known newspaper adage, "The editorial page belongs to the publisher. The news pages belong to the readers." This expresses the widely respected tradition that news reporting and presentation should be kept fair, impartial and free of bias and that expressions of opinion should be clearly identified as such and confined to the editorial page or to columns closely identified with the columnists' names.

Editorials, in The Telegram, were not intended to express the personal opinions of the Associate Editors. They were meant to convey the collective opinion of the newspaper, as decided upon by the editorial board. This august body met five days a week at 11 A.M., with the Publisher in the chair. Also present as members were J.D. MacFarlane, the Editor in Chief, Arnold Agnew, the Executive Editor, the four Associate Editors and the Editorial Cartoonist, Yardley Jones. The Publisher usually led off each meeting by introducing some topic in which he had a special interest and asking for the opinions of the board members. From the ensuing brief but incisive discussion, a position to be taken by the newspaper usually emerged. Bassett would summarize this position and then assign one of the Associate Editors to write an editorial on it. Completed editorials had to be read, edited and approved by either the Executive Editor or the Editor in Chief. Occasionally Basset himself would ask to see an editorial before it was printed.

Each Associate Editor was assigned an area of responsibility in which he was expected to carry out in-depth research and keep up with news reports. At every board meeting, the Publisher would ask each of us to introduce subjects that we thought might merit editorial comment. We would outline the background, state the position we thought The Telegram should take, and present our supporting arguments. Everybody was invited to comment either for or against the position. No formal votes were taken, but a consensus was usually reached fairly quickly. Bassett made the final decision as to whether we would run an editorial and, roughly, what it would say. The appropriate Associate Editor would then write the editorial and give it to the Executive Editor for approval.

As the new boy on the board, I kept very quiet for the first few weeks and then began cautiously introducing a few topics. Besides urban affairs, I was given responsibility for education, on which I had some firm opinions.

One of the first topics I introduced was the very low percentage of Ontario high school graduates who qualified for university entrance. At this time, it was well below ten percent. I argued that it was hard to believe that fewer than ten percent of Ontario kids had the mental capacity to benefit from university training. But the fact was that more than ninety percent of those who completed five years of high school were barred from university because of the rigid entrance requirements. These demanded a high standing in all of the main high school subjects, including mathematics and science. But new research had shown that different people had widely different areas of brain development. And everybody knew that a boy or girl could have great difficulty in maths and science but be brilliant in communication, art and music and have a high I.Q. score.

Drawing from my own school experience, I kept gently hammering at this and finally got the board to agree. The Telegram began to run editorials calling for a review of university entrance requirements. The Ontario government began to take note. Educators, it appeared, had been worrying about the same thing. After much discussion, Bill Davis, as Minister of Education, introduced the "credit system", which introduced a higher degree of flexibility in university entrance requirements. For some programs, mathematics would still be required. For other programs, however, kids like me who had math phobia could qualify by acquiring enough credits in subjects other than mathematics.

Editorial board meetings were sometimes fun. Once in a while, Bassett would devote ten minutes to medical case histories and we would all talk about our ailments. He also hoped to hear the latest jokes.

Besides keeping up research for editorials on my assigned subjects, I continued with reading and research on my other interests: conservation, geology, forestry and archaeology, and I frequently contributed columns on these topics for the Op-Ed Page. Of course I also continued writing a Trip column every week.

The Associate Editor position was the most prestigious job I ever held. It widened my reputation and my circle of friends. It involved lots of travel. I went to England several times to research pieces on how London was coping with its horrific population increase. I visited "New Towns" which the national government was building to divert people from the London area. I also made visits to Kenilworth, in

Warwickshire, the home of my mother's family. I met lots of cousins who looked like me, short and blonde and jovial. On one memorable New Year's Eve at the British Legion clubhouse in Kenilworth, I hit the jackpot on a slot machine and called for "Drinks for the House"—a once in a lifetime experience.

Back at the Tely, I grew to enjoy the editorial board meetings. I felt I was building a reputation for myself as a capable editorial writer, and I was becoming more relaxed in discussions with Publisher Bassett. He had a good sense of humour and was surprisingly kind and considerate in his attitude toward his subordinates. He disliked pretension and self-importance.

On one occasion, I persuaded Bassett to change his mind. The issue involved Bill Dennison, the NDP mayor of Toronto. Through regular lunches with the mayor, as part of my job, I had come to like Mr. Dennison as an unpretentious and honest civic official. On the other hand, The Telegram had disliked him, mostly because he was leftist in his politics. This was a reflection of the old-time Telegram's rigidly rightist WASP attitudes. Now, with a civic election looming and several important issues at hand, Mayor Dennison began hinting that he intended to quit. His wife was ill and he would not run again for mayor. The problem was that there was nobody suitable to replace him. I brought this up at an editorial board meeting when we were discussing which candidate The Telegram was going to support for mayor in the coming election. Bassett polled the editorial board members on the matter. Nobody could suggest a suitable choice.

I mentioned Dennison's good record and the fact that he had not tried to force his NDP opinions upon Council. I said, "It's really too bad we're going to lose him. Toronto needs a man like him for the next two years." Bassett reacted as I thought he would. "There's only one answer," he thundered. "Bill Dennison will have to run again." He then told me, "I want you to take the mayor to lunch. Tell him I have changed my mind and The Telegram has changed its mind. We think he owes it to his city to run again and we will support him in the election campaign."

I immediately phoned the mayor and asked him to see me on an important matter. He agreed to have lunch that day on the 54th floor of the Toronto-Dominion Centre, then Toronto's smartest restaurant. I phoned and made a reservation and hurried over to the TD to tell the Maitre D' to expect the mayor of Toronto in a few minutes.

Mayor Dennison arrived in his city limousine and was whisked up 54 floors to our table. When the Maitre D' asked what wine we'd like with lunch, Bill Dennison asked, "What's the sweetest wine you have?" The Maitre D' shuddered but replied, "Leave it to me. I'll bring you something you'll like." The wine waiter shortly appeared with a nice bland Italian white. I then had to give the mayor my message from John Bassett.

"This is certainly a surprise," said Mr. Dennison. "The Telegram has not been very kind to me in the past."

"I know that," I told him. "Things have changed, and Mr. Bassett is big enough to be able to apologize and change his mind. If you agree, there'll be a lead editorial in tomorrow's paper urging you to run again, recognizing your contributions to Toronto and promising our support."

He thought for a moment, then agreed to run again. His wife was feeling better, he said, and she would not object to another—final—term for him as mayor.

I wrote an editorial headed "Mayor Dennison must run again". Bassett read and approved it and Bill Dennison was subsequently elected with a huge majority.

Bassett, I should point out, could be very bull-headed and stubborn sometimes, and this characteristic evidently led to a final disastrous clash between him and J.D. MacFarlane. It happened when I was on vacation in October, 1969. I came back to find that JDM had left The Telegram. Whether he had quit or been fired, I never found out. All I was told by Arnold Agnew was that there had been a flaming row and that JDM was gone and Arnold had been named Editor in Chief. There was no new Executive Editor.

In his book about his father entitled *Canada's Newspaper Legend: The Story of J. Douglas MacFarlane*, Doug's son Richard wrote that Bassett fired MacFarlane with the words: "We're retiring you. You're running out of steam." If anyone was running out of steam, I'd say it was Bassett rather than MacFarlane. In his book, Richard MacFarlane quoted me correctly as saying, "I always felt that the heart had gone out of The Telegram after Doug left." This was true. The paper survived only two years after JDM's departure.

Chapter 49
The Twilight Of The Tely

Despite the sadness I felt at the departure of Doug MacFarlane, I enjoyed the next two years at The Telegram and felt that I did some good writing for the paper. It was in this period that my second book of Trip columns was published by the Musson Book Company. It was entitled *More Trips Around Ontario*. My first Trip book, *Thirty Trips Around Ontario*, had sold 20,000 copies in the late 1960s. The second book also came close to that figure.

While I was Associate Editor, Andrew MacFarlane vacated the post of Managing Editor to become Director of Research and Development. I felt that he was "kicked upstairs". Art Cole had left the City Desk in 1967 to become The Telegram's New York correspondent, covering the United Nations; he was unhappy about the move. Doug Creighton succeeded him as City Editor. When Andy MacFarlane moved out of the Managing Editor's office, Creighton became Managing Editor and John Downing became City Editor. One autumn month, Downing asked me if he could hold a City Desk staff conference at my Lake Josephine cottage, near Parry Sound. I agreed and the conference was held. I don't remember that it accomplished much.

As an Associate Editor, I had a nice office with a window—a real luxury in the new Tely building. The window gave me a view of the McGregor sock factory. I also had a reserved spot with my name on it on the second floor roof parking area.

In October 1968, I was asked to carry out the kind of travel assignment I liked. To celebrate completion of Highway 401 from Windsor to the Quebec border, I was told to drive the entire 816-km (510-mile) length of the highway in one day. Just a day or two earlier, the last section of the highway to be completed, near Gananoque, had been opened to traffic. I went down to Windsor and started my journey heading eastward, having arranged to pick up engineers, officials and Ontario Provincial Police officers at various spots along the 401. I collected a mass of material about the superhighway, construction of which had been started in 1952 and had taken sixteen years to complete. As I drove, I talked to my official passengers and I also dictated notes into a tape-recorder microphone fastened to my shirt collar.

At the far end of the trip, at a place called Lancaster, I took time out from the highway story to gather material for a Town and Country Trips column on a country inn nearly two hundred years old. When I got back to the Telegram building, I sat down to spend the better part of a day hammering out a "401" story that occupied a whole page of the newspaper. It was on the Friday before Thanksgiving, and I was anxious to finish the job so the family and I could take off to Lake Josephine for the holiday weekend.

For my lead paragraph, I wrote: "They're still calling it Highway 401." This was to emphasize the fact that the official attempt to call Ontario's main street the "Macdonald-Cartier Freeway" was proving to be a failure. Nobody I met called it anything but "the 401".

For more than two years, I was to enjoy life as an Associate Editor of The Telegram and a member of the editorial board. My office was next-door to that of Reuben Slonim and we became good friends, arguing about religion and morals in a good-natured way. I also enjoyed the company of Arnold Agnew. He was the son of a prominent doctor and was married to one of the Eatons. As Executive Editor, Arnold was my immediate boss and edited my copy. He was a good professional editor and helped hone my skills as an editorial writer.

Arnold had experienced many European assignments. When I was going to England to write about London's massive population problems, I asked him where I should stay in London. He recommended Brown's Hotel. I found this antiquated establishment to be straight out of an Agatha Christie novel. The bathtubs were enormous but the rooms rather gloomy. A personage known as the Hall Porter ruled the lobby and could get you anything from theatre tickets to a London cab. I remember one evening I was about to step into a cab when a big imperious woman who looked like a duchess jumped in front of me and was about to steal my cab. Somehow the Hall Porter happened to be out front. He deftly cut the duchess off with the words: "Madam, that cab belongs to this gentleman. I shall get you another cab." I boarded the cab. As we drove off, the cabbie remarked to me, "He certainly told off that old trout, didn't he, Guv?"

Back at The Telegram, I found that negotiations between Bassett and the reporters' union, the Toronto Newspaper Guild, were becoming more hostile. The Guild was demanding large salary increases. Bassett was emphatically stating that he couldn't meet the union demands because the newspaper was losing money. To prove this, he opened the newspaper's books to accountants hired by the Guild. The union refused to relent, however, and called for a strike vote. Basset bluntly stated that he would not go through another strike. Rather than face a strike, he would close the newspaper and sell off its assets.

Most of us on the management side believed him. He was increasingly interested in CFTO, the TV station he had successfully started. The feeling was that he was tired of worrying about how to keep the Tely afloat. Moreover, the Eatons were thought to be restless about the fact that they were backers of Bassett and did not want to become liable for Telegram debts.

As 1971 arrived, the atmosphere became gloomy and astute staffers started looking around for other jobs. I was among them, and began to regret that I had not accepted the offer to go to Humber College.

The final blow came in September, 1971. The union took a vote in an emotional atmosphere and voted to go on strike. Bassett replied with a devastating announcement that The Telegram would close and would cease publication on October 31, 1971.

I was plunged into gloom. The newspaper had

been my only employer for my entire adult life. I had gone to work there in 1939. The Telegram had been my university. Now, after thirty-two years, I was being cast adrift.

For the past few months, I had been trolling for other job possibilities. The outlook was not all bad, but it appeared that whatever new job I took would lead to family inconvenience and possibly a move to another city.

People I had worked with and helped in previous years started hunting on my behalf. Fraser Kelly and Peter Ward, both in Ottawa at this point, came up with solid offers from federal government ministries. The Federation of Ontario Naturalists and the Metro Toronto and Region Conservation Authority both made offers as well, but the salaries offered were lower than what I was getting from The Telegram and I had heavy mortgage payments to meet on our new house. As for the Ottawa positions, they offered satisfactory salaries but involved a move to Ottawa and the requirement that I take a course of French language instruction.

Most promising was an offer from Doug Creighton to join a group of Tely friends in starting a new Toronto morning tabloid newspaper to be called The Toronto Sun. Amazing advances in photo typesetting and printing would mean that the typography and printing of the new paper could be contracted out to three photo printing companies on the east, west and north sides of Toronto. Bassett had generously offered to give Tely street-corner newspaper boxes to the new paper. Tely truck drivers were planning to rent trucks to deliver the Sun on a contract basis to stores and other outlets.

The Sun's outlook looked fairly bright, but I had serious doubts that any new paper could survive. All across North America, old established papers were going out of business. I didn't want to make an investment of money and time in a new ship, only to have it sink under me.

It turned out that I was wrong. The Sun did survive and prosper because new print technology made it possible to produce newspapers at much lower cost. Massive linotype machines producing molten lead type were no longer needed. Lead stereotype plates became a thing of the past as did the huge presses with heavy lead plates for each page. I did not know all this in October, 1971, however.

The new job I did take came to my notice almost by accident. Around the last week of October, just as I was about to be forced to make up my mind, I noticed an ad in The Globe and Mail stating that the Etobicoke Board of Education was looking for an Information Officer. The job looked interesting. I clipped the ad and dashed off a letter addressed to T.D. Boone, the Director of Education for Etobicoke. I mailed the letter, figuring that it would probably be lost in a maze of bureaucracy. The very next morning, I was surprised by a phone call from T.D. Boone himself. He said to me, "It sounds as though you might be the kind of person we are looking for. Is there any chance you could come to see me today?"

I agreed to visit him that afternoon. I gathered up some clippings of my recent work for The Telegram, copies of the four books I had written, three citations for writing awards I had received from the Outdoor Writers of Canada and one from the Toronto Police Association. After lunch, I drove to the new Etobicoke Education Centre, just a few blocks from my house.

I was favourably impressed as soon as I walked into the lobby of this handsome building. A receptionist left his desk to conduct me up one floor to the office of the Director where I was immediately ushered in. T.D. Boone proved to be the kind of teacher and principal that I wished I had encountered as a student. He greeted me warmly and said, "Just give me a minute to look over the material you've brought me."

After five minutes, he asked me why I thought I would like to work for the Etobicoke Board of Education. I told him what had happened at The Telegram and that the newspaper was folding at the end of the month. I recalled that both my daughter and son had gone through the Etobicoke elementary school system and had been very happy in Etobicoke schools, and that my wife and I had got to know their teachers and principals. I confessed that I had never worked at public relations myself but had been on the receiving end of a lot of P.R. efforts and thought it should not be difficult to present a good image for a first-class school system such as we had in Etobicoke.

Tom Boone explained to me that the Etobicoke Board had experienced somewhat unsatisfactory relations with the press, mostly due to misunderstandings with local weekly papers. It needed someone who knew newspapers and knew what reporters wanted from schools. The Board had earlier hired an Information Officer but he did not seem to fit in well with the administrative organization and had made little impression before he left for another job.

After a few more words, Mr. Boone offered me the job. He had already made some inquiries about me, had read my Trip columns in The Telegram and thought we would get along well together. He offered me a salary somewhat higher than I was getting at The Telegram, with the promise of a raise at the end of six months if I proved satisfactory.

There ensued a brief exchange that cemented my decision to take this job. Mr. Boone asked, "What would you like in the way of holidays?" Up until then, I had been getting four weeks' annual holidays at The Telegram. I decided to go for broke and said, "I'd settle for six weeks." (I was thinking of being able to spend almost a whole summer at my beloved Parry Sound cottage and woodlot.) To my delight, T.D. Boone replied, "That would be satisfactory. This place almost closes down during the school holidays in July and August."

The deal was made. Mr. Boone explained that the appointment would have to be approved by the Board's twelve elected trustees but he was sure they would accept his recommendation. (One of the trustees happened to be my old mentor, Hugh M. Griggs. After serving as mayor of Mimico, he had retired to become an Etobicoke school trustee when Mimico and Etobicoke had amalgamated in 1967.)

Satisfied that I had made a good deal, I drove a few

blocks home to get approval from Josephine. I told her about all the offers I had received and said that it really came down to deciding between the new Toronto Sun and the Etobicoke Board of Education. She immediately opted for the Board of Education, with the comment: "You'll be able to walk to work instead of fighting traffic for an hour every day. You will live a lot longer."

Chapter 50
My Career In Education

At the beginning of November, 1971, I turned up at the Etobicoke Education Centre to begin my new career in education.

The preceding weekend had been an emotional period. On Saturday October 30, The Telegram's last edition had appeared with a huge Page One headline proclaiming: "This is It—Our Last Day". There were parties all weekend but I didn't attend any of them. I did not feel like drinking, and I knew there would be a lot of liquor flowing at all the wakes being held to mark the demise of my true alma mater. Instead, I stayed home with Josephine.

The next day, Sunday, I went out to gather material for my first Trip column in the new Toronto Sun. It was about Edna Blackburn's Caledon Hills farm and was due to appear in The Sun on Friday, November 5, 1971. The lead paragraph read: "To step into Mrs. Edna Blackburn's kitchen up in the hills of Albion is like stepping back into the early 1800s."

I had earlier told Doug Creighton that I would not be working full-time for The Sun. He expressed regret at this and asked if I would continue my weekly Trip column for the new paper. I accepted this offer and was elated at the thought that my column was not going to die along with The Telegram.

The first morning I walked into the two-year-old Etobicoke Education Centre, I felt at home in the place. Tom Boone welcomed me and introduced me to Paul Buddenhagen who then showed me around the building and introduced me to the top officials and department heads. Mr. Boone informed me that as Information Officer and Public Relations Manager I would report directly to him but I should try to help any official who needed assistance. I promised to produce a tentative public relations action plan later that day and started out to tour the big four-floor building with Mr. Buddenhagen.

Paul and I became friends that day and remained friends for the rest of his life. He began by showing me my office, a big bright room in what the staff called "Millionaire's Row" on the executive floor. I would be assigned a secretary in a week or so, but in the meantime I should give any typing work to Mrs. Lillian Bannon, the Director's secretary. I met a lot of pleasant people that morning. Many of them said they had read my work in The Telegram and looked forward to working with me.

The afternoon was devoted to a long meeting with Tom Boone, the Director, and a fuller explanation of my duties. It appeared that the details would be mostly left up to me. But Mr. Boone did outline to me some of his hopes and wishes. He wanted the school system to have better relations with the local weekly newspaper, The Etobicoke Guardian. He wanted to have some form of regular report sent to all citizens of Etobicoke, not just to the parents of students in the schools. He wanted to have a staff newsletter go out regularly to staff members, teaching and non-teaching. And he would be happy, he said, to see the odd mention of Etobicoke schools in the Toronto daily papers.

I told him I thought that all these expectations were reasonable and could be met quite quickly. I promised him brief regular written reports. He invited me to attend meetings of the Executive Committee, held every Monday morning, and to feel free to put items on the Committee's agenda by giving notes about them to his secretary.

As I recall now, the Executive Committee consisted of the major department heads: Jack Baker, Curriculum and Program; Paul Buddenhagen, Academic Personnel; George Clarke, Finance; Bill Moore, Planning and Plant.

In 1971, the Etobicoke system had 93 schools: 73 elementary and 20 secondary. It was the biggest employer in the Borough of Etobicoke and, I think, one of the ten largest school systems in Canada.

That same day, my first at the Board, I tackled the matter of relations with the local weekly paper. I called Muriel Duncan, the paper's editor. I knew her slightly from my days as Suburban Editor at The Telegram. I asked her, "Have you ever met Tom Boone, the Director of Education?" She said, "No, I've never had the chance."

"Would you come to meet him?" I asked.

"Sure," she replied. "I'd like to meet him."

I walked into Tom Boone's office and asked when he could meet with Ms. Duncan. I told him that newspaper people find it easier to write nasty things about people they've never met than about those they know as individuals. He said he would clear an hour that Friday morning and I said I would try to set up a meeting for 10 A.M. I called Muriel and she agreed to the time. I told her to bring her assistant, Barry, who also happened to be her husband. Lillian Bannon ordered coffee and sticky buns. We arranged to hold the meeting in a committee room, not in the Director's office. I didn't want the boss to meet the press from behind a big official-looking desk.

The atmosphere at the meeting was cordial. We ironed out a lot of trivial things that had been bothering the newspaper, including a belief that school principals were not authorized to talk to reporters without permission of the Director. Tom Boone said, "There's no such rule. If a principal is considered competent to run a school, he's competent to handle the school's relations with the press. If you have any trouble in that regard, call Mr. Currell here. He'll make sure you get through to the principal." That meeting ushered in a new era in our relations with The Etobicoke Guardian.

The next thing I started thinking about was a regular education report to the taxpayers of Etobicoke. I decided on a four-page newsprint tabloid to be produced quarterly and distributed to every home in Etobicoke. As an Etobicoke ratepayer, I felt that citizens would not approve of an expensive-looking magazine on glossy paper but would accept and read a small newspaper-type publication about their school system. I quickly drew up a rough plan for such a paper and took it to the next meeting of the Executive Committee where I asked for suggestions about story topics. The Executive members liked the idea and gave me many ideas for stories. Included were items about our excellent middle-school instrumental music program that gave every kid in Grades 6, 7 and 8 the chance not just to learn to play a musical instrument but also to play that instrument in a school orchestra.

The new publication, named *Education Etobicoke*, was ready for distribution by the post office a month after I started work. I had every story in it read and approved by the Director. Included was a layout of photographs of the twelve elected trustees who made up the Etobicoke Board of Education.

Something Tom Boone had said to me about school trustees stuck in my mind. He said, "As a Board, a collective body, trustees have all might, majesty, dominion and power. The Board's word is law. As individuals, however, they have little power or importance. We must try to keep them happy, but they do not, as individual trustees, give orders to staff."

After the launching of *Education Etobicoke*, which was to be published four times a year, I started to think about a staff newsletter. My predecessor as Information Officer had come up with a name for such a publication: *News Across the Board*. He had even designed a front-page heading for it but had evidently never produced a first edition.

I began by getting out a letter to all of Etobicoke's ninety school principals, introducing myself and asking for items of school news that would interest teachers. I soon received scads of material. Quickly, I had my new secretary start typing a newsletter on ordinary letter-size paper with headings in capital letters. I began with an editorial-style introduction, briefly mentioning who I was, and inviting teachers and other staff members to send me bylined items about ideas they had found useful in teaching. I also asked for examples of good writing by students, giving credit to individual boys and girls for their work.

It had been arranged that the Director of Education should read and approve every edition of *News Across the Board* before printing. I felt this to be necessary. Everyone's writing benefits from editing, and on The Telegram there had been an iron-clad rule that everyone's work, even the Publisher's, should be checked and edited before printing.

Over the months and years that followed, I put out an edition of *News Across the Board* ten times a year. It was improved over time by newspaper-style headings, produced by a photo-type heading machine, and by being typed in narrow newspaper-style columns.

Not long after I went to work for the Board, I was assigned a very competent secretary. Right from the beginning, I had been generating a large volume of typing work. The secretaries on the second floor soon began complaining that they couldn't get their own work done because I was always at their elbows with some typing job that I insisted had to be done A.S.A.P. To protect himself from these complaints, Bill Hall, the Personnel Manager, quickly found me a very capable assistant. She was Gwen Buckle, an Etobicoke woman of Scottish ancestry who had graduated from

Thistletown Collegiate. She proved to be a real jewel of a secretary as well as a very sympathetic and kind person in dealing with the public and with news reporters. As I recall, Gwen stayed with me about five years. She and her husband finally moved out of town so that they could afford to buy their own home and have a baby. I greatly regretted losing Gwen and once tried to coax her to come back to work. She declined. She thought it was more important to stay at home and be a mother.

After my first six months in education, Tom Boone announced that he was thinking of retiring after a lifelong career as high-school teacher, principal, superintendent, and then five years as Director. I had enjoyed working for him. He had a unique way of making an employee feel good about his work. Whenever I met him at a party after his retirement, he would loudly proclaim: "Well, I did at least one thing right as Director. It was hiring you."

After Mr. Boone announced his retirement effective in June, 1972, the twelve elected trustees of the Board enjoyed a period of supreme power. It was up to them, and them alone, to select a new Director. They advertised the position in the Toronto newspapers, with applications and résumés to be directed to the Chairperson of the Board, Mrs. Nora Pownall. (I refuse to call her "the chair". She was, and is, far too nice a person to be named like a piece of furniture.) Following some private meetings, the Board selected Jack Baker as Director and Paul Buddenhagen as Associate Director. It was a decision that everybody approved.

Jack Baker, born in Lindsay, Ontario, had begun his high-school teaching career at Beaverton, Ontario, married a Beaverton woman and then moved to North Bay. There he became such a popular teacher and vice-principal that The North Bay Nugget newspaper ran an editorial deploring his departure when he accepted a principal's position to open the new Alderwood Collegiate in the early 1950s. From Alderwood, Jack moved to open another new Etobicoke high school, Thistletown Collegiate, in the north end. After a few years there, he was made a superintendent.

Jack Baker was an ideal choice as Director. I worked for him for five years and enjoyed every year of it. After he retired in 1977, we became close friends. He often drove with me to gather materials for my Trip columns for The Toronto Sun, and he was a regular guest for Saturday night dinners with Josephine and me.

Soon after Jack took over the Director's job, I proposed to him that we hold a public relations seminar for all Etobicoke principals and the Toronto press. We would invite all the principals and the education reporters from newspapers, TV and radio stations to meet for a whole day at the Education Centre. They would hear a talk in the morning by the Public Relations Officer for the New York City Board of Education, then have lunch and then spend the afternoon in discussion groups with the objective of encouraging the reporters and principals to get to know each other.

In planning sessions, the question of a location for lunch came up. I said to the Executive Committee,

"If we're going to get reporters to come, we'll have to have a bar."

"That rules out the Education Centre for lunch," Jack Baker replied. "A Board bylaw forbids the serving of booze on Board property."

After some discussion, it was decided to have lunch, with a free bar, at the Valhalla Inn, across Hwy 427 from the Education Centre.

The morning session of the seminar was a great success, with Jack Baker re-affirming the principle that principals were free to conduct their own public relations for their schools. He did stress that the principals should carry out this important duty themselves and not delegate it to teachers or vice-principals. The New York P.R. guy was a big hit and gave principals and reporters lots of useful tips.

Lunch time rolled around. Jack Baker and I went over to the Valhalla Inn together. When we walked into the big room assigned to us, I noticed that all the reporters were busy at the bar on one side of the room. All the principals were in a line on the other side. None had gone near the bar. Jack quickly took in the situation. He strode over to the bar, announcing in his well-known loud voice, "I'll have a J and B on the rocks." At these words, a tidal wave of principals descended on the bar. After that, everything went as "merry as a marriage bell" and the seminar was pronounced a great success.

During Jack's five years as Director of Education, he and I developed a good working relationship. I soon realized how difficult and tiring the Director's job must be. He spent a full day in his office, making decisions on hundreds of complex questions. His evenings were seldom free; he was back at the Education Centre nearly every night for meetings of the Board, committee meetings with trustees or staff meetings. When he was not busy in Etobicoke, he was in downtown Toronto for meetings of the Metro Toronto School Board or contract negotiations with teacher or caretaker unions.

Turning now to speeches, I had never written speeches professionally although I had made a few impromptu speeches myself. In my new job with the Etobicoke Board of Education, I began writing speeches, first for the Director and then for the Chairperson of the Board. I found it surprisingly easy, provided I knew exactly what the speaker wanted to say. Before sitting down to write, I always insisted on a brief interview which I would begin by asking, "What are the points or arguments you want to make in this speech?" From attending Executive Committee meetings, Board meetings and committee meetings, I was usually familiar with much of the subject matter being covered. I acquired a reputation as a good speech writer, so much so that Jack Baker had to caution me, "Don't start writing for every principal in the school system or you will not have time for anything else." He established a kind of unwritten rule that I could write speeches on request for him, for the Associate Director and for the Chairperson of the Board, but demands for other speeches should be made and cleared through him.

On one occasion there was a speech-writing request from none other than Tom Wells, the Ontario

Minister of Education. He was scheduled to speak to all the public school trustees in Ontario at a convention in Windsor. The subject was how to consult with communities before closing schools because of falling enrolment. This had become a very hot topic in Etobicoke where the post-war baby boom had abruptly ended and we had many schools nearly empty.

To take parental heat off our trustees, the Etobicoke Board had developed a unique procedure: When enrolment at any school dropped below a hundred students, a Community Review Committee was formed with representatives of parents, neighbourhood taxpayers, teachers and Board officials. The Committee was given three months or so to examine the school's situation and make recommendations about its future.

I was the one considered responsible for this idea. At an Executive Committee meeting one morning, discussion centred on the fact that trustees and officials were taking a lot of parental flak over a decision to close a very small school. I asked, "Why don't you do what the provincial and federal governments do when they get a nasty problem? They appoint a royal commission or other independent body to investigate and make recommendations."

The idea took root. Tom Wells, the Minister of Education, heard of it and wanted a speech about it. (I had known him from my Telegram days.) He offered to pay me for the speech. I said I could not take money since I would be writing the speech on Board time. Jack Baker asked me to write the speech. I gave it to Jack to read over. He approved it and it went by courier to the Minister's office with a note from the Director to consider it a gift from the Etobicoke Board.

About this time, I got an offer from Doug Creighton, Publisher of The Toronto Sun, to come to work for The Sun as Associate Editor, writing editorials and "think-pieces" for the op-ed page. I was tempted to accept until I talked to Ed Monteith, an old Telegram friend who had become Managing Editor of The Sun. As a friend, he advised me *not* to come. There was a struggle going on for control of the editorial page, he said, and he feared that I would be caught in the middle.

I told my boss, Jack Baker, about the offer. He begged me to stay with the Board of Education. I told him that sometimes I felt a little out of place with my lack of formal education amid flocks of Bachelors of Education, Masters of Education and even a few Ph.D.s. Jack said "You can forget about that. We consider you a professional. You have writing skills and other skills that we need and haven't been able to find in anyone else. Nobody here is going to question your qualifications. I sincerely hope you will stay with us."

I thanked Doug Creighton for his offer but declined the move. My old friend Ron Poulton took the job at The Sun and later told me he was unhappy there. The only important thing he ever got to write was a book about the start of The Sun. It was entitled *Life in a Word Factory* and proved to be a best seller. A couple of years later, I got a second offer from Doug

Creighton, this time to write a daily Queen's Park column. I also turned this job down.

From 1973 to 1984, however, I did write an education column every week for The Sun, first under the nom de plume of Bob Anstruther, and later under my own name. I gave it up because by 1984 I had begun getting a lot of flak about having a conflict of interest.

I also took a certain amount of criticism from newspaper friends about the fact that I had abandoned the newspaper business to become a public relations officer or "flack". I shrugged this off. I was happy with what I was doing and had financial security, with no fear of another newspaper sinking under me.

Owing to John Bassett's generosity, Josephine and I were able to pay off the mortgage on our house with my severance pay from The Telegram. We began putting the money that had previously gone for monthly mortgage payments into Canada Savings Bonds, which we later converted into other sound dividend-paying investments. We were very pleased that we now owned outright our house for which we had paid $26,900 in 1963. I was to work at the Etobicoke Board of Education for sixteen happy years, from age 49 to age 65, and then retire with an adequate pension and a good investment portfolio.

An account of my duties would occupy many pages, so I shall just list a few that I liked the most. I was happy to get to work every day and happy to be writing about teachers and others who I knew were providing excellent education for thousands of good happy kids. My major duties included:

- Producing the staff newsletter *News Across the Board*. An important feature of this was a monthly teacher profile, an extended story about an excellent teacher nominated by a principal and a regional superintendent.
- Writing and producing **Education Etobicoke**, a four-page newsprint tabloid sent to every home in Etobicoke four times a year.
- Publishing a combined Annual Report and Night School Calendar.
- Attending all Board and Board committee meetings to assist news reporters and the public.
- Keeping in touch with reporters and editors of the local weekly newspapers and with the education reporters of the Toronto dailies. I got to know lots of young reporters and became friends with many of them.
- Sending out press releases and notes about picture possibilities and news to all the Toronto-area newspapers and TV and radio stations.
- Arranging radio and TV appearances for principals, teachers, officials and trustees.
- Clipping education items from all the weekly and daily newspapers, photocopying these and sending them to Board officials and trustees.
- Holding press conferences about important developments such as the opening of the Etobicoke School of the Arts, the first such high school in Canada.
- Writing and publishing many small attractive information booklets about special programs available in Etobicoke schools such as instru-

mental music, French immersion, advancement classes for gifted students, the School of Experiential Education, and special education for kids with learning problems.

- Issuing a "Welcome" booklet for families moving to Etobicoke. Greeting such families when they turned up at the Education Centre and introducing them to appropriate principals.

Above all, I think, the Education Centre valued my ability to produce clear, concise writing. Like any competent newspaper reporter, I could take a mass of information, analyze it into sections, list the important conclusions and quickly produce a clear understandable summary. Consquently, I soon found myself much in demand for writing briefs.

Elected school trustees, for some reason, love to fire off briefs to various government bodies, committees and commissions, setting forth the positions of their Boards on all kinds of issues. Board officials dreaded the mention of briefs because preparing them could take large amounts of time. Many highly qualified people could take several days, sweating over the wording of a brief directed, perhaps, to the Ontario Minister of Education. Writing such a document was considered a serious matter, and it had to be just perfect for presentation to the Director of Education and the Board before going to Queen's Park.

One day, Jack Baker asked me, "Have you ever written a brief?"

I replied, "I have written sermons and even an inscription for a granite monument but never a brief."

"Would you like to try writing one?" he asked.

I agreed to try. He handed me a mass of material. I quickly skimmed through it and asked for a meeting with the officials most involved. I found that writing a brief was much like writing a speech—you had to find out what the Board wanted to say. I cleared my desk, spent a couple of days researching the data and presented my first brief, in handwritten form, to my secretary to be typed. The Director and the Executive Committee were astounded to get a brief so promptly. They made a few minor changes and then ran it before the Board for approval. The trustees quickly OK'd it and off it went. I think the recipients were the federal Minister of Transport and the Members of Parliament for Etobicoke. The subject, as I recall, was a series of gripes about the harmful effects of aircraft noise on schools located under the flight paths leading to and from Toronto International Airport. I was asked to go to Ottawa as a member of the delegation that presented the brief to the Minister.

After that, I was much in demand as a brief writer as well as a speech writer.

Chapter 51
Struggling Through Another Strike

When I left the defunct Telegram, closed down because of a strike threat, I thought I was through with labour strife. Alas, it was not to be. In the autumn of 1975, secondary school teachers across Metro Toronto went on strike and were out for twelve weeks, from the middle of November to the middle of February. This led to all the usual conflicts, tensions and encounters that result from any strike.

But this particular strike was a major one because of the fact that negotiations for teachers' salaries were carried out on a Metro-wide basis with a uniform salary scale for all teachers in the Metro area. (The latter extended from Scarborough on the east to Etobicoke on the west, including, of course, the cities of Toronto and North York.) What happened was that the elected trustees opted to exert their real power. As individual Boards of Education and through the Metro Toronto School Board, they solidly voted to fight the secondary teacher salary demands and to keep the high schools open. Elementary school teachers had earlier settled with the Boards for a wage increase.

I was drawn into the conflict at both the local and the Metro level. In Etobicoke, I wrote many speeches for the Chairperson and the trustees.

Our Board kept all of its secondary schools open, with the principals and regional superintendents in charge. The trustees decided to set up a massive printing operation at the Education Centre; it used rented photocopy machines to produce course outlines for all important subjects at all grade levels. Students were told to come to their schools to pick up the course outlines and to use them to continue their studies. Some parents formed neighbourhood study groups and appointed volunteers with teaching experience to supervise and assist students.

At the Metro level, information officers from all the local boards were summoned to working sessions at the headquarters of the Toronto Board of Education on College Street where William Ross, Chairman of the Metro Board, had assumed command of the united trustee forces. In what we called "The War Room", the information officers were set to work composing newspaper ads, posters, press releases and speeches for the trustees to use. We took turns responding to calls from reporters.

On many days, we were taken to lunch by Chairman Ross—he later became a provincial judge—at La Scala, an upscale restaurant. I can remember that La Scala served a wonderful vichyssoise. Expenses for the Metro campaign were paid out of the savings realized from non-payment of teacher salaries during the strike.

The strike dragged on over Christmas into a bleak cold winter. At the local level, I had to cope with teacher picket lines to get in to work at the Education Centre. These were fairly peaceable. Jack Baker told staff, "Let's not be nasty about small delays in getting to work. Remember, these people on the picket lines are still our colleagues. When this is all over, we'll be back working with them."

On one occasion when I was in his office, Jack looked out the window into a snowstorm and said to me, "There's poor old Norm out there. He's too old to be exposed to this kind of weather. I can't do it myself, but would you do me a favour and quietly take some coffee out to him and the others." I took the coffee out with the message that Jack Baker had sent it. The pickets received it gratefully.

One day during the strike, a CBC news reporter phoned to ask if there had been any "incidents" on the picket lines which had been placed around every Etobicoke high school. I told him, "No. Actually it has been a rather gentlemanly strike." He replied, "Well, in Etobicoke, I suppose it would be."

After twelve weeks, the strike ended with the teachers being sent back to work by a special Act of the Ontario Legislature and with the appointment of a judge as an arbitrator to decide on a settlement binding on both parties. He gave the secondary teachers exactly the same settlement that had been won by the elementary teachers without a strike. The universal opinion was that the high school teachers had lost twelve weeks' pay for nothing.

After the strike, a political rhubarb ensued over the $100,000 in expenses run up by the Board negotiators at the Royal York Hotel. Included was $75 for a shrimp pyramid ordered one midnight. The trustees fiercely defended the expenditure, pointing out that the team of Board negotiators had been away from home for many long days and many long evenings, attempting to reach a settlement while the strike dragged on. They argued that the negotiators had saved several million dollars for taxpayers by fighting the strike to a conclusion. The expense account became an issue at the next municipal election, but the voters did not seem much concerned and no sitting trustee was defeated over it.

After the teacher strike, the high school teaching staffs returned to work with enthusiasm, evidently determined that no student should lose a year because of the work stoppage. They achieved this objective, and by the end of June the whole thing had been largely forgotten.

From the start of my employment with the Board, I was agreeably surprised at how warmly I was welcomed and how much I felt at home. I made friends at every level of the organization, from Ted Maginn, the head caretaker, to Doris Biggart, the "Queen Bee" or senior secretary at the Education Centre, and Lillian Bannon, the Director's secretary. I was warmly welcomed in all the schools. The elementary principals association immediately invited me to their annual three-day conferences. These were enlivened by skits poking good-natured fun at the Education Centre officials. I was once portrayed in one of these as the "Grand Vizier" of a mythical kingdom.

After my first secretary, Gwen Buckle, retired, I had a succession of other excellent secretaries including Barbara Fenske, Jackie Darling and Josephine Li. Jo Li stayed with me until my retirement in 1987. All of them were enthusiastic about public relations work and got to know the reporters who used to call me and come to my office. They were all fast, accurate typists who turned out beautiful clean transcript from my handwriting, which one secretary described as being like "ant tracks on paper".

Among the close personal friends I made at the Education Centre were Bill Moore, the Superintendent of Planning and Plant, and Sam Mackinlay, the Superintendent of Finance. They took an interest in my work and often gave me helpful suggestions. I introduced them to the news reporters who covered education. After a year or so, the three of us began holding lunches for the reporters twice a year, in June and at Christmas, at the Villa Borghese. This is a very good Italian restaurant in Etobicoke, famous for an Italian version of bouillabaisse, a rich fish stew. We paid for the lunches ourselves; they were not put on expense accounts. Bill and Sam gave me many ideas for my Trip columns for The Toronto Sun, accompanied me on many of the trips, and visited Josephine and me at Lake Josephine, our cottage near Parry Sound.

One of the public relations tools that I especially valued was the school newsletter. When I arrived, most elementary school principals were already sending home monthly newsletters from their schools. I set out to help principals make these more attractive and interesting. I prodded successive Directors into mentioning the importance of regular newsletters in their speeches to principals. I got them to suggest that *every* school should have a newsletter and that it was a good idea for each principal to appoint a vice-principal or senior teacher as editor of the newsletter.

From the Education Centre, I offered to supply design service for newsletter mastheads, and cartoons from a syndicate service to which we subscribed. School newsletters soon began blossoming out with examples of good writing by teachers and students and sometimes even by parents. Copies of all newsletters were sent to me at the Education Centre and also to the trustees of the wards in which the schools were located.

Soon after I came to work at the Board, I got in touch with the community channel director of Maclean-Hunter Cable TV which supplied service to Etobicoke. I asked him if he would like to videotape meetings of the Board of Education and show them on channel 11, the community service channel. He was enthusiastic about this, so I next took the proposal to the Director of Education. Jack was equally in favour but wisely commented, "Since this concerns the whole board, we will have to take it to the trustees, convince them that it was their idea and let them run with it." Jack mentioned it to the Chairperson who mentioned it to a trustee who brought it up at the next Board meeting. After a somewhat lengthy period of argument and discussion, the Board instructed staff to carry out the proposal, and TV broadcasts of Board meetings soon became a popular feature of cable TV in Etobicoke.

Colin Musson, Director of Community Service for Maclean-Hunter, quickly arranged most of the broadcast details, but one important problem remained. He could supply all the needed electronic equipment (cameras, lights, cables, videotaping equipment and so on) from a van to be parked at the front of our building on meeting nights. He could also supply a crew boss, but we would have to provide camera crews and two helpers. He suggested we use students.

I took this matter to the Director. He knew that one of our high schools, Silverthorn Collegiate, had an after-school TV club mentored by a teacher. Jack said I should contact that teacher and ask him to name six students for our TV crew. Jack came up with another good idea. He suggested that the student crew members should be paid for their work. The Board approved this, but then another problem appeared. Instead of the six names we needed for our TV crew, the school sent me a list of twelve students.

We needed only six. Somebody would have to select six out of the twelve. The school refused to do this, and nobody at the Education Centre would take the job. The Director said to me, "I guess it will have to be you." I disliked the idea. Since I was not a teacher, I felt I should not have to have any contact with students. Jack finally persuaded me to make the selection. I asked the school to send the twelve applicants over to my office and I interviewed all twelve, finally selecting three girls and three boys. It reminded me of my days as Suburban Editor when I had hired aspiring young people as Telegram reporters. To soften the rejection for the six who were not chosen, I told them that the decision had been made on the basis of experience and that they would be given jobs if any of the selected crew dropped off during the season. I also told them they would probably be hired in the following year.

The TV screening of Board meetings went well. We advertised the broadcast times, and the shows attracted wide audiences. Some trustees were tempted to show off their oratorical skills.

One unfortunate but minor incident occurred in the first year. A boy and girl from the camera crew started "fooling around" while carrying a camera through the Education Centre lobby. The camera crashed through a glass door, breaking the glass. The indignant Maclean-Hunter crew boss demanded that I fire the pair for endangering his camera. Remembering what it was like to be a teenager, I was reluctant to do this. I finally placated the crew boss by telling him that we were deducting the cost of the door glass from the pair's pay. I then phoned the principal of Silverthorn Collegiate, and suggested he call the pair into his office for a stern reprimand.

A couple of days later, one of the ladies on the Education Centre cafeteria staff tearfully told me that the girl involved was her daughter and that her principal had told her she owed her job to me. I later heard that the young woman had gone on to a career in television production.

One other way I helped a student was through a design for the cover of the Board's Annual Report and Night School Calendar. When I first went to work for the Etobicoke Board, these were two separate publications. I considered this a waste of money. I told the Executive Committee that the mandatory annual financial report should be expanded to include stories about innovative programs introduced during the year as well as promotion material about our night school along with the lists of night courses offered. I argued that each of the sections should re-inforce the other. The Executive Committee agreed, but we had a difficult time convincing Terry Hanes, the Superintendent of Continuing Education.

For the cover of the combined report, I wanted an attractive colour design. From talking to regional superintendents, I got the name of an art teacher at Burnhamthorpe Collegiate. I can't remember his name but he was said to be an outstanding teacher of commercial art. I contacted him to ask if he could recommend one of his students to create a cover illus-tration. He came up with the name of Nancy Zboch and sent her over to the Education Centre to see me. I told Nancy what we wanted, and she then produced an excellent cover design. We used it, featuring her name as the artist in an explanatory note in the com-bined report. We also paid her for her work. I hope this helped her get established in an art career.

Altogether, I worked for five Directors of Education at the Etobicoke Board, all of them outstanding. They were Tom D. Boone, Jack E. Baker, Paul Buddenhagen, Hadden Gillespie and Silvio Sauro.

I was to go through two more strikes between 1971 and my retirement at the end of 1987. The first was a strike by school caretakers, the second by school secretaries.

Trustees personally fought the caretaker strike. They formed teams of trustees and supervisory of-ficers to clean the schools, including washrooms, and they kept all the schools open. They gave amusing names to the cleaning teams which worked at night. One of the team names I remember was "The North End Plungers"! I was not asked to join any of these teams and did not volunteer. Ultimately, if I remember correctly, the strike ended with a negotiated settlement.

As for the school secretaries' strike, it did not last long and it also ended with a negotiated settlement. The secretaries picketed the Education Centre and, surprisingly, came up with quite a few ribald comments as we crossed their picket lines to go to work.

When Jack Baker became Director of Education in June, 1972, one of the things he proposed was that I should attend the convention of the Canadian Education Association, held every year in a different provincial capital. Usually a small delegation from Etobicoke attended, including the Director, some interested trustees and one or two officials. I welcomed this opportunity to see more of Canada. In the next few years, Josephine and I went to Halifax, Quebec City, Winnipeg, Saskatoon, Edmonton and Vancouver. The Board of Education paid my transportation and hotel expenses. I paid all Josephine's expenses.

I faithfully attended the various sessions of these conventions, but in my free time I gathered information for my Trip columns for The Sun. After the first year, I was often asked to speak at convention seminars about public information plans that had proved successful for the Etobicoke Board. I found that our Etobicoke school system enjoyed a good reputation across Canada for its schools and programs.

At the C.E.A. conventions, I met information officers and public relations people from school systems across the country. I suggested to Bob Blair, Executive Secretary of the C.E.A., that we should form a Canadian education public relations association. He thought this a good idea and offered to help. Back home in Toronto, I floated the plan at regular monthly luncheons of the Toronto area school board P.R. officers. At these meetings, we all paid for our own lunches. My fellow "flacks" all liked the idea, and a national association was formed under what I thought was the somewhat self-important title of the "Canadian Association of Communicators in Education" or C.A.C.E. I never held any office in this association. But after I retired, I was presented with a life-membership plaque for my part in getting C.A.C.E. started.

While I worked for the Etobicoke Board, I sometimes had to defend my decision, made in the 1960s, to send my daughter and son to private secondary schools.

Judith became a day student at St. Mildred's College, a small school operated by an Anglican order of nuns in a connected complex of old buildings at Lowther Ave. and Walmer Rd. in Toronto's university district. Judith enjoyed it, received five years of excellent education and had no trouble gaining admission to Huron College at the University of Western Ontario in London to earn her B.A. Later, St. Mildred's sold its downtown property and united with a private school in Oakville, Ontario.

The decision to attend St. Mildred's for high school was largely Judith's choice. We took her to visit the school while she was still in Grade 8 at Islington Public School. She liked the principal and the atmosphere. Attending as a "day girl" involved a ride downtown by bus and subway five days a week, but Judith coped with this like a young adult.

I suppose my bias towards private schools for our kids was largely a result of my own unhappy high-school experience. I wanted our daughter and son to receive individual attention and to have good secondary-school memories in later life. Also, Jo and I were somewhat disturbed by what we had heard about high-school drinking, drugs and sex in the turbulent period of the 1960s.

In the choice of a secondary school for Bob, we had no worries. He solved the problem for himself. For his last year of elementary school, Bob had been considered a "gifted" student and had been placed in advancement classes (which had been pioneered by the Etobicoke Board). Guided by a wonderful teacher named Mrs. Purdy, the advancement students spent half the school day on the regular curriculum and the other half in group and individual research on topics they themselves had selected. Bob flourished in this atmosphere and looked forward to getting to school every day.

I had been doing some quiet research myself on private schools, influenced by the records of private-school grads who had worked at The Telegram. I was especially impressed by Pickering College, a Mennonite-based school at Newmarket. A number of Pickering grads had worked for me at The Telegram, including Russell Cooper and Duncan Cameron.

They exhibited a fierce love for their old school and admired Joe McCulley, its headmaster.

The problem with Pickering was that it was a boarding school. I didn't like the idea of boarding schools; I thought kids should grow up at home with their families. Also, the fees were fairly high. Bob solved the whole problem by opting for U.T.S.—the University of Toronto Schools. This was then a private secondary school operated and subsidized by the Faculty of Education of the University of Toronto. Entrance was by a competitive written examination.

Bob registered to write the exam for entrance to Grade 9, and was accepted from among the brightest kids in the whole Toronto region. He had a good five years at U.T.S., learned to work hard at his studies, had summer jobs on "portage crew" at Quetico Provincial Park in northwestern Ontario and was more than ready for university when the time came.

As the 1980s rolled along, I enjoyed my work for the Etobicoke Board. I was accepted and valued as one of the education "family", and my salary kept increasing as administration salaries were adjusted in line with teacher pay scales.

I began to think of retirement, which for me would happen at age 65 in 1987. I figured out that my OMERS pension would be adequate for Josephine and me, along with the Canada Pension Plan and Old Age Security (OAS) payable at age 65.

OMERS is an acronym for Ontario Municipal Employees Retirement System. Board of Education employees not covered by teacher's contracts come under it for pension purposes along with police officers, firefighters, caretakers and all other municipal workers in Ontario.

Although I would have worked for the Etobicoke Board of Education only sixteen years at retirement, I would get credit for nineteen and a half years for pension purposes. This happened because somewhere around 1980, OMERS had announced a plan whereby employees who had served in the Canadian Forces in World War II were invited to buy credit in the pension plan, for their years in the services.

I had served only three years as a soldier. At the end of August, 1945, I had then been released on six months' leave to resume my job at The Telegram. My formal discharge certificate however, credited me with 3½ years of service. It cost me a couple of thousand dollars to buy credit for my war service years but this added substantially to my eventual pension in 1987.

By 1987, I was ready to retire. I was not tired and still had lots of energy, but I had begun thinking about how nice it would be not to have to get up early every morning. I was looking forward to having more time to travel on my Trip columns for The Toronto Sun and perhaps, eventually, to write another book.

Also, Josephine, my much-loved wife, was having health problems with severe arthritis and osteoporosis. I wanted to have time to care for her and to keep her comfortable.

I had been working full-time since age 17—for forty-eight years—when I finally cleared out my office just before Christmas, 1987, and quietly slipped out of the Education Centre for the last time.

There had been a series of parties, receptions and dinners to mark my retirement, climaxed with a big public affair at the Shaver House, a restored 19th century farmhouse on the West Mall in Etobicoke. Dozens of old newspaper friends turned up for this as well as several hundred teachers and principals.

Staff at the Education Centre had contributed to a fund to buy me my first computer, a wonderful device on which I could type my columns and transmit them to The Sun by plugging into a telephone jack.

Some groups in the school system took up their own collections for presentations, including the elementary-school principals. The Outdoor Education Department gave me an inscribed cherry-wood canoe paddle.

I was especially grateful that the secretaries on the second floor, the Executive section of the Education Centre, also insisted on making their own presentation to me. I had many good friends among the secretaries and had always insisted that they get credit for good work.

Chapter 52

New Trips And New Memories In The Making

In the first few weeks after retiring from the school system, I began casting my memory back to my earlier job at The Telegram where I had worked for thirty-two years. Many of my old Telegram friends now worked at The Toronto Sun. Some of them would come with Josephine and me to Lake Josephine, the property I had bought near McKellar, in Parry Sound district. Many would phone me with suggestions for my Trip columns.

Among them was Bob Vezina, an acerbic but wonderfully generous character from North Bay. For a time, Bob was City Editor of The Toronto Sun. Bob insisted on high performance standards for reporters and had little patience with incompetence. When I was Suburban Editor, I once asked him if he thought I should hire a certain reporter who had applied for a job. Vezina knew the applicant. He replied, "Don't hire him. He's lazy, he can't write and he wouldn't know a story if it bit him in the ass."

It was through Vezina that I got to know Don Delaplante, a competent free-lance reporter-photographer who became known right across northern Ontario. Don used to tell about how a new Telegram night editor phoned him at home in North Bay one night and asked, "Don, could you drop over to Thunder Bay and cover a story for me?" Delaplante told him, "If you look at the distance table on an Ontario road map, you'll find that Thunder Bay is 1091 kilometres, or nearly 700 miles, from North Bay. It would take me more than two days to drive there. You'd better find someone closer to drop in on your story."

It was Delaplante who introduced a small group of Tely editors to a mining venture. He phoned a story in one morning to Ed Monteith, our Ontario Editor, about a rush to stake copper claims in a roadless area north of Sudbury. One of Delaplante's informants was a prospector who wanted to get in on the claims but was temporarily out of funds. He had no money to buy the canoe, camp outfit and food he would need. He told Delaplante that if a few guys at the Tely were willing to raise $300 and wire the money to him, he would stake claims for us, and they might some day turn out to be worth something.

Monteith called five of his cronies together. Because Don Delaplante vouched for the honesty of the prospector, we each put up $50 and sent the total off to North Bay. A couple of weeks went by. Word came down from the north that claims had been staked for us, but now we had to send one of our number to Sudbury to take out a prospector's license, go to the site and carry out certain legal requirements. Sam Crystal, a member of our little syndicate, volunteered to go if we bought him a ticket and lower berth on the night CPR train to Sudbury. We collected more money and sent Sam off. He satisfied the legal requirements and we sat down to wait.

More weeks went by, and then months. Word finally came that a mining speculator wanted to buy our claims, form a company and sell stock to the public. For the claims, he offered to pay each of us $100, as I recall, and give us each a few thousand shares of company stock. We received the money and the share certificates but had to wait a year or more before the shares were worth anything. After the company's shares did go on the market for a few cents a share, the company founder offered to buy us out. We accepted. I think I received a couple of hundred dollars. As I remember, my total profit from the venture turned out to be under $500. I saved the money and finally used it as part of the purchase price for my Lake Josephine property.

I retired from my Board of Education job at the end of 1987. Friends had been warning me that I should have lots of activities planned for my retirement years or else I would quickly grow old and die. I told them that I already had a satisfying job lined up: continuing a Trip column every week for The Toronto Sun. With lots of time on my hands, I felt free to travel farther afield. That first winter of my retirement, Josephine and I drove down to Myrtle Beach, South Carolina, for a winter holiday. For the Sun travel pages, I wrote a Trip column every week about interesting places we found along the way.

It was in that winter of 1988 that Josephine began to develop severe arthritis, complicated by osteoporosis. By the time we arrived at Myrtle Beach, she needed a wheelchair to make it possible for her to get from our car into restaurants and hotels. We were able to rent a wheelchair for our stay at Myrtle Beach. When we arrived home, I bought one for Jo. We also had chairlifts installed on two stairways of our split-level house so that Josephine could easily get to three of the four levels and could exit and enter by way of a ground-level entrance at the side of the house.

When spring came, we moved to our cottage which was all on one level, accessible by wheelchair and by a walker. A wonderful summer followed when we experienced every cottager's dream: being able to spend a whole summer in the north without ever having to endure traffic jams back and forth on weekends.

I easily found Trip destinations to write about within 160 km (100 miles) or so of Parry Sound.

I had learned to use the computer that my colleagues at the Board of Education had given me as a retirement gift. Powered by our cottage's 12-volt solar-electric system, the computer stored my columns until I was ready to plug its modem into our telephone jack and speed them on their way into The Toronto Sun's computer system which set my words into phototype for printing in the travel section.

It hurt me to see my beloved Josephine become more crippled every year with arthritis. I made it my most important task to try to keep her comfortable and happy. She could, with my help, get in and out of our car and she enjoyed riding with me to all the places I selected, with her help, for my Trip columns.

On several occasions, Josephine had to be admitted to Parry Sound General Hospital: once for a hip fracture after a fall and twice for pneumonia. We were both extremely grateful for the excellent medical and nursing care Jo received at the hospital. By 1997, we had been spending summer holidays in the Parry Sound area for 50 years, and some of the nurses at Parry Sound Hospital knew us as summer neighbours. When I finish writing this book, I hope to write another one about my experience as a Parry Sound tree farmer and how I became the owner of my own small wilderness lake.

Josephine's health continued to deteriorate and I continued to care for her. Both at home in Toronto and at our cottage, the excellent Ontario health system provided caregivers to stay with Josephine one day per week when she could no longer go with me on my trips.

By the late 1990s, Josephine was not only badly crippled by arthritis but had developed symptoms of Alzheimer's Disease, an insidious process that destroys brain power and personality. She experienced hallucinations and delusions in periods when she no longer knew me. I continued to care for her with the help of visiting nurses. Then after a fall in April, 2001, our family doctor said she had to be hospitalized. She no longer recognized any of her family, could no longer speak to anyone and was in a perpetual coma. She was admitted to hospital for a few weeks and finally to a nursing home.

It was a traumatic time for me—the first time that Jo and I had really been separated since our marriage in 1945. We had celebrated our golden wedding anniversary in 1995 with a party at the Montgomery Inn in Etobicoke.

Josephine was in Central Park Lodge nursing home from April 2001 to November 11, 2003. Except for periods in July and August when I was at Parry Sound, I went to see her every day and to feed her lunch. I met many people who were providing the same service to family members. We provided a little company and support for each other. On sunny summer days we would take our loved ones outdoors for periods in the shade of big trees.

Josephine finally lost the ability to swallow food in November, 2003. The doctors said her heartbeat had become very slow. Early in the morning of November 11, Remembrance Day, 2003, it stopped. Josephine had left me at eighty years of age.

My daughter and son, Judith and Bob, helped me get through the next few weeks. From a sense of duty, I continued to write my weekly Trip column for The Toronto Sun, although my heart was not really in it. I stopped doing the column in March 2007.

PART SIX: TWELVE MORE TRIPS

Chapter 53

Observations On How Ontario Is Changing

This section of the book is devoted to twelve more Trip columns that I think will interest present-day readers. There are some trips I would like to have included but cannot do so because the places no longer exist or because the persons involved have moved on to new activities and new locations.

I have seen Ontario change a lot in the fifty years since I wrote my first Trip column for The Toronto Telegram. Population has increased greatly, not only in cities but throughout the province as a whole. Tiny hamlets that had almost disappeared have grown again into busy communities. Quiet roads have become four-lane arteries. Historic mills have burned, been demolished or changed ownership.

There have been many changes for the better. Around 1960, I wrote that I knew of only one country restaurant within 100 miles (160 km) of Toronto. It was the Terra Cotta Inn, beside the Credit River. Up until then, if you were on an Ontario car trip and wanted lunch, you had to look for a restaurant on the main street of a town or sizeable village. Nowadays, there are dozens and dozens of good restaurants in scenic country locations. The pioneer Terra Cotta Inn is still in business, although under new management. There are other places like Mrs. Mitchell's at Violet Hill, the Globe Hotel at Rosemont, the Cataract Inn at Cataract on the Credit, the Millcroft Inn at Alton, and the Elora Mill on the Grand River at Elora.

By the 1950s, craftsmen and artists had almost vanished in rural Ontario. There were very few potters and woodcarvers left. Around 1960 I knew of only one Ontario glass blower. Stained-glass artists were few and far between. All this has changed, largely, I think, because of the establishment of community colleges which have given young people renewed chances to relearn ancient arts and crafts. Many hundreds of individuals and young couples have become skilled craftspeople, have left the cities, have set up studios and have managed to make a living as painters, potters, silversmiths, wood sculptors and furniture makers in the hills and valleys of rural Ontario. They've brought new life to remote backwoods areas. Along with many good country restaurants, they provide destinations for interesting trips.

Chapter 54

Grant's Woods—Forest Giants Live Here

Before Europeans discovered America, southern Ontario's rich soil had provided a seed bed for millions of monster trees, very tall and very old. Today, less than one percent of Ontario is covered with old-growth forest, made up of trees more than 120 years of age. To see a few of them and to walk in their summer shade, you can go to Grant's Woods on the outskirts of Orillia.

Grant's Woods are one of Ontario's natural treasures. There's no charge to visit them and no parking fees. They are open seven days a week from dawn to dusk all year, because of the generosity of one Ontario citizen and the work of an organization called the Couchiching Conservancy. Made up of a few hundred Simcoe County citizens, the Conservancy is a publicly-owned non-profit trust concerned with the preservation of natural resources. It is associated with the Nature Conservancy of Canada and owns, protects and manages more than 3,116 hectares (7,700 acres) of conservation land in the Orillia region.

The original giant trees of Grant's Woods somehow escaped the attention of the lumber companies that logged Ontario in the 1800s. Around 1909, the 21-hectare (52-acre) property, with its trees still intact, was bought by an Englishman, Lewis John Mason Grant, and his wife, Daisy. Lewis Grant was a "remittance man" who evidently had got into the bad books of his aristocratic family. He was sent a lifetime monthly "remittance" on condition that he not return to England. Quite a few remittance men are mentioned in early Canadian folklore and literature.

Lewis and Daisy must have loved the huge old trees they found on their property. They raised three sons and taught the boys to protect the trees. For nearly one hundred years, the Grants cut only a few trees for firewood. The huge trees continued to grow taller and wider. In the year 2000, William Grant, the only surviving son, donated the farm to the Couchiching Conservancy. William was living in an Orillia retirement home when I inquired about him in 2008.

Grant's Woods is a great place for a summer detour destination off Hwy 11 if you're driving to Muskoka or Lake Nipissing. Here you'll find the Couchiching Conservancy Office, a gazebo and a 5-km (3-mile) network of walking trails under the huge trees: maple, white ash, red oak, white pine and American beech. I particularly remember the Three Sisters, a trio of white pines that are probably the oldest in Ontario.

The only other place in the province where I've seen trees this big is the Backus Woods, near Port Rowan, on the Lake Erie lowlands.

Ron Reid, a biologist, is the executive director of the Couchiching Conservancy. His office is at Grant's Woods, 705-326-1620.

To get to the Woods, take Hwy 400 to Barrie and then Hwy 11 to Orillia. Exit from 11 onto Hwy 12

West (Coldwater Rd.) for 1.5 km to Fairgrounds Rd. Go right on Fairgrounds Rd. to Division Rd. and right on Division about 200 metres to Grant's Woods on the right.

In winter, the trails are open for snowshoeing or skiing but are not groomed.

Chapter 55

Explore The Bonnechere Caves—Your Chance To See A Stalactite

True caves are rare in Ontario. I know of only two places where you can walk through real caverns deep underground. One is at Niagara where you ride down in an elevator for a journey behind the falls. The other is near Eganville in the upper Ottawa Valley region. Here you'll find the Bonnechere Caves where Chris Hinsperger makes a living by conducting tours through a cavern that dips 25 metres (82 feet)under a limestone bluff to emerge beside the fast-flowing Bonnechere River.

From the ceiling hang stalactites that look like stone icicles. Don't hold your breath while waiting for them to get bigger. It takes about 150 years for a stalactite to grow 2.2 centimetres (less than 1 inch). They owe their growth to dripping water loaded with dissolved limestone.

This is a trip for summertime. The caves are open only from the Victoria Day holiday weekend in May until Thanksgiving in October.

When I met Chris Hinsperger, owner of the caves, he said to me, "I suppose you could call me a troglodyte. That's a cave dweller." He grew up in the region and has been in and out of caves all his life.

While barely a teen he went to work as a guide for Tom Woodward, who bought the cave property in the 1950s, explored the caves and mapped them and opened them to the public.

Chris graduated from an outdoor education program at Sir Sandford Fleming College, worked for the Ontario government for a few years and took over the caves in 1991. He likes to conduct tours himself, but in peak visitor periods he also employs ten student guides who give visitors a mini-education in Paleozoic and Pleistocene geology.

Dating back hundreds of millions of years, the Paleozoic era saw Ontario covered with shallow tropical seas, swarming with trillions of primitive life forms such as gastropods, crinoids, cephalopods and trilobites. You can see their fossilized remains imbedded in the walls of the caverns. This really was a period of global warming.

The Pleistocene period included the last ice age. It ended a mere 10,000 years ago after miles-thick glaciers had covered Ontario and created most of our present landscape.

Student guides also tell about the adventures of the first owner, Tom Woodward, as he explored and mapped the water-filled caves. Woodward later installed a pumping system, stairs, walkways and electric lights.

To take a tour, you should be able to walk without difficulty; the caves are not wheelchair-accessible. You should wear stout shoes and a sweater or jacket and not be afraid of bats. A few are sometimes seen flying through the caves. They're harmless. I've caught and liberated many of them from summer cottages. Also, don't forget your camera.

While you are in the area, Chris Hinsperger suggests you also visit Bonnechere Provincial Park and the Eganville Museum.

I think you'll like Eganville (pronounced Aiganville) with its friendly Irish-French flavour. When I was last there, I enjoyed lunch at the Granary Schnitzel House at 57 Bonnechere St. On its wall there's a mural depicting the child prodigy Mozart peering across a changing world. The restaurant's original owners were from Salzburg, Mozart's birthplace.

For information about the Bonnechere Caves, call 613-628-2283 or visit www.bonnecherecaves.com. Prices for cave tours are $14 for adults, $11 for teens and seniors and $10 for children.

To get there, take Hwy 401 east from Toronto to Exit 579 at Napanee. Go north on Road 41 to Hwy 7 at Kaladar. Here Road 41 becomes Hwy 41. Continue north on 41 about 119 km to Eganville. Lined by great forested hills and many lakes, this is a scenic route. At the entrance to Eganville, follow signs about 7.4 km along back roads to the Bonnechere Caves.

Chapter 56
The Wooden Roo At Burks Falls

Newspaper reporting can be stressful and even downright dangerous at times. Reporters often have to talk to people who are in trouble or experiencing serious difficulty. I once had a lady threaten to shoot me because of an error in a story I had written. We ran a correction that satisfied her and she later apologized.

It's not like that with travel writing. Whenever I showed up to gather information for a Trip column, people were happy to see me. I still remember the warm welcome I received from Mike Grima when I first visited the Wooden Roo. It's a furniture and woodworking shop on a high hill overlooking the town of Burks Falls and the Magnetawan River. If you phone the shop for information (1-705-382-3812) you'll get the same joyful greeting on the answering machine in Australianese.

Which reminds me of a joke about Australian English. A Canadian visitor, after an accident, regained consciousness in an Australian hospital. Feeling terrible, he said to a nurse, "My God, was I brought here to die?" She replied, "Oh no, Luv. You came in yesterdie."

I found Mike Grima and the Wooden Roo in 1999

while on an autumn colours drive. I liked Mike's furniture so much that I ended up paying $235 for an oak library ladder that converts into a chair.

Travel information agents call the area around Burks Falls the Almaguin Highlands. The town itself is at a waterfall on the Magnetawan River. In summer, the falls provide beautiful picture possibilities. In autumn and winter, they are almost dry because water is diverted through a power plant.

The Magnetawan runs from Algonquin Park down through Lakes Cecebe and Ahmic and eventually reaches Georgian Bay at Byng Inlet. After a railroad from Toronto went through Burks Falls in the 1800s, steamships provided passenger service from the town to the village of Magnetawan and to resorts and cottages on the two lakes.

To get back to the Wooden Roo, I can recommend a stop there because of the warm and friendly personalities of its proprietors, Mike and Brigitte, (pronounced Bridget) and the very good furniture made by Mike. You'll recognize the place by its hilltop location and the leaping kangaroo on its sign. The building also serves as a showplace for the work of other district artists and artisans.

Mike was born in Melbourne, Australia, where he trained and qualified as an electrician while picking up woodworking skills from his father. He also took college courses in woodworking. Brigitte was born in Toronto. She and a girlfriend started on a working trip around the world. They got as far as Australia where Brigitte met Mike. Her friend, Laura, met Mike's best friend, Alan. They went no further. Both couples married.

After they had two daughters, Mike and Brigitte came to Canada to visit her parents at their cottage on Little Doe Lake. Mike liked the Almaguin area so much the pair decided to stay. They bought the hilltop location in Burks Falls. In stages, they built a house, a gallery and a workshop.

Besides building a reputation as a skilled furniture maker, Mike has also become known as a worker in community efforts. The local Lions Club selected him for a Helen Keller Fellowship.

For information about business hours at the Wooden Roo, call 1-705-382-3812. If you visit, don't feel you have to buy. You're welcome to browse. The merchandise on display ranges from small gift items to big furniture pieces such as three-mirror oak dressers and mouse-proof cottage cupboards.

Burks Falls is 260 km (162.5 miles) north of Toronto. Take Hwy 11 up past Huntsville to Hwy 520 on the right. It becomes Ontario Street in Burks Falls. Just past the Magnetawan River bridge, Hwy 520 goes left. To get to the Wooden Roo, you continue north on Ontario Street. Look for the shop on the left atop a hill.

Chapter 57
The Hunt For The Dyer Memorial

Hidden in deep forest beside the Big East River about 12 km (7.5 miles) northeast of Huntsville, there's a four-hectare (ten-acre) landscaped park and garden with a lofty stone spire in its centre. The park and monument are a memorial to a loving marriage. Detroit lawyer Clifton G. Dyer built them more than fifty years ago in memory of his wife, Betsy. Over the years, the forest has closed in around the Dyer Memorial so that it takes an adventurous spirit to find the spot. If you own a rugged vehicle and like to explore backwoods terrain, you might like to devote a day to finding your way into the Dyer Memorial. Picnics and camping are not allowed, but visitors are welcome and the site has picture possibilities.

I first went there and wrote about it for The Toronto Telegram in 1965. I went back for The Toronto Sun in 2004 and had to hunt to find the spot; roads had changed and vandals had moved direction signs. I'll give my 2004 directions and you can try to follow them at your own risk, but first here's the appealing story of Clifton and Betsy Dyer.

Clifton and Betsy first came to Muskoka and Algonquin Park by train in 1916 on their honeymoon.

They didn't return for many years but never forgot the Muskoka scenery. On their 20th anniversary in 1936, they came back, camped beside the Big East River, bought 400 forest acres (162 hectares) and built a cabin as their Canadian retreat. After fourteen years of winter and summer vacations at the cabin, Betsy died in 1950. Clifton spent his retirement years planning a park, gardens, steps and a lofty stone spire as a memorial to his wife. Betsy's ashes were placed in a copper urn atop the tower. When her husband died at age 74 in 1959, his ashes were also deposited there.

Clifton left a trust fund he thought would provide income to assure perpetual care for the memorial, but inflation has evidently reduced the effectiveness of the plan. When I was there in 2004, one part-time retired custodian was caring for the gardens.

The Dyer Memorial is now within the extended boundaries of Huntsville, but as far as I've been able to find out, it is not a Huntsville park. The memorial is also close to the boundaries of Arrowhead Provincial Park but was not part of the park in 2004. If you're interested, you could make inquiries by calling Huntsville City Hall at 705-789-6421.

Although finding your way to the place can be a bit of an adventure, the Dyer Memorial rates as one of Ontario's wilderness beauty spots. Couples sometimes make the journey to have their wedding ceremonies there and to have pictures taken on a terrace at the top of the seventy stone steps. When I was last there, family and friends of Art Payne, a workman who had helped build the memorial, showed up for a visit. I took a picture of them on the terrace.

Here are the road directions I used for my 2004 visit to the Dyer Memorial. Local roads may have changed, may have improved or may be worse by now. I took Hwy 11 to Hwy 60 at the north end of Huntsville. I went right on Hwy 60 to Muskoka Road 3 at the second traffic signals. I turned north (left) up Road 3 for 2.8 km to Williamsport Road. I went right on Williamsport Road for 5.3 km to Harp Lake Road. I went left on this road for about one km over a bridge. Past the bridge, I finally found a small sign on the right to Dyer Memorial Road. I went right here to a small parking area on the right, overhanging the river and stone steps on the left leading up to the memorial.

Chapter 58

For A Taste Of Luxury, Try The Benmiller Inn, For Scenery, See Benmiller Falls

Benmiller is a picturesque pioneer mill community in the valley of the Maitland River, about five km (three miles) upstream from Goderich. Until the 1950s it was noted for Benmiller blankets, made by the Gledhill family's woollen mill. Now it's noted for two modern features:

- The Benmiller Inn, located in the rebuilt massive old limestone building that used to house the woollen mill.
- The Falls Reserve Conservation Area where, in high-water periods, the river becomes Benmiller Falls as it thunders over a 1.8-metre (6-foot) ledge of limestone that stretches in a wavering line across the wide valley.

When I first visited the Benmiller Inn in 1975, shortly after it opened, I wrote that I was adding it to my short list of good Ontario country inns. The owners at that time were Peter Ivey, of London, Ontario, and Mrs. Joanne Mazzolini, of Toronto. They had bought the old woollen mill in 1970, had poured piles of money into it and had opened it in 1974 after taking three years for remodelling. The conversion job was outstanding.

Nearly thirty-five years later, the old building remains one of the most comfortable, interesting and pleasing country inns I've seen in Ontario. Many of the floors are flagstone, beautifully fitted and finished. The comfortable dark leather and wood furniture was custom-designed and fits perfectly into the stone-and-timber interior. Old oaken gear wheels from the mill have been fitted unobtrusively into the décor as rails or room dividers. The grounds around the building have waterside terraces for tea, private trout ponds and walking trails.

When I stayed there for a night in 1975, the main mill building had twelve guest rooms with fourteen more ready to open in a separate gristmill building. Now the inn offers a total of fifty-seven rooms in five buildings, with conference rooms available in a sixth.

In 1975, I wrote that lunch with a drink would likely cost between $3 and $5.50; dinner with a drink from $12 to $15. Today, the average three-course lunch will run you around $35, with dinner costing from $49 to $59.

There was a dress code in 1975. Men were expected to wear jackets with ties, ascots or turtlenecks. Nowadays, you're only expected to wear "dressy casual" clothes in the dining rooms. Reservations are required for meals and rooms. The toll-free number is 1-800-265-1711. Children are welcome.

Now known as the Benmiller Inn and Spa, the place has many new features. It is owned by a consortium of five Ontario owners and is managed by

Sequel Lifestyle Hotels and Resorts. Room rates go from $169 to $369 per night.

To reach the inn, go through Stratford and Clinton on Hwy 8. About 13 km (8 miles) past Clinton, look for Huron County Road No. 1. Go right on this road and 3 km will take you to Benmiller and the inn.

As I mentioned, Benmiller's other attraction is the Falls Reserve Conservation Area, a 1,100-hectare (2,700-acre) camping and picnic park, operated by the Maitland Valley Conservation Authority. The area is called Falls Reserve because the land around Benmiller Falls was not sold when the Canada Company, an early 19th century land-speculation group, was offering land to settlers in Huron County. It was reserved for mill sites.

In the 1960s, the site was acquired by the Conservation Authority to be preserved as public open space around Benmiller Falls. The community, by the way, was named for one of the district's first settlers. He was Benjamin Miller who arrived in the area about 1830 and ran a tavern in the village. It became known as "Ben Miller's Place" and later just Benmiller.

To get into the Conservation Area for a summer picnic will cost you about $10 a car, depending on how many people you have in the car.

This is a favourite camping ground for families with big trailers, campers and other elaborate recreational vehicles. There are about 230 campsites. About half of them have electric connections and water taps. If your trailer is satisfied with 15-ampere electric power, you pay $33 a day to camp here. If you need 30 amps, you pay $35 a day. When I last talked to Geoff King, parks superintendent for the Conservation Authority, he told me that some owners of big mobile homes were asking for 50-amp electric power. If you don't require any electric power at all and are content to sleep in a tent, your camping cost is $28 a night. There are lots of modern washroom buildings with flush toilets and hot showers.

The phone number for Falls Reserve Conservation Area is 519-524-6429. For the Conservation Authority Office in Wroxeter, the number is 519-335-3557.

To get to Falls Reserve, go to Stratford and take Hwy 8, the Huron Road, westward from Stratford through Mitchell, Seaforth and Clinton. About 6.5 km past Clinton, take Huron County Road 31 to the right. Follow it about 9.6 km to Benmiller and up a hill on the far side. At the top, you'll see the United Church on the right. Go past the church to the first road on the left. Go left on this road to Falls Reserve.

Chapter 59

Tony Bianco, Creator Of Coins

Have you ever wondered about the people who create the designs that are engraved on millions of Canada's handsome big coins? I'm thinking in particular of the polar bear and cubs on the Toonie; the Georgian Bay pines on the $20 coin; and a hockey game between Royal Military College and West Point on the $100 gold piece. Here's your chance to meet the artist who created those images. His name is Tony Bianco. He lives and works in the hills of Oro-Medonte near the tiny hamlet of Fair Valley, about 140 km (87.5 miles) north of Toronto. If you make an appointment, you can visit his studio and get to know one of Canada's most promising artists.

I first went to see Tony and wrote about him for The Toronto Sun in February 2006. I found his success story heart-warming and amazing and his talent surprising for its brilliance.

This modest self-taught artist was born in Newmarket, Ontario, to an Italian artisan father and a Dutch mother. He graduated from Newmarket High School where he had immersed himself in art books from the school library and from the Newmarket library. At age 13, he had begun to paint on his own.

At one point, a staff member from the Newmarket Library saw his paintings and asked him to display some at the library. The paintings attracted such widespread attention that a local real-estate agent—to whom Tony will always be grateful—presented him with a set of professional oil paints and brushes. A couple of artists gave him informal lessons and encouragement and his paintings began to sell. Tony's first real break came when he entered five wildlife paintings in a show at the Buckhorn Art Festival. To his surprise, they all sold quickly for a total of $6,000. That convinced him that he could make a living from art.

He married in 1988. He and his wife, Linda, moved to Orillia. Later they moved to their present country home; friends had to back a loan to buy the house because the banks wouldn't give a mortgage to an artist.

In 1991, Tony hit the Big Time. Ducks Unlimited, an international conservation foundation, selected him as its North American Artist of the Year and published his painting "Black Ducks at Tiny Marsh" across the continent.

His work, which he describes as mostly realist but partly impressionist, now sells at galleries across Canada. He likes to paint wildlife and the outdoors but is also attracted to people and to cities. I love his cityscape showing Yonge and Queen Streets, Toronto, at dusk in light rain.

The Royal Canadian Mint discovered Tony after one of his shows at Algonquin Park. The Mint invited him to submit designs for coins, and up to 2008 it had used ten of them. Tony is especially proud of his coin designs. In 2008, he was completing two coin scenes to commemorate the 2010 Winter Olympics at Vancouver. One depicts speed skating and the other a luge race.

Recently the Biancos have been travelling across Canada with their young son and daughter. Tony has been painting scenes from Canada's National Parks and has completed one hundred and fifty of them for a book and show backed by an anonymous donor. When I talked to Tony at the end of 2008, the show was scheduled for the fall of 2009 at the Columbus Centre in North York.

Visitors are welcome at the Bianco Studio, Monday to Friday. To make an appointment, call 705-835-3870 or e-mail fairvalleystudio@rogers.com.

Tony sold his first painting for $5. His originals now bring from $800 to $20,000. When I was there, he had a few prints priced at from $20 to $175.

To get to the Bianco studio, take Hwy 400 from Barrie to Exit 131 at Mount St. Louis Rd. From 400, go east on this road for 2.9 km to the Ninth Line. Jog right on the Ninth Line and then go left again on the Mount St. Louis Rd. for another 4.6 km. Just past the Twelfth Line, the studio is No. 1640 on the left.

Chapter 60

Port Elgin's Pampered Pumpkins

What do you do with a pumpkin that weighs around 550 kilograms (a little over 1,200 pounds), occupies your whole veggie patch and keeps growing bigger and bigger? You cosset and protect it, make it a special bed on a wooden pallet and cover it with an electric blanket on frosty nights. Around the first of October, you carefully load it onto a truck and haul it over to the Lake Huron town of Port Elgin. Here you enter it into the great Ontario Pumpkin Weigh-in at Port Elgin's annual Pumpkinfest. If yours turns out to be Top Pumpkin—heaviest in the show—it brings you a prize of $5,000. After the show, you carefully collect and dry every one of its seeds. Champion's seeds have sold for up to $750 per seed!

Even if you don't grow pumpkins and don't have a vegetable garden, you might want to drive over to Port Elgin, about 240 km (150 miles) west of Toronto, and join the fun of Pumpkinfest. More than 55,000 spectators and hundreds of growers pour into this attractive lakeport community for the two-day festival. It's held every year on the first full weekend in October to identify the biggest pumpkin grown in Canada in the current year. The 2008 winner was a monster of 1,395 pounds (634 kilograms) grown by Darrell Leonard, of Wyevale, Ontario.

Growing immense specimens of *Cucurbita pepo*, the common pie pumpkin, has become an international sport with a worldwide organization, a newspaper, and twenty-three official weigh-ins at sites scattered around the globe. The world record pumpkin up to press-time for this book weighed in at 1,689 pounds. It was a pumpkin grown in Rhode Island, U.S.A., in 2007. Growers confidently expect that some year soon a pumpkin will hit 1,700 pounds. (For international competition, pumpkin weights are measured in pounds, not kilograms.)

Port Elgin got on the giant pumpkin train in 1986 when Mayor Fred Worth, a hobby gardener, challenged his friend, the mayor of Elora, to a pumpkin-growing contest. Mayor Worth won with a 240-pounder (109 kilograms) and his town organized a small impromptu festival to celebrate.

Since then, the annual Pumpkinfest, like the pumpkins, has kept on growing. Every autumn it includes forty to fifty events over Saturday and Sunday, including the Canadian championship weigh-in on Saturday, a local weigh-in for smaller pumpkins on Sunday, a celebrity seed-spitting contest, giant tomato and other vegetable contests, pumpkin carving, scarecrow making, a haunted house, an elephant tug-of-war, elephant rides, a classic car show, a motorcycle show, an artists' village craft show, an antiques show, live music and entertainment, a Legion breakfast, a United Church dinner and lots and lots of food and vendors.

Organized by Lisa Irwin, who works year-round at it, this is the biggest annual event on the Canadian shore of Lake Huron. Weekend tickets for it cost $9 for adults, $4 for kids and $7 for seniors. This includes most of the events. One event, a wall-climbing contest, charges an extra $5.

Driving into Port Elgin from either the south or north on Hwy 21, you park free in cornfields just outside town and board free shuttle buses for the Pumpkinfest village on the high-school grounds.

On the Saturday morning of the first complete weekend in October, growers and their trucks, with pampered pumpkins swathed in blankets and foam rubber, will have been lined up at the gates since 4 A.M. Starting at 8 A.M., the pumpkins are carefully unloaded by eight forklifts and weighed on big official scales. Their weights are then recorded on huge Olympic-size scoreboards.

When I went to Port Elgin in 2002 to write about Pumpkinfest for The Toronto Sun, I heard many stories about how growers nurse their giant veggies through the growing season with homemade greenhouses, blankets, special foods, warm water and fertilizers. A real winner can put on ten pounds (4.5 kilograms) a day at the peak of the season.

Joanne Robbins, co-ordinator of that year's festival, gave me two seeds from what she described as a near-champion. I carefully took them home. The following spring I gave one to my daughter, Judith, at Madoc, and the other to my son, Bob, at Sault Ste. Marie. Both planted the seeds and reported that huge pumpkins resulted. Judith's grew as big as a doghouse until one night some deer invaded her garden, discovered the pumpkin and gradually ate it over the next few weeks. Bob's pumpkin got so big it was crowding out his vegetable garden and raspberry patch. Neighbours came to admire it until it aged and fell apart.

To drive to Port Elgin, about 240 km (150 miles) from Toronto, go to Orangeville, and then go west on County Road 109 which in some areas becomes Hwy 9. Go through Arthur, Teviotdale, Harriston, Greenock and Kinloss to Hwy 21 at Kincardine. Go north on Hwy 21 for 34 km to Port Elgin.

For information about Pumpkinfest and Port Elgin generally, call Lisa Irwin. The toll-free number is 1-800-387-3456. In daytime this puts you in touch with a real human voice, not a machine.

Chapter 61

Winter Fishing Near Hamilton

Comfortable winter camping may seem like an oxymoron—a contradiction in terms— but staff at Valens Conservation Area, just north of Hamilton, try to offer a few comforts to the hardy souls who rent winter campsites in this 283-hectare (700-acre) park on Valens Lake. In 2008, for $29.40 a night you could rent a tent site or trailer site with an electrical outlet that lets you run lights and a small electric heater—you bring the heater. Some campers even bring electric blankets. Close to your campsite is a heated washroom building with hot showers, flush toilets and laundry facilities.

Most winter campers come to Valens for the relatively comfortable ice fishing. You can rent a fishing hut with a propane heater that keeps you warm and also lets you cook hot dogs and make tea or coffee.

Twenty minutes from downtown Hamilton and about 75 km (47 miles) from Toronto, Valens—along with six other conservation areas, a string of smaller parks and a hiking trail network—is operated by the Hamilton Region Conservation Authority.

An 80-hectare (200-acre) lake at Valens was created in the 1960s when the Conservation Authority built a dam on Spencer Creek to maintain summer flow and control spring floods at the downstream town of Dundas. Originally the lake was stocked with large-mouth bass. They have taken hold and now naturally reproduce to provide summer fishing. In winter, anglers catch northern pike, a few perch, bluegills and crappies; all of these fish somehow got into the lake and have multiplied. Bluegills and crappies (pronounced croppies) are panfish, similar to sunfish, that are good to eat if you take the trouble to de-bone or fillet them. Many kids and dads catch them just for fun and return them alive to the water.

Open seven days a week and offering groomed cross-country ski trails, Valens is a favourite spot for outdoor-minded families because it's not too distant for city dwellers and has milder weather than northern ice-fishing lakes and provincial parks. Park operations officer Ted Doyle told me that on a winter Saturday there'll be two hundred or more adults and kids on the lake, fishing through the ice. The park staff check the ice every day for thickness safety.

Some fishers rent heated huts. Some bring their own improvised plastic shelters. Most just bundle up warmly and stand with their backs to the wind. Last time I checked (in early 2009), it cost $20 per adult per day to rent a heated hut. You can buy fishing bait at the park. You bring your own rods, lines and hooks or buy them here.

The winter entrance fee to the park, including fishing on the lake, is $8 for a car with driver. The total fee can go up to $12, depending on how many others are in the car. The park is open seven days a week. When there's no staffer at the gate, you pay at machines like those devilish ones that charge you for public parking in Toronto.

For information, call 905-525-2183 or visit <u>conservationhamilton.on.ca</u>

To get to Valens, take the Queen Elizabeth Way and Hwy 403 to Hwy 6 north at Hamilton. Go north up Hwy 6 for 16.2 km to Regional Road 97. Go west (left) on Road 97 for 9 km to the park gate on the right.

Chapter 62

You Can Be Married At This B And B

Some guests go to the O'Kane Bed and Breakfast at Hillsdale, 24 km (15 miles) north of Barrie, to enjoy the ambience of a century-old house and a quiet Ontario village. Others go for skiing at nearby resorts or for hiking and bird-watching in the Copeland forest. Still others go to get married. Proprietors Mike and Carol O'Kane are licensed marriage officers, empowered under Ontario law to perform marriage ceremonies.

Mike is a former high-ranking Roman Catholic missionary priest who served many years in the Amazon rain forest of Brazil, in the Caribbean and as an administrator in Canada. Carol was a teacher nun of the Sisters of St. Joseph in Guatemala and the Bahamas, and a hospital chaplain in Canada. Both left their orders over matters of conscience—chiefly disagreements with Catholic Church policies that appeared to them to support cruel and repressive regimes in Central and South America.

Mike wrote a book about his experiences. Entitled *Beyond our Vision: Journey of a Married Priest*, it was published in 2003 by Tomiko Publications, Ottawa. It is now out of print, but you can see a copy at the Bed and Breakfast.

Both Mike and Carol were born in North Bay. They met briefly in Guatemala in 1968 and then later in the Bahamas when Mike was Superior General of Scarboro Missions, Canada's major Catholic mission order. By 1987 they had both independently decided to leave the Church, and in 1988 they were married by a United Church minister in the chapel of Hart House at the University of Toronto. Mike sums up his experience succinctly: "I fell out of love with the Church and fell in love with Carol."

They bought their house at Hillsdale in 1988, rented it out for a while and renovated it for four years. Mike did much of the carpentry work himself. They moved there in 1992 and opened as a Bed and Breakfast the same year, because they both like to be surrounded by people and they needed income.

I enjoyed meeting this warm-hearted couple and liked their modestly priced, compact and comfortable home. I have since read and liked Mike's book.

Room rates at the end of 2008 were $55 single and $65 double, with a full breakfast. The O'Kanes will sometimes prepare dinner on advance requests.

The O'Kanes perform many marriage ceremonies each year, both at their home and at spots selected by wedding couples. They have even married couples atop the Mount St. Louis ski hill. They told me that in recent years the Ontario government has been licensing marriage officers, sponsored or endorsed by churches and religious organizations. This has been prompted by the reluctance of judges and justices of the peace to officiate at weddings because of heavy court work.

Most O'Kane weddings are in summer. Couples can choose a non-denominational religious ceremony or a civil form of marriage. Most choose some form of religious ceremony. Mike speaks Spanish and Portuguese and has served as an interpreter for Ontario courts.

For information about the O'Kane Bed and Breakfast or about weddings, call 705-835-3554 or visit okanesbb.com. To meet the O'Kanes, please phone to make an appointment. To get there, take Hwy 400 north from Barrie for 16 km to Exit 121 at Hwy 93. Go left (north) on Hwy 93 for 8 km to Hillsdale. The O'Kane house is No. 4609 at the corner of Albert Street and Hwy 93.

Chapter 63
Live In A Lighthouse At Cabot Head

Cabot Head is a picturesque lovely point that juts eastward from the Bruce Peninsula a few kilometres south of Tobermory and 256 km (160 miles) north of Toronto. Every summer, interested married couples, most of them from cities, pay $350 a couple to live for a week in the old Cabot Head lighthouse and act as Assistant Lightkeepers. The Assistant Lightkeeper program is run by historic-minded Bruce Peninsula citizens who make up a non-profit organization called the Friends of the Cabot Head Lighthouse.

Together over the years, the Friends have saved and restored the 1800s lighthouse and turned it into an attractive museum. It tells the story of shipping and shipwrecks along the Bruce as well as the saga of settlement on this rugged limestone peninsula. The Assistant Lightkeeper program is one way the Friends raise money to keep the lighthouse alive and attract visitors to it.

If you sign up far enough ahead and are accepted for the program, you move in on a summer Monday and live until the following Sunday in three rooms and a bathroom in the four-storey lighthouse. You are expected to carry out a few duties such as acting as guides for museum visitors and helping out in a small shop. In return, you have a unique vacation experience as you steep yourselves in the history of the light on Cabot Head.

I first went to Cabot Head in 1969. A road to the lighthouse had been completed just three years earlier. Two men, employees of the Canadian Ministry of Transport, tended the light in shifts of six hours on and six off. They welcomed visitors for tours of the site for a few hours each week from May to November.

In the 1960s, the original light, in a tower atop the house, had been replaced by a steel beacon tower with an automatic light. Federal government plans were underway to eliminate lightkeeper crews and perhaps demolish buildings at lighthouse sites up and down the Lake Huron shores. That's when historic-minded citizens started to organize to preserve the Cabot Head lighthouse. Many of them were descendants of people who had worked at building the towers in an 1800s government program to provide navigation aids on the Canadian portion of the Great Lakes.

Over the years, the Friends of the Cabot Head Lighthouse have restored a good portion of the premises, including: the main lighthouse building which now has a new cupola on its top level, fitted up to look like the lantern room of an old-fashioned lighthouse; a pioneer room, a nature room, a marine heritage room, and a timber room; and an apartment for the Assistant Lightkeepers. From the cupola on the top floor, you get a wonderful 360-degree view of the Bruce coastline.

A shed that once housed powerful foghorn machinery has been converted to an art gallery.

Every year from May 1 to October 31, the lighthouse is open seven days a week. There's no formal admission charge, but the Friends of the site are happy if visitors donate $3 a person to help with expenses. The two resident managers are Guy and Kathleen Langman. Ina Toxopeus is president of the Friends of the Cabot Head Lighthouse, 519-795-7769. For information about the site, a map and the Assistant Lightkeeper program, she suggests you go to Google and type in Cabot Head Lighthouse. You can also log on to www.cabothead.ca.

When I talked to Ina Toxopeus in November 2008, she told me that placements for the summer of 2009 in the Assistant Lightkeeper program were being filled rapidly.

The Canadian government still operates the modern beacon light but leases the rest of the site to the municipality of Northern Bruce Peninsula, which in turn rents it to the Friends organization.

To get to Cabot Head, turn east off Hwy 6 onto the Dyer Bay Rd. Drive east about 8.4 km along this road to an intersection. Here you turn right, following signs to Dyer Bay. The road goes down a winding pass through the limestone cliffs, emerges at shore level and turns left through the community of Dyer Bay. Past Dyer Bay, drive along the shore road. On your left will be high white cliffs; on the right will be Georgian Bay. On some parts of the road there will be cottages, on others stony beaches. You'll cross, about 15.2 km from your starting point, a stream tumbling down to the bay. Continue on past the stream and past Boulder Bluff and Centre Bluff. Finally at 21.2 km you'll come to the road leading in to the lighthouse.

You'll find that Cabot Head is not a sheer cape but a low plateau. Beyond it is Wingfield Basin. A popular yacht harbour, the basin is one of the few protected inlets on the east side of the Bruce Peninsula.

If you're interested in lighthouses, you might try to locate a book entitled *The Light on Chantry Island* by Mary Weeks-Mifflin and Ray Mifflin, published in 1986 by Boston Mills Press. It's the story of one historic lighthouse near Southampton, Ontario.

Chapter 64

Exploring The Historic French River

For scenery, history and romance, the French River ranks as a queen of Ontario's inland waterways. Draining Lake Nipissing and a watershed area of 19,000 square km (over 7,000 square miles) into Georgian Bay, the French was the first and most important water highway into Canada's interior. First Nations war parties, French explorers, missionaries, fur-trade brigades, trappers and lumbermen all travelled the French River by canoe before there were roads to the interior.

The largely francophone people who live along the river's 120 km (75 miles) love the French, its many falls, bays and tranquil stretches. They know the names of its twenty-three rapids and they know the legends surrounding the river. Nobody knows them better than Rene La Haie, of Noelville. Born beside the French, he has lived and worked there all his life except for a spell he spent at the former Ontario Forest Ranger School at Dorset. He has worked as district roads foreman, has served as mayor of the municipality of French River, and has dived, fished and canoed along the river since he was a small boy. Now he spends his summers taking visitors on cruises aboard his stable but not-too-fast pontoon boat that seats up to nineteen people.

Until 2003—even though I'd heard and read about the French River all my life and had crossed it many times—I had never been on the French. When, in the summer of 2003, I asked about the best way to see the river, people started telling me to see Rene La Haie. That July, I went on one of Rene's cruises and absorbed more river lore in a couple of hours than I'd picked up in a lifetime of reading.

With Rene, you realize that the French is not really a mad rushing river all the way, although it does drop 20 metres (66 feet) between Lake Nipissing and Georgian Bay. For most of its length, the river is actually a chain of long, wide, deep lakes falling into each other over falls, rapids and chutes. Some of these can be dangerous, like the Recollet Rapids. Here, in the 1700s, a party of Recollet Order missionaries all drowned because they tried to run the rapids instead of portaging around them.

Writing this reminds me of a story and leads to a brief digression. When my son, Bob, was working summers as a student on "portage crew" in Quetico Provincial Park, Ross Williams, the Park Superintendent, issued an order that if the portage crew kids wanted to run rapids, they must do so in empty canoes. To avoid expensive losses of time and money, all their camp equipment and food must first be carried down around the rapids. This reduced considerably their teen-age enthusiasm for rapids shooting. Portage crews were also forbidden to ride on the backs of moose swimming across lakes.

To get back to my column about the French, I was

about to say that many stretches along the river are accessible by road and have been occupied by lodges and cottages since the 1920s. Other locations are reachable only by water. Summer residents depend on barges to bring in gasoline and diesel fuel for generators and propane for heat and cooking. Many, like me, are also starting to use solar panels to provide 12-volt electric power in their cottages.

Much of the forested shore of the French River is crown land, part of the French River Provincial Park, or owned by First Nations communities.

Wearing a colourful voyageur sash with a handmade filleting knife at his belt, Rene brings history to life. He tells his passengers how the Dokis (pronounced Doe-kees) native people wisely kept their timber from 1800s lumber barons and have profited from it in modern times.

Ranging from two to five hours in length, Rene's cruises start at Totem Point at the head of Wolseley Bay on the river's north side. Fares range from $20 to $30, depending on the length of the cruise. Rene provides two-hour introductory cruises, 3½-hour trips to the Five Finger rapids for a picnic and swimming, a sunset cruise for dinner at Lochaven Lodge (where you pay extra for your dinner), and a maxi five-hour excursion to several rapids. Rene gives a live commentary in English, French or Spanish. His boat, La François, can carry nineteen people but he usually limits the number to twelve to avoid crowding. The La François is wheelchair accessible but has no washrooms.

For information and reservations, call 705-898-2971.

Cruises are available from May to October. Before going on one of Rene's trips, it's a good idea to visit the new Ontario government French River Visitor Centre on Hwy 69 just south of the French River bridge at the Recollet Rapids.

To get to Totem Point where Rene's cruises begin, take Hwy 69 north from Parry Sound for 99 km to Hwy 64, 10 km north of French River. Go right on Hwy 64 for 28.5 km to Hwy 528. Go right on 528 and 528-B to the end of the road at Totem Point Lodge.

Chapter 65

An Excellent Inn At The Mouth Of The Severn

Hidden away on the Severn River just a kilometre east of Hwy 400, Gloucester Pool (pronounced Gloster) is where Muskoka begins. This long tranquil lake, formed by a dam and canal lock at the Georgian Bay mouth of the Severn, has been known for some eighty years to a relatively few cottagers and boaters as a quiet retreat for good fishing and vacations. Now "The Pool" is also gaining a reputation for fine dining, luxury accommodation and spa service because of the opening in 2004 of the rebuilt Inn at Christie's Mill.

The original Christie's Mill was a big sawmill which was taken over by a local lumberman named Bill Christie after the American-owned Georgian Bay Lumber Company went broke around 1900.

After three Toronto Sun readers phoned me and sent me e-mails about the inn, I first went there for lunch in 2004 and have been going back regularly ever since. I rate it as the best dining destination in the area centred around the towns of Barrie, Orillia and Coldwater. It's also a great place to stay, if you can afford the rates. The last time I checked, they were $195 for a double room, with breakfast, and up to $450 for one of the luxurious whirlpool suites. You can get up-to-date rates by calling 1-800-465-9966, by logging on to www.christiesmill.com or by e-mailing info@christiesmill.com.

The place is owned by a German industrialist count, Graf Ruediger Von Goertz. If you really want to blow a bundle, you could book a reservation for the Graf's personal suite. It was going for $555 a night in 2004. The Count, or Graf, lives in Germany and comes to Canada once or twice a year to visit the inn.

Draining Lakes Simcoe and Couchiching from Washago down to Georgian Bay, the Severn River, almost 48 km (30 miles) long, is a waterway gem. With canal locks, power plants and a marine railway, it forms the western leg of the Trent-Severn Canal system which took almost one hundred years to build. Cutting across southern Ontario for 384 km (240 miles), from Trenton on Lake Ontario to Port Severn on Georgian Bay, the canal was intended as a short cut for freight ships to avoid the long haul via Lake Erie and Lake St. Clair to Lake Huron.

By the time the canal was opened, however, railways, trucks and the enlarged Welland Canal had made it obsolete for freight traffic. Today it's a wonderful pleasure craft route. Yachts sailing the Trent system can tie up at the Inn at Christie's Mill. From the inn's two dining areas, you can watch boats crossing Gloucester Pool to and from Lock 45, the western gateway of the canal system.

From my first visit to the inn, I have been impressed by three things: the food, the French-country design of the buildings, and the service. I usually time my trips to and from Parry Sound so that I can enjoy lunch at the inn. It is just a short distance off Hwy 400 which has finally been completed to four lanes all the way to Parry Sound.

A favourite item of mine on the lunch menu is Georgian Bay pickerel fillet with a salad of organically grown greens and fruit. Dinner entrees often include breast of chicken stuffed with apple, caraway and currants; roast sirloin of lamb; and roast halibut with lobster tail.

The inn is open all year. In busy seasons, reservations are recommended. The toll-free phone number, again, is 1-800-465-9966. To get there, take Hwy 400 north to Exit 156 at Port Severn. Go right here, following inn signs for about one kilometre to the inn on the left.

Chapter 66
Au Revoir And "30"

This is the chapter where, among other things, I thank those who have helped me in various ways all through my long life.

First, I thank God for the many wonderful things given to me. Yes, I do believe in God. I also believe in evolution. Through my adult life I have read and studied the natural sciences: botany, zoology, geology, forestry and so on. The development of life on planet Earth has proceeded so perfectly that I have concluded that it can't have all been by accident, that there is evidence of a master benign intelligence, permeating all forms of life and all forms of energy and matter. Of course I can't understand it, but I am confident that it does exist.

I have many, many things to be grateful for.

I am supremely grateful for Josephine and our years of love together. I am grateful beyond words for having been a parent of our wonderful daughter and son, Judith and Bob. They were truly children from Heaven and helped keep our home and family life full of love.

To young parents, I'd like to say: Remember always, you do not own your children. They are just loaned to you for a few years. Your greatest job in life is helping them become mature and independent of you so that they can live happy and productive lives of their own. As they're growing up, try to realize that they are unconsciously assuming and adopting the attitudes they observe in their parents and others closest to them. In the natural sciences, it is called "imprinting".

Through my period of fatherhood, I've frequently recalled a couple of lines by the Scottish poet Robert Burns: "To make a happy fireside clime for weens and wife. That's the true pathos, and sublime, of human life." If you do a good job of parenting and allow your kids to become independent as they grow up, they'll return to you as true friends in a new loving adult relationship.

Next to my wife and family, I am truly grateful for my long, happy and satisfying career as a reporter, writer and editor. I realize I have never been a great writer, but I have tried to be a clear and competent one, always remembering that the task of a journalist is to convey accurate information, not to impress readers with the writer's cleverness and ability. J.D. MacFarlane used to express it well: "Good writing slips down like honey. Bad writing sticks in the throat."

I'm grateful to all the editors who gave me work that would educate me. I have come to realize that working on a good newspaper is like studying at a good university. It produces "generalists": people who know a little about a great many subjects.

I'm grateful to all the younger people who so loyally worked with me during my term as Suburban and Regional Editor of The Telegram. In recent years, many have written and called me to say that they enjoyed those years when we operated together as a team and that they learned a lot from them.

To the many teachers who struggled to pierce my layers of apathy at elementary and high school, I owe a special debt. I have retained a surprising amount of what they dispensed. I have found Latin to be one of the most useful subjects that I was exposed to; it has helped me understand English more fully. At Northwestern University, I learned a lot about many things, including "critical paths", "labour intensive" and "capital intensive" projects and Abraham Maslow's "hierarchy of needs".

The successive Directors and the staff at the Etobicoke Board of Education welcomed me as a refugee from the closing of The Telegram. For sixteen years, they made me feel an important part of their team and family. (I believe that former premier Mike Harris made a mistake in throwing Etobicoke and the other Metro Toronto suburbs into the melting pot of the monster City of Toronto. Much community spirit has been lost and many innovative programs have been forgotten.)

About The Toronto Sun: Although I never really became part of The Sun's editorial team, I am grateful for the opportunity The Sun gave me to write Trip columns for thirty-six years. As Travel Editor, Robin Robinson was most kind, efficient and helpful.

Carolyn and Grant Leigh, of Etobicoke, have helped and encouraged me in the preparation of this book. Carolyn is a professional typist and computer operator. She turned my ant-track handwriting into beautiful typescript and kept up my morale during the writing process by telling me that she looked forward every week to reading more of my narrative. Grant, a retired hotel accountant who now delights in guiding visitor tours of Toronto, is an important member of the Toronto Bruce Trail Club. He has helped and encouraged me with much research. He even succeeded in finding for me a scarce copy of my first book, *Where the Alders Grow*, written in the 1950s.

There is another group of people to whom I am indebted: the residents of the Parry Sound area where I have spent vacations and summers for sixty-two years. I admire these wonderful people. Many of them are my closest friends.

Now that I've finished writing this book, I hope I'll have the energy to produce another one: about my adventures, experiences and mishaps as a cottager and tree farmer in McKellar and Ferguson Townships (in the Parry Sound area). I've even dreamed up a title for it. I think I'll call it *Lake Josephine Journals*.

A warm Thank You to my readers who have read my columns and taken my suggested trips over forty-nine years. I have welcomed and enjoyed your letters, phone calls and suggestions.

Instead of Adieu, I am concluding with Au Revoir. At the end, I'll also just write the traditional end of a news story. For now, it's "30".